Teacher as Writer

REDWOOD WRITING PROJECT

Teacher as Writer

Entering the Professional Conversation

Edited by

Karin L. Dahl
The Ohio State University

with the Committee on Professional Writing Networks
for Teachers and Supervisors

National Council of Teachers of English
1111 Kenyon Road, Urbana, Illinois 61801

Project Editor: Michelle Sanden Johlas

Cover Design: Barbara Yale-Read

Interior Book Design: Doug Burnett

NCTE Stock Number 52686-3050

© 1992 by the National Council of Teachers of English. All rights reserved. Printed in the United States of America.

It is the policy of NCTE in its journals and other publications to provide a forum for the open discussion of ideas concerning the content and the teaching of English and the language arts. Publicity accorded to any particular point of view does not imply endorsement by the Executive Committee, the Board of Directors, or the membership at large, except in announcements of policy, where such endorsement is clearly specified.

Library of Congress Cataloging-in-Publication Data

Teacher as writer: entering the professional conversation / edited by Karin L. Dahl with the Committee on Professional Writing Networks for Teachers and Supervisors.
      p. cm.
   Includes bibliographical references.
   ISBN 0-8141-5268-6
    1. Authorship—Handbooks, manuals, etc. 2. Teachers as authors. 3. Teaching. 4. Educational publishing—Handbooks, manuals, etc. I. Dahl, Karin L., 1938– . II. National Council of Teachers of English. Committee on Professional Writing Networks for Teachers and Supervisors.
PN147.T328 1992
808'.02'024372—dc20
                                               92–4182
                                                 CIP

Dedicated to the memory of Eileen Tway

Eileen Tway served as a charter member of the Committee on Professional Writing Networks for Teachers and Supervisors, the National Council of Teachers of English. She supported the committee's early work and advocated its production of a book that would support the writing of teachers. For many of the contributing authors in this volume, she served as a mentor and guide. She is remembered as a teacher who shared her knowledge with others through writing and as a steadfast advocate for aspiring authors.

Contents

Contents

Foreword

Thomas Newkirk
University of New Hampshire

Where was this book when I really needed it? My own professional writing proceeded by trial and error (mostly the latter): trying to fathom why some work was published and some was not, trying to read my rejection letters without feeling totally inadequate—or just plain mad. *Teacher as Writer* is not only a book of sound advice; it is a book of moving stories by teachers who recreate themselves as they discover that their own earned knowledge and insight can matter to other teachers. It calls to mind my own first publication in *English Journal* and editor Stephen Tchudi's letter, which I must have read twenty times—I even ran my hand over the paper. And then to see my name (in what seemed like huge marquee-size letters) in the journal a few months later was a thrill that later publications could not match.

I have watched other teachers take that step, and through edited collections like *Understanding Writing* and *Breaking Ground* I have coaxed a number into print. Yet while collections of teacher essays are more common now, and while journals are doing more to seek out teachers' writing, the process of writing has never been as well explained as it is in this volume. The National Council of Teachers of English and members of its Committee on Professional Writing Networks for Teachers and Supervisors, especially committee chairs Gail Tompkins and Karin Dahl, should be congratulated on producing (and in many cases contributing to) this fine collection.

The book caused me to consider the lives teachers lead, particularly the impediments to the kind of professional involvement that this book encourages. The stories of the teachers here are testimony to the possibilities of reflective work even in the midst of hectic job demands. But I would guess that even for many contributors to this book, it took some extraordinary juggling to find the time and energy to write as they have. To mix my metaphors, it took considerable swimming against the current, which in most U.S. schools is not in the direction of professional reflection. Schools, by and large, are not good places for teachers to learn.

Teachers surely need to be encouraged to swim against this current, but we also need to work to change that current. I believe that the questions about reflective practice and professional writing (handled so well in this book) need to be embedded in the broader questions of structural change in schools, particularly the high school. For example, I recently received a letter from a graduate of our master's program who is in her second year of teaching high school English; the year is going well, but she is nearly overwhelmed with her 171 students. Another New York City teacher in our program is going back to classes as large as 40 students. What mental energy—let alone time—is left for these teachers to write professionally?

These high teacher-student ratios are partly due to budget problems, but they are also caused by the school structure that segments a day into seven, eight, or nine short time periods. Sizer's *Horace's Compromise* (1984) suggests promising ways of restructuring time in the school day by consolidating subjects into four areas, thereby reducing the number of students seen by a teacher—and increasing the time spent with each. If the current is to move in the right direction, the possibility of reflective practice—including teachers writing about their work—must be connected with the issue of structural change in schools.

The same issue is relevant for the elementary school. Does the structure of the school day enable or impede teacher learning and reflection? Certainly one impediment is teacher isolation. When I taught in a high school I was amazed at how infrequently teachers visited each other's classes; surely the situation was better in the elementary school. I'm now convinced, however, that the situation is worse in many elementary schools: teachers rarely visit each other, even within the same school. If teachers are to write, they must believe that what they do matters to other teachers; so long as they are isolated they will never gain this sense of having something to contribute. Isolation also tends to "naturalize" the practices of teachers; when we only see our own way of doing things, that approach comes to seem as inevitable as the August collapse of the Red Sox.

A number of writers in this collection speak of creating positive learning environments for students in their classrooms. How can we make schools into the same kind of productive learning environments for teachers? In my view, this will necessitate teachers questioning the anachronism of the typical school schedule and seeking alternatives. It will mean creating opportunities for teachers to teach teachers. It will mean the end of inservice programs that treat teachers as passive receptacles, and it will mean more opportunities for them to develop their creative abilities as so many have done in national and local writing projects. All of these are political issues, and at its root I feel the issue of teacher research and publication is a political one. It deals with what counts as knowledge and who, in Glenda Bissex's words, can claim "to know, and be known as an authority" (Bissex & Bullock, 1987, p. 17).

Even the stories we tell may need to be more political. A number of the authors here advise prospective writers to focus on the specific, on stories of their work with students. Good advice, surely. But one limitation of teacher research is the way the world outside the classroom has often been bracketed out. It is as if the classroom is a separate island of learning, unaffected by the institutional setting. I want to raise the question whether this bracketing can play into a very conservative and minimal model of school change, one that leaves the basic structures (subjects, schedule, grading, grouping) intact. Let me explain.

I believe that conservatives love the archetypal story of the teacher hero; movies like *Dead Poets Society* and *Stand and Deliver* or, a while back, *To Sir with Love,* have particular appeal because they suggest that a kind of teacher heroism can resurrect learning without any major structural change in schools. We simply need more teacher heroes. These stories do inspire and they are important, but I worry that they can also lead to a political quiescence (in the same way that George Bush's "thousand points of light" are a substitute for fundamental political change). If our teacher research becomes another version of the teacher heroism story and does not look beyond the classroom, by default we will leave the system intact and unquestioned, or, worse, we will leave reform in the hands of politicians and administrators eager to centralize authority.

I hope this book will be a step in not only empowering teachers to describe their own practices, but to speculate and work toward schools that are good learning environments for teachers, schools where the kind of reflection and writing described in this book is the norm and not a heroic act. Politicians with their vacuous talk of standards and vouchers cannot create these environments. Teachers can.

In *Horace's Compromise*, Sizer describes a dinner with Horace, a high school English teacher. Horace is bitter about the "Outside Influentials" who will decide on the solution to "the Current High School Crisis." He's seen these crises come and go. But Sizer writes:

> The empowerment of Horace would make a difference. Underneath his defensiveness, he knows that. For some reason, we start comparing the U.S. Army's top-down activities to the Viet Cong peasant army.

> Could Horace be a peasant soldier? We slide off the analogy: it isn't right. But he persists in this direction. If I had my way . . . he goes on. It all rings right, because Horace knows he could find a way to improve each student's self-esteem, how standards could be raised, how sloppy routines could be shaped up. I leave our dinner knowing Horace is the key. (Sizer, 1984, pp. 200–201)

Teachers are the key, and *Teacher as Writer* will help and encourage readers to take that major step toward empowerment by asserting the significance of knowledge gained through daily work with students. My hope is that readers won't stop there, that they will form the peasant army Horace spoke of, that they will work to create schools that are good learning environments for students—and for teachers.

References

Bissex, G.L., & Bullock, R.H. (Eds.). (1987). *Seeing for ourselves*. Portsmouth, NH: Heinemann.

Sizer, T.R. (1984). *Horace's compromise*. Boston: Houghton Mifflin.

1 Introduction: Old Habits, New Conversations

Karin L. Dahl
The Ohio State University

Habit is habit, and not to be flung out of the window by any man, but coaxed downstairs a step at a time.

Mark Twain, *The Tragedy of Pudd'nhead Wilson
and the Comedy of the Extraordinary Twins*

The time has come to coax some old habits of thinking downstairs, ways of thinking that have become costly and unproductive. Two candidates come to mind, both being habits that have prevented our learning from each other. The first is the separation of educators' roles, seeing teachers as exclusively school-based practitioners and professors as theory-bound researchers separated from the reality of schooling. The second is differential valuing of knowledge, privileging only the knowledge gained in the classroom or trusting only information that is tagged "research-based." The first habit has kept us from working together with ease and the second from broadening our ways of knowing.

This book is about moving from these old habits and engaging in new conversations. It invites teachers to share their knowledge and suggests that professional journals are a likely catalyst for expanded exchanges of information. Our journals serve as a kind of professional conversation in print, a conversation that requires the voice, perspectives, and insights of teachers. Teacher writers tell the educational community information it simply does not hear from other sources (Bloome, 1989; Goswami & Stillman, 1987). The published observations, reflections, and responses of teachers expand the profession's sense of the realities of teaching and enable educators to see learners in action. Such writing allows the field to consider the information it needs and sharpens understanding of classrooms and learning.

From a teacher's perspective, writing for educational publication provides a way to reach beyond the walls of the classroom and not only share insights but make sense of new information. While some would argue that professional writing is an unrealistic expectation and that teachers have neither the time nor inclination to write (Jost, 1990), others suggest a different perspective. Rick Monroe, a teacher from Seattle, explains, "I write because I need to understand myself and others, because I want to be a part of, even help shape, the printed professional conversation" (Chapter 8, this collection).

As teachers place themselves in the role of writers, they become consumers of professional literature and creators of new information about teaching. To participate in the professional conversation is to shape its topics and focus—to change and be changed by its information and differing points of view.

This book, therefore, is directed to the expanded professional conversation. Rather than being a handbook for teachers about writing for publication, the book directs its attention more broadly. Our purpose is to suggest possibilities for teachers interested in writing for professional journals, to coax educators away from old habits, and to encourage teacher voices in the new conversation.

The contributors to this volume are teachers, professors, directors of writing projects, editors, and researchers; each has extensive experience in writing for journals. Some teach in elementary schools, others in secondary schools or universities, and all are writers with a history of dedication to the writer's craft.

From the Author's Perspective

The book begins with well-published teachers describing their writing experiences. Their chapters are about personal journeys as writers and individual ways of writing.

Tom Romano writes about voice, tracing his own history as a writer of poetry across adolescence and through teaching and parenting. Nancy Gorrell accounts for her work by considering writing as a renewal process. She recounts her growth as various articles were written. Betty Van Ryder provides an account of her writing progress within a writing group. She illustrates the kinds of help she receives with an evolving draft and shows the revisions she makes based on group members' suggestions. The chapters by Cora Lee Five, Jay Simmons, and Vera Milz examine the interplay between teaching and writing for publication. These teacher writers describe how they combine their roles and how they manage the process of writing in the midst of their classroom obligations.

Thinking Like a Writer

The collection continues with a general rationale for writing professionally. Chapters describe the contributions that teacher writers make and also explore the impact of writing on teachers' professional lives. Drawing on literature about teacher writers, Chris Crowe describes what teachers gain when they write. He interviews several writers and presents their responses to being published. Among the benefits of writing, he explains, are a deeper understanding of the writing process and increased credibility with students.

Rick Monroe and Rod Winters, both classroom teachers, describe their reasons and motivations for writing. Across Rick Monroe's history of publications the theme of writing to resolve professional issues is important. Monroe documents his growth as a writer through the issues that emerge in his teaching. Rod Winters contends that teachers write for themselves, for their sense of identity, and for professional growth as they confront their own professional uncertainties. He presents a redefinition of teaching as learning and addresses the questions of who professional writing is for, what it is, and how it relates to personal writing and a teacher's sense of self.

The section closes with Alan Frager's piece about thinking like a writer. Moving beyond reasons for writing, Frager addresses the kinds of reading prospective writers need to do. He suggests that professional writing entails reading professional journals with an author's eye. Extensive critical reading in journals is recommended for insights on topics, writing purposes, audiences, and stylistic devices.

From the Editor's Perspective

Shifting to the journals' perspective, the third section presents information from current and past editors of national and regional journals. Ken Donelson, former editor of *English Journal*, summarizes what makes a good article and suggests an array of topics that teachers might consider. Ben Nelms, current editor of *English Journal*, outlines what *EJ* looks for in articles and provides advice about preparing manuscripts. William Teale, current editor of *Language Arts*, describes how editors consider and make decisions about manuscripts. He presents information about a year's worth of *LA* manuscripts, describing acceptance and rejection rates and rationales. And finally, Alice Swinger, an affiliate journal editor, describes what happens to a manuscript when it reaches an editor—the reviewing process and guidelines for authors.

Essential Information for Teacher Writers

The next section presents a range of information and strategies for teacher writers. Taking the reader from the inception of an article to the point where the piece is ready for submission, Gail Tompkins walks the writer through each phase. Details for submitting an article are described, including what to say in a cover letter (a sample is provided) and what to send along with the manuscript.

Chris Anson and Bruce Maylath describe the process of choosing an appropriate journal for a particular piece. They argue that journal selection needs to occur when the author is getting ready to write, and they describe ways to select wisely. Recognizing the vast number of journals from which to choose, they categorize journals by audience and general range of topics, then provide a comprehensive listing of information about a wide range of journals—the kinds of pieces published, intended audience, rejection rates, and typical length of published articles.

Margaret Deitrich offers strategies for beating the odds—not only choosing journals wisely, but using other reference materials, building one's own list of journals, and making writing more vivid with classroom vignettes and examples of student work.

Recognizing that many writers work at the computer, Thelma Kibler describes how she manages the drafting and revising process. Rather than scratching out drafts on yellow legal tablets, she fast-drafts and revises on the computer, taking bigger risks and combining information from several files. Kibler, a computer convert, lists the ways computers support the writer's craft and provides guidelines for generating and preserving text.

The Craft of Writing for Publication

The fifth part of the book addresses practical considerations for teacher writers—selecting a topic, crafting leads, making decisions, revising drafts, and even coping with rejection. The section begins with a discussion of what teachers write about, that is, where they find their topics. Renée Casbergue and Patricia Austin survey well-published teacher writers and recount the ways they select topics.

Eileen Tway, in her chapter on "beginnings," outlines some ways to write leads. She offers four alternatives: anecdotes, provocative questions, quotations, and challenges, and provides examples of each. Showing how writers go about drafting and choosing among these alternatives, she addresses not only how leads get written, but also how writers begin writing.

Four additional chapters in this section address the writer's concerns during drafting and revising. Doris Prater asserts that writers have decisions to make: what the article will be about, how the piece will be organized, who the audience is, and who the speaker is. Using an article published in *Language Arts,* Prater shows how each decision is resolved.

In their chapter on revision, Lea McGee and Gail Tompkins describe specific strategies that writers use to distance themselves from their texts and shape the writing into finished manuscripts. They argue that revision includes rethinking a piece: seeing the text that is actually written in light of the one intended, and thinking about the text that could be written.

Karen Feathers continues the conversation on revision by demonstrating specific ways to add, delete, substitute, and rearrange text. She lists the questions that she asks herself as she considers particular revisions and shows how her text changes.

Another important aspect of the writer's craft is coping with rejection. Alice Swinger presents the coping strategies of successful writers throughout the country. Her chapter reports how these authors handle rejection, what rejection contingency plans they make, and what happens to the rejected manuscript itself. Rejection responses range from "I sulk for a week" to "I do not take rejections too seriously. . . . The piece itself may be very good, only sent to the wrong place at the wrong time." Most writers say that they read reviewers' suggestions and use them in rethinking the manuscript, and many writers report having three to five additional journals in mind as alternatives in case of rejection.

Teacher Writer Communities

The final section of the book presents a variety of support systems and roles that influence and often motivate writing. These include writing communities and writing projects as well as various collaborative relationships. The section presents information about writing groups, pairs of writers collaborating, and teachers working in the role of teacher researcher.

Chapter 26 traces the development of the Bay Area Writing Project as one of the more significant influences upon teacher writing. Mary K. Healy presents this history and also describes her experiences in the University of California English Credential Program and the Puente Project.

Noting that various collaborative relationships support the writing process, Russel Durst, in his chapter on writing groups, and Jill Dillard and I, in our chapter on collaborative writing, describe the benefits of working together. For teachers wishing to write on a continuing basis, writing groups create internal deadlines and a context for writing. Durst describes his own writing-group experiences and outlines specifically how teachers can establish and participate in such groups. He notes that writers learn about revision as they make recommendations about the writing of others.

Working as collaborating authors, Jill Dillard and I describe specific drafting strategies that collaborating writers use. Our chapter includes techniques for writing together used by five well-known pairs of writers: Jane Hansen and Donald Graves, Lisa Ede and Andrea Lunsford, Chet Laine and Lucy Schultz, Cora Lee Five and Martha Rosen, and Chris Clark and Robert Yinger.

Shifting the discussion to still another kind of support community, Marilyn Cochran-Smith and Susan Lytle suggest that teacher researchers have special needs as writers. They present a definition of teacher research and discuss obstacles that constrain this activity in schools. They also develop a conceptual framework for creating communities for teacher research and outline the kinds of writing that are involved as such communities function.

An Invitation for Teacher Writers

Looking across the book as a whole, these authors assert that writing for publication is a promising avenue for teachers. In thinking like a writer, teachers experience personal growth and increased professional influence. In exploring new roles as teacher researchers or writing-community members, teachers find support for their writing and gain an expanded sense of what can be written. And finally, in looking toward the journals themselves, teachers find a consistent pattern of interest in teacher-written pieces.

References

Bloome, D. (1989). Introduction. In D. Bloome (Ed.), *Classrooms and literacy* (pp. 1–29). Norwood, NJ: Ablex.

Goswami, D., & Stillman, P. (1987). *Reclaiming the classroom.* Upper Montclair, NJ: Boynton/Cook.

Jost, K. (1990). Why high-school writing teachers should not write. *English Journal, 79*(3), 65–66.

I From the Author's Perspective

2 Evolving Voice

Tom Romano
Utah State University

Voice. I should have known that my look into teacher as writer would come at last to voice. After many years writing and almost as many years working with writers—children, teenagers, and adults—voice has always been in the forefront. Sometimes bold, sometimes timid, even using a lowercase *I*, voice defines a writer. It is a point of growth. It changes and evolves. Voice follows the contours of the talk surrounding us, of the talk we engage in with others. Voice is shaped by our reading—the early books of our childhood through the books we read today. I believe this, because my mother sent me a notebook I'd owned as an adolescent and I got a look at an early evolutionary stage of my voice.

The words in that notebook brought to life a me of more than twenty years earlier. I remembered that I had loved poetry as a high school student. I didn't spread the word about that, of course, not as a member of the football and baseball teams. When I read poems, though, I connected with language and rhythm and sound and meaning. In my favorite poems the words meant something deeply to me, and the saying aloud of those words was pleasurable. When my high school English teacher presented us with her favorite passages of poetry to memorize, I took to the task gladly, even though the words she had responded to were not always the ones I had responded to. To meet my personal needs, I picked out my own passages to learn by heart. On tests, after I'd written the lines my teacher needed us to memorize, I added the ones that I needed to memorize. Although Mrs. R never awarded me bonus points for my extra-duty memorizing, she didn't object to it.

On one occasion, however, I thought she might object, so I didn't write down one of the passages I'd learned. The voice and the meaning of the lines were meant for me alone, anyway. I was eighteen then, and in serious, dangerous love. The girl I was in love with had broken up with me in February of that year and left me in a prolonged, spiraling funk. When I read John Keats in English class, he who had died so young—too soon, like my own father—John Keats, who had loved Fanny Brawne more than she had loved him, Mrs. R didn't have to assign me lines to memorize. I had already picked some out. I memorized the closing lines from the sonnet "Bright Star" that John Keats, dead nearly 150 years, had surely written just for me in 1967:

No—yet still stedfast, still unchangeable,
    Pillow'd upon my fair love's ripening breast,
To feel for ever its soft fall and swell,
    Awake for ever in a sweet unrest,
Still, still to hear her tender-taken breath,
And so live ever—or else swoon to death.

This voice spoke hard, eloquent truth to me, as though Keats had suffered my teenage loss and pain and longing and knew exactly how to use words to articulate the depth of my feelings. His words have stayed with me more than twenty years now, and I've never forgotten what *swoon* meant.

How had Keats reached me a century and a half after he'd written "Bright Star"? Like me, he also had cared for a girl with a consuming, constant love. He had known the powerful fusion of flesh and intellect. But Keats hadn't reached me merely because my experience was similar to his. There was something more involved, something that made experience live, something that made it ever new. Keats had quickened my pulse because he had "given primary allegiance to the language" and to his own experience with it (Stafford, 1986, p. 59). "Bright Star" had been true for me in 1967 because John Keats had been true to language in 1819. Because of that allegiance, his experience assumed life. His perception attained urgency. And his voice traveled years.

When spring came during my senior year of high school, I still dwelt in a fairly common—but very real—brand of teenage melancholy from losing my girl. May arrived and we began our senior English projects; I did mine over John Keats, naturally, throwing myself into the research and writing, the work both homage to Keats and tribute to the girl I loved. Years later, I realized that, above all, I had done the project for myself. In learning about John Keats maybe I could learn about Tom Romano. And maybe I could begin to meet the deep need I had to work out my loss—the loss of the girl, the loss of my father three years earlier, maybe also the loss of a time of my life

"Bright Star" reprinted by permission of the publishers from *The Poems of John Keats* edited by Jack Stillinger, Cambridge, Mass.: The Belknap Press of Harvard University Press, Copyright © 1978 by the President and Fellows of Harvard College.

I was leaving forever. And it was through reading and writing that I rode out of the slough. Those spring days marked a passage, both brutal and crucial, my personal adolescent experience of coming through slaughter.

I wrote my first poem a week after graduation. In school I'd had only one classroom opportunity to write poetry, and that came in fifth grade when the teacher instructed us to write poems. I don't remember reading any poetry in her class. No immersion in poetic voices. We'd had no talk or teaching about choosing topics or how to write verse. All we had was the directive to write poetry. When the day came for us to read our poems, no boy had written one except Davy.

> Davy, who couldn't hit a softball out of the infield
> couldn't catch a ten-yard screen pass
> couldn't run without splayed feet.
> Davy.
> It figured, I thought.

And Davy would have raised his eyebrows in smug surprise had he seen me seven years later, a week after high school graduation, sitting at a small desk in the kitchen, laboring to express some truth I felt about love and loss. For months I had been unconsciously rehearsing the subject matter. And when it came time to write, I called upon the rhythms and language that were in my head from three years of reading poetry in high school, all of which had been written by poets before 1900, with the exception of Robert Frost and Joyce Kilmer. No Whitman, though, or Dickinson, but plenty of Longfellow, Whittier, and Poe, Poe, Poe.

As I sat at that tiny desk in grim seriousness, I grappled with genuine emotions of grief and loss and regret. The emotions arose from unique experience, unforgettable images, and one-of-a-kind language that the girl and I had spoken to each other. The emotions were timeless, and they were mine. The language and rhythms and notions of poetry in my head, however, were from another time. The poetic voices I'd come to know as models were not ones that validated my 1967 adolescent voice:

> He who has tasted wine,
> Can never be satisfied with less,
> So whatever be my life's success
> My heart shall always be thine.
> Though I am not the first to pine
> For a love that had been so divine,

The longing and sorrow which around my heart is lain
Has become the foundation for unending pain.
Her touch was as soft as a new fallen snow
And her radiant smile was surpassed by an inner glow.
Since the days of her wine all others are sour
And my mortuous despair increases by the hour,
O for a basic mind and a heart of stone
That I may live peacefully alone.

Recently, I shared this poem with high school seniors as we began three weeks of concentrated work writing poetry. I placed the poem on an overhead transparency and read it aloud. There followed noticeable silence, a few smiles, some snickers, and a number of serious faces.

"*Unending pain,*" Rosanna finally said. "Man, that's a long time!"

"What's this *thine* and *pine* business?" asked Stephanie.

"*Mortuous?*" said Eric. "I never heard that before. Is it a real word?"

Krissy articulated the central problem. Though the despair behind the poem had been honest enough, the voice had come right out of Mark Twain's Emmeline Grangerford school of poetry writing: "You know," said Krissy, "that doesn't sound like *anybody* I know."

It didn't sound like anybody I knew, either. And it certainly didn't sound like anybody I had known twenty-odd years earlier.

In her book about teaching poetry writing, *For the Good of the Earth and Sun* (1989), Georgia Heard often asks children if what they have on the page matches what they have in their hearts. In 1967 I probably would have answered that yes, I'd created a match, for the voice that I'd written in was a sincere attempt to emulate the poetic voices my required reading in high school had sanctioned.

James Britton has written that "trying other people's voices may for the adolescent be a natural and necessary part of the process of finding one's own" (Britton, 1970, p. 262). That is instructive and comforting to me, both as teacher and evolving writer. And, it makes me take on greater resolve to include contemporary poetic voices as a significant part of the literary experiences of students.

When I became a high school English teacher in 1971, though, I taught many of the same poems I had been taught. The traditional canon—at least the bit of it a textbook company had decided upon—lived on in my classroom. I couldn't teach the entire canon, of course. I didn't have time, in fact, to teach the entire textbook—which was, back then, the course of study, too.

Neither did I read contemporary poetry, nor did I invite students to write poems. Frankly, I was afraid of poetry I had to face without a teacher's manual. College education had awakened that fear in me. Louise Rosenblatt's transactional theory of reader response was not the dominant pedagogy of my college literature classes. I learned to keep my mouth shut to avoid looking foolish. The professor, I knew, would reveal to me what a good English major ought to think.

Although as a teacher I lectured on traditional poetry, I didn't teach the writing of poems. I was smart enough to shy away from such fraudulence. I didn't know the first thing about poetic composition. I wasn't a participant myself in writing contemporary poetry. I didn't have an inside view of what it was like to launch forth and make a poem.

In 1977 one of my former students spent her senior year at Interlochen Arts Academy in Michigan. She studied music there and also took a course in feminist literature. She sent me a copy of the *Interlochen Review*, a book-like journal of poetry and fiction by the high school students. After reading fifty pages, I rose from my chair, went to my desk, took out my journal, and wrote a draft of a poem I'd been prewriting for thirteen years, ever since the death of my father. I wrote of the events in his life, imagining his days as a boy in Italy before he and his family emigrated to the United States. The composing let me comprehend things about my father that I'd been trying to understand since his death. It was language that let me do this, that let me ride its rhythm to personal meaning. And it was the reading of contemporary voices that had set free my voice to do it.

My Interlochen connection—and thank the Muses that our students help us to see—spurred me to more reading when she loaned me two volumes of poems by Marge Piercy. Her precise, metaphorical voice and modern subject matter enabled me to see possibilities for my own writing. I began reading more modern poetry, bought small-press poetry publications, and learned that it was only in truly good bookstores that I could find them. So much good writing is published by these small presses, like the University of Pittsburgh Press, the Carnegie Mellon University Press, Milkweed Editions, and the University of Massachusetts Press. Yet few people experience the excellent poems such publishers gather.

Before I began the habit of reading contemporary poetic voices, I was daily in the company of a natural metaphor maker, an unpretentious poet who saw the world new each day with responsive eyes. For her the world was a marvelous curiosity shop. When I served hamburgers for supper, I learned that the catsup-soaked top of the bun was a delicious "sweet lid." I learned that smoke rings were doughnuts, that umbrellas were more properly termed "rainbrellas," and that the fountain in the middle of the shopping mall was not a fountain at all, but rather "jumping water."

My young daughter was trying to let me see. In my journal— the place where I was reckless and honest and unfettered with language and thinking, the place where I learned to write—I wrote down her metaphorical connections. Her inventiveness was enriching and revitalizing my own conventional way of seeing.

In *Language and Learning* James Britton noted that young children have no choice but to be poets:

> There are other similarities between poetry and young children's speech. Poets tend to look for significant, evocative detail— something straight out of life—to carry their meaning, and to avoid the vaguely general or abstract term. . . . With young children it is not a matter of choice: their ideas must take a relatively concrete form of expression because they have not yet mastered the art of making and handling abstractions. A five-year-old boy in an infants' class once said to a colleague of mine, "Oh, yes, I know Geography. It's polar bears at the top and penguins at the bottom!" (Britton, 1970, p. 155)

I slowly absorbed the implicit poetic model my daughter so effortlessly provided. And I began writing poems that reflected the contemporary models I was reading. I found a rhythm in my voice and tried to follow it with faith and fearlessness.

These days, I often will a poem into existence when I write along with my students. In such instances, nothing is particularly gnawing on me to be written, but I join students in brainstorming ideas and mapping out possibilities, nonetheless. Sometimes, however, a poem wells in me from an intense moment of emotion; sometimes an image stays with me like a color slide stuck in a projector; sometimes a metaphor blazes in my mind, suddenly obvious and true; sometimes a memory looms up vividly after years of dormancy, and I must write to discover what it means.

However the spark of an idea arrives, I try "to write in a gush," as Whitman recommended (Wallace, 1982, pp. 284–286), with little regard to anything but meaning. Later, after this stage of acceptance and growth, I gladly take Maxine Kumin's advice to "pound and hammer the poem into shape and into form" (Kumin, 1979, p. 23), an organic form that language and I collaborate upon as we both evolve. Over the course of days or weeks, often months, the poem changes under my pen.

The writing changes me, too. I am different from having written poems. A better man, I think.

Although I often will poems when I write with students, the poems I'm most satisfied with evolve from a line that says itself to me. A whisper in my ear. A quiet voice deep in my mind. Meaning and rhythmical language come together. The voice beckons to be explored and elaborated. Unlike the first lines of articles, proposals, or reports that I usually alter during revision, the first lines of incipient poems that say themselves to me I do not change. At least I haven't yet.

One such opening line that I listened to was this: "My daughter wassa poem." I heard it just like that, orthographic variation and all. I knew that soon I would join my students in a day of drafting, of excavation into the psyche with language as our working tool. I knew that the subject matter of that first line was my daughter's use of metaphorical language some thirteen years earlier. And, of late, I had felt a link between that time and her life now as a teenager, the last ingredient that enabled my subconscious to meld language and meaning.

The link had been forged when my daughter brought home an assignment from school. She had responded in writing to a chapter from her history book. Here is an excerpt from the paper: "The American people just seemed to be a group of unruly children. Nothing the king said really bothered them much at all. There were civil wars between different colonies, because of petty disputes over boundaries. Even different sections of colonies were at odds. The government sat back and watched like a lazy babysitter."

For days I mentally carried around "My daughter wassa poem." I let my subconscious work with language, image, and meaning. Something—a poem, I hoped—was building in me. When the day came to write with the class, I sat down in one of the student desks, wrote the first line at the top of a yellow legal pad, and proceeded to catalog the metaphors my daughter had made as a child, the ones I'd written in my journal years before. I didn't worry about how the figurative language fit together; I just produced in a gush. And in trying to catch my daughter's serious playfulness, I found myself playing with language and images.

The students and I worked on our poems for several days, conferring with each other, expanding and deleting, developing focus, thinking twice about word choice. Finally, I took a number of the poems-in-progress, including mine, typed them without the names of the poets, and made photocopies for the class. We read the poems aloud, and talked about language and rhythm and meaning. Occasionally, the author of the poem joined the dialectic, and we talked about how the poet's language matched her or his vision and the responses of the flesh-and-blood readers.

We talked about my poem, too, about the delightful metaphors my daughter had created. I found myself saying why her speech and insights as a child were so important to me. The talk with the students and their questions made me articulate my experience—emotion and intellect combining for the best kind of cognition. This evolving poem embodied what I believed about language, creativity, and individual vision. It was the most recent example in a long line of personally important subject matter that I'd written about as my voice evolved over the years. Whether I wrote a poem about my Italian immigrant father I'd barely gotten to know or about teenage writers I'd come to know well, the interaction of language, perception, and experience provided exercise for my voice and furthered its development.

Seeing the words of my poem typed and put before the eyes of my students made me think that *wassa* was no longer important in the poem and that, perhaps, it distracted the reader from the larger playfulness of the figurative language. I decided to drop it. Even though the word wouldn't be part of the final product, I wasn't sentimental about seeing it go. I knew the great worth of *wassa*. It and the line it helped form had played a crucial role in the process of launching the poem. That was noble enough work for any word.

I told the students about my word choice plan. After class, several of them trooped up to my desk and informed me that they thought *wassa* worked very well and that I should keep that childlike spelling in the poem. I listened to the talk, and like Peter Elbow's owl that eats a mouse whole, digests only what is good for it and gets rid of what isn't (Elbow, 1973, pp. 102–103), I took in all the comments, not defending, but listening. Ultimately, I would decide for myself what to do.

As an ending for the poem, I had used the entire excerpt from my daughter's homework assignment about the colonists. At home I read the poem to her while she sat on the floor, listening patiently, even though she was overdue to make a telephone call to a friend. She liked the poem, she said, but thought the ending was too long, "too dragged out," as she put it. As soon as she said that, I knew it was true. She had given words to an imbalance I'd felt in my bones.

I worked with the poem for several weeks, deleting and adding words, altering rhythm, and shaping meaning with the voice I'd come to after nearly forty years. It's a voice I know well, a voice that has grown from my reading, my perception, my place in life. It harks back to the speech of my childhood. It reflects the current speech of my adulthood. With this voice I am able to see and learn and write. The voice is not just the sound of my speech or the cadence of my words on a page. My voice is the way I think, too. It limits me; it empowers me. And it's mine. As years pass, it will continue to evolve, just as life does, ever onward and outward. Respected and nourished and used, voice is a source of pleasure, insight, and invention for us. Voice enables us to write our letters, plays, essays, fictions, and poems. Language collaborates with flash of image, with unmistakable felt sense, with sudden sound or smell or taste. And if we respond to the urging of language and experience, our voice gets on the page.

Poetics
for Mariana

My daughter was a poem.
She'd waken early, kneel near my
sleepface, wait for my eyes.
One flutter and milkbreath whispered,
"Papa, will you get me cereal?"

Yes, my daughter was a poem.
"Get your pipe," she'd say.
"Get your pipe and blow doughnuts."

That was eons ago, before fashion,
when she knew without doubt that
the shopping mall held
but one point of interest:
the spout and splash of the
jumping water.

Oh, she was a poem, all right.
We walked the neighborhood then,
she knew enough to clasp my finger.
The daisy's petals, she told me, were eyelashes,
then asked the name of the drifty-looking tree.

Yes, my daughter was a poem and I swear that
she
    (along with all poems that age)
should win perpetual Pew Lit Surprises.
When she was three feet (with no rhyme),
she saw that Saturday morning pancake flour
was really dust of snow.

"Poetics" by Tom Romano first appeared in *Language Arts, 65*(8), p. 810. Copyright © 1988 by the National Council of Teachers of English. Reprinted by permission.

On wet days we opened rainbrellas.
To soothe sore throats we sucked coughdrips.

Yes, my daughter was a poem
and may still be . . .
you see, her heart,
though carefully incognito now,
lets slip glimpses of that older identity.

She drags her weary teenage bones
home from expository school,
punches on the stereo, tables
books, folders, and a jumble of papers.
Amid the turmoil,
sticking from the pages of her history book,
a tattered fragment from a hurried essay:
"The colonists fought among themselves
like unruly children,
and King George sat back and watched—
just like a lazy babysitter."

Is a poem.

References

Britton, J. (1970). *Language and learning*. Harmondsworth, Middlesex, England: Penguin Books.

Elbow, P. (1973). *Writing without teachers*. New York: Oxford University Press.

Heard, G. (1989). *For the good of the earth and sun*. Portsmouth, NH: Heinemann.

Kumin, M. (1979). *To make a prairie: Essays on poets, poetry, and country living*. Ann Arbor: University of Michigan Press.

Stafford, W. (1986). *You must revise your life*. Ann Arbor: University of Michigan Press.

Wallace, R. (1982). *Writing poems*. Boston: Little, Brown and Company.

3 A Teacher's Story of Renewal

Nancy Gorrell
Morristown High School, New Jersey

Have you ever published anything?" The eyes were expressive and probing.

"No, I really haven't," was all I could reply. The question was natural. I had just given a pep talk to my creative writing class about the value of publication. I had posted on the back bulletin board all the major writing competitions and literary magazines for high school students.

"Why, Mrs. Gorrell? Why?"

"Well, I guess I haven't tried." My response startled even me. I felt a sudden sense of shame and hypocrisy as the "practice what you preach" adage quickly came to mind.

"But your writings are so good," the student persisted.

For over ten years I had been writing along with my students in this creative writing elective. I had frequently used my own writings as models for their memory pieces, stories, and poems. Yes, they had always been an appreciative audience. I knew they liked my childhood memories, especially when eighth-period students would beg me to read what third period had heard "about the time you wrecked the garden with Herbie." But I had never recognized my own value as a writer. They were my students, so naturally I assumed they enjoyed hearing my work. Would they have said otherwise?

Shortly after that unsettling episode, I was sitting in the department office gazing over a colleague's desk when I noticed a photocopied poem I had distributed to my classes the week before. Curious, I asked, "Mary, where did you get that poem?"

"Oh," she exclaimed with rare enthusiasm, "this is a fantastic poem. We just spent a whole period talking about it!" When I mentioned that this poem was central to a lesson I taught the week before, she was surprised. Apparently a rather unassuming student, one we both taught, brought it into Mary's class to share during a poetry lesson. Mary was quite impressed and wondered where the student had found it. I explained that the verse was a special kind of poetry called found poetry, and that for years I had been using "Parents" to introduce poetry to my classes. Mary continued to ask for more information, and as I explained my entire lesson, I could see by her expression that I was talking about something valuable. "You know," she said as she got out of her seat to go to class, "you really ought to write that up."

And so the seed was planted. Yes, I thought to myself, maybe I should. I had never considered professional writing before. Full-time teaching while raising two small children had occupied all my time. But this was 1987, and I suddenly realized my children were older and more independent. Perhaps I could find the time. But when and how? Thus began a two-year journey of self-discovery and personal renewal, a journey that would help me evolve as a teacher writer, a journey that would transform my thinking.

Although I was a beginning writer full of insecurities and self-doubts, of one thing I was sure. I knew I was going to send my article, if written, to *English Journal* for possible publication. I had been an avid reader of *EJ* for nearly a decade and had used many ideas from other teachers. I felt inspired at the thought I might be able to contribute an article, but I wasn't sure of the best approach. Should I just write up my lesson and submit it? Or would it be better to respond to a specific *EJ* call? With that thought in mind, I looked at the 1987 calls and noticed a category involving "Responding to Literature." My lesson certainly taught how students could respond to poetry, but it was through a special kind of poetry, found poetry. Should I focus on reader-response or the genre approach of found poetry? This dilemma troubled me, and I wrestled with it. But I also felt I had to be practical and seize the moment. Why not write for the call? What did I have to lose?

I did not begin right away. After all, I was teaching 125 students, buried perennially under all those paper corrections, in addition to taking care of a family and home. How could I find the time to write? Looking back, I realize the "wait" time was critical in my evolution as a writer: strange things started to happen to me while driving to work in the morning, cleaning the house, or doing the dishes. My article, an embryo of an idea, started to grow in my consciousness. It developed a life of its own, coming to me at unsuspected moments, and I began what I felt was a dialogue with myself. The passages I composed in my mind stayed with me, and I could retrieve them and think about them again and again. I had discovered an inner world, and I began to feel a pleasure I had never felt before. I realize now it was the pleasure of connection with oneself, of finding one's inner voice. But I had not yet expressed it. No pen was set to paper, no notes typed.

It was not until mid-June, when my husband and I took a trip to Toronto for a reunion with friends, that I actually took some notes. It happened spontaneously, during one of those "dead" moments we all find ourselves with while traveling. I began to jot down bits of text—on the plane, in the car, and in the hotel room. For the entire trip, my article was "with me," and I felt the coming together of ideas in a way that I knew was preparing me to write.

When I returned home, I realized I had to hurry if I were to make *EJ*'s August 1 deadline. Early one evening, after making supper and settling the children, I sat down at the typewriter in my study. I remember the feeling I had at that first drafting session because it surprised me. The words flowed the way I had been hearing and thinking them all along, and I wrote with an ease I never thought possible, not stopping for a minute for fear I would lose momentum:

> When I first began teaching in an upper-level creative writing elective well over a decade ago, I engaged in a rather short-lived fantasy. My passion was poetry, and I dreamed of sharing my favorite poems with excited and receptive students. We would discuss poetry, inspire each other, and write poems together. I would sit in our then popular sharing circle (credits to Ken Macrorie), reading passages from T.S. Eliot's "The Love Song of J. Alfred Prufrock" while the boys' chests swelled and the girls all sighed. The reality? Silence . . . that dreadful silence, when we know in the classroom we are talking more to ourselves than anyone else. Why was it so difficult to talk about poems? Students I knew capable of animated discussions of music, film, politics, and even literature seemed tongue-tied when responding to poetry. At best, students might express "I liked it" or "I didn't like it," but they were rarely ever able to explain how or why. I knew all this had to change, but how was I to begin?

It was an odd, comforting feeling, working until 3 a.m. with the sounds of my family asleep around me. I relished the solitude, the privacy, the uninterrupted moments of thought. I was where I wanted to be, in front of that typewriter, writing, and I felt at once a sense of productivity and inner peace. When I was finished, I had written the introduction and drafted the first lesson, a comparison of the found poem "Parents" with the news article it was based upon.

I did not realize at the time the importance of the step I had taken. I only knew I had begun, and I felt a growing confidence that I just might be able to finish the task. But I was also a committed mother, and summer loomed ahead. Would I be able to do both? That July, while I sequestered myself at the typewriter, my children did just what they wanted. Those writing days turned out to be rewarding for all of us. I stopped organizing my children's lives and just began to write. They knew where they could find me if they needed me, but they rarely did. I realized we were all "growing up," and I felt a new sense of freedom and self, my writing self.

By mid-July I had completed a fifty-page manuscript entitled "Found Poetry: An Approach to Developing Poetic Response." The introduction presented a reader-response approach to poetry and the value of beginning such an approach with a particular found poem, "Parents" by Julius Lester. In the body of the manuscript, I included four lessons. The first helped answer the question, "what is poetry," through a comparison of "Parents" with the news article it was based upon. I concluded that lesson with a found poetry writing assignment for the students. Lesson two continued developing a poetic by establishing criteria upon which to base poetic response. In lesson three, a follow-up response, I compared the "not-so-poetic" found poem "Parents" to Robert Frost's highly poetic "Out, Out—." Here I suggested students paraphrase "Out, Out—"to imagine the news article it was based upon. In lesson four, I explained strategies for students to share found poems they had written. The manuscript concluded with a final note on the issue of response, as well as with several pages of students' found poems and paraphrasings.

I had written more than I had ever anticipated, and I was proud of my accomplishment. I really *did* want the article to get published. Was it possible? And suddenly, I developed the strangest fear. I hadn't done my homework. My article was based on the use of one poem. Had anyone ever written about that poem before? And what about found poetry? Had anyone ever written about its use in developing an understanding of poetry? I was overcome with the thought that I just might not be able to mail my article after all.

The word *research* now took on new meaning. I needed to know, and I needed to know quickly. The August deadline was rapidly approaching as I found myself at the reference desk of the Somerset County Public Library. "I'm writing an article on found poetry, and I need to know everything that's been written on the subject in the last thirty years." Those words were a startling revelation for me.

No sooner had I said them than I realized the meaning of my public declaration. I was a writer, and the librarian took my request seriously. She acquainted me with numerous indexes, the *Educational Index* in particular, and while I was sorting through the collection, she recommended we do a databank search on the subject. I had not conducted serious research since I completed my master's degree in history seventeen years earlier, and I was completely ignorant of computer technology.

For the next two weeks, I reveled in amazement at the advances. Within days, I had a twenty-page computer printout of all the articles written on the subject of found poetry, going back to the early 1960s. Through interlibrary loan, I had the most important monographs and manuscripts in my hands within the week. Although there were several pertinent articles, not one addressed the use of found poetry as a starting point for poetic understanding and response. Most important, no one seemed to mention "Parents." But what if someone had? How could I know? The databank search included only certain journals within the field, not every possible publication.

At this juncture, a solution presented itself in a way that still amazes me. I had read somewhere that acceptance of an article might be expedited if all the information regarding serial rights were included for the editors. I knew "Parents" would require such rights. Perhaps I could get the information? After several phone calls, I discovered the original publisher no longer existed, and the rights had been taken over by a new press. I immediately called and was referred to the person in charge of serial rights. "My," she exclaimed, "we haven't had such a request in over ten years!" Those were the words I wanted to hear. I felt assured I would be bringing something "new" to the attention of the *EJ* audience. I mailed the completed manuscript, typed by my husband's secretary, on August 1, 1987. I included a brief cover letter about myself, information concerning serial rights, and a detailed bibliography of the literature. "Even if it never gets published," I told my husband, "I know I accomplished something."

Yet, at the time I was truly unaware of the extent of that accomplishment. As a writing teacher, I knew the ability of writing to renew oneself, but I never imagined it happening to me. After mailing the manuscript, I felt a sudden down feeling. It was "over." I didn't realize I had started the workings of some inner world that would now take on a life of its own. My mind kept composing, and I felt compelled to write. I began keeping a notebook on my night table, and I found myself (a morning person) rising at 5:00 a.m. to lines of poetry. I longed for the quiet haven of my study and the clicking of the typewriter keys.

In the midst of this hiatus, a friend called just to chat. In exchanging small talk over what we were doing over the summer, I mentioned writing an article. "I didn't know you wrote!" she exclaimed. "Why don't you write an article for us?" (She was the editor of our synagogue's literary review.) "Oh no, I couldn't," I replied reflexively, "everyone will read it." To this day, I am amazed those words came out of my mouth. What a revelation: I still didn't think of myself as a writer in a public arena. And nothing could be more public than writing something personal for my local community. Yes, everyone would read it—and that scared me. But my friend persisted. The focus of the issue was travel experiences in Israel. She knew I had spent three weeks in Israel visiting my husband's family on a major kibbutz. Would I please write about it?

That week I packed my portable electric typewriter and proceeded with my family to our vacation spot in Lake Placid, New York. My typewriter sat on the kitchen table facing Mirror Lake. There were noisy moments when I wrote while my children played around me, and there were quiet moments in the early morning when I wrote gazing at the fog lifting off the lake. Nothing could be better than writing a story about family with my family all around me. I no longer felt the conflict of mother/writer. I was accepting my new self, my writing self. And my family seemed to accept it as a natural occurrence, like cooking or cleaning. In a week's time I wrote a six-page article entitled "Afi Kim: One Family's Ongoing Story." It was an introspective piece of personal reminiscence, and I remember how vulnerable I felt at the thought of public exposure. I had to reassure myself that it would receive a sympathetic audience. This too, I realized, was part of writing, and with some trepidation, I mailed it.

That fall my mailbox became an overwhelming preoccupation. Coming home from school was exciting, since I poured through the heap of mail hoping to find a letter of acceptance from *EJ*. But no letter came. Now I knew how writers felt. By the end of October (*EJ* had indicated decisions would be reached within three months), I could no longer contain myself. I picked up the phone and called. I simply asked the female voice on the other end if she knew the status of my manuscript. "Hmmm," she said, "I think it's in some committee." Just the thought they might still be considering it thrilled me. Shortly thereafter, the phone rang. It was Ben Nelms, the editor. I was more than surprised. Although my article was not accepted for the "Responding to Literature" call, he wanted me to know that everyone on the committee "thought very highly of your work." Those words were the confirmation I needed to feel I had written well. Colleagues liked my work. I felt I needed nothing more. But he continued, "Your article might be better for our February 1989 issue focusing on literary genres." I was so delighted to still be under consideration that the thought of publication a year and a half away didn't even faze me. I barely heard his final comment about the Frost poem being very costly to publish. I was soaring.

Several days passed before I realized the import of what had happened. Yes, "they" were positive, but did I really have a guarantee of publication? I knew revisions were necessary for a genre approach. If only I had done that in the first place, I thought to myself. I wrote a letter to Ben Nelms confirming our conversation, indicating several changes for the February 1989 call. I mentioned, in particular, cutting the Frost poem and the follow-up lesson which would no longer be pertinent to an article on found poetry as a genre. And then I waited.

A month later, my article on Afi Kim was printed in *Shir L'Sholom Literary Review,* and for the first time I felt the reaction of a public audience. People were interested in my family and my travels. I got many calls of inquiry about the kibbutz. But most important, I was enlightened. I learned about members of my own congregation who also had relatives living in Afi Kim. My writing had put me in touch with my community. I had a voice, and I was reaching an audience.

But it had only just begun. I continued to be an avid reader of *English Journal,* scrutinizing every call for manuscripts I could find. That year I noticed a call by the Committee on Classroom Practices of the National Council of Teachers of English for manuscripts on helping students respond to literature. Perhaps the poetry unit I had developed for my literature classes would be appropriate? Although based on teaching strategies I had developed successfully over ten years, I taught my poetry unit differently that year. In anticipation of the article, I developed a before and after poll to assess attitudes toward poetry. With the eye of a researcher, I evaluated my own teaching methods and instructions, refining the lesson for universal application. As we proceeded, I queried my students: "What worked today? What did not? Do you think other students would like to learn poetry the way I have been teaching you?" The more my students became part of my writing life, the more I felt revitalized in my teaching.

During that school year, I drafted a ten-page article about how to engage students with poetry. While teaching, my mind was composing the article, and I would steal precious moments to write, occasionally in the evenings (if I still had the energy), but mostly on the weekends in the early morning hours when I was "fresh." I finished drafting "No-Fail Poetry Unit Strategy: Teaching Aesthetic Appreciation" during April vacation when I was able to write for an extended period of time. It incorporated a reader-response approach in a four-week comprehensive unit plan. I felt pleased with the manuscript, but most important, I realized that writing was a natural consequence of my teaching. I *could* teach and write at the same time, and I felt a growing sense of myself as a teacher writer.

By June, I started to feel restless about my *EJ* article. I hadn't officially heard anything about publication, and my self-doubts started to surface. If the article were going to be accepted for a genre approach, I knew it had to be revised. I also knew it was way too long. I kept reading over the February 1989 call for manuscripts on "Writing in Literary Forms," realizing anyone else could submit an article as well. I had no guarantees. "You're not going to work on that again!" my husband pleaded. "If they want it shorter, they can edit it themselves." Although I didn't realize it at the time, I was at a critical juncture in my evolution as a writer. My husband assumed it was "work" to write all over again. He wanted to spare me. The truth was, I had no choice. My mind had been thinking through the revisions for months. I was a writer compelled to write. I couldn't wait.

That summer I learned a lot about revision. I retitled the manuscript, "Let Found Poetry Help Your Students Find Poetry," and I wrote a new introduction focusing exclusively on the poem "Parents."

> The found poem "Parents" by Julius Lester never fails to excite, provoke, and inspire my students. This gem has become the starting point for poetry reading, writing, and appreciation in all my high school English classes ever since I discovered it well over a decade ago. My students react strongly, often directing the discussion themselves. They empathize with the subject, they raise factual and poetic questions, and they respond by wanting to write their own poems. In the course of three lessons, we arrive at a poetic which provides the basis not only for instruction but for a lifetime of pleasurable response.

I also cut the manuscript in half, omitted the Frost poem and the follow-up lesson which seemed to trouble Ben Nelms, and I wrote a new conclusion stressing the enduring value of found poetry:

The enduring quality of found poetry lies in its ability to forever change students' attitudes, values, and sensibilities. Because it challenges them to find poetry in all the "wrong" places,
it continues to thrill them with those rare and elusive encounters. One year after engaging in the "Parents" lesson, a student
of mine surprised me with his own found poem discovered
while reading the *Wall Street Journal*. Just the thought that he
would continue to think poetically outside the strictures of teacher
and classroom attests to the enlightenment and sheer fun of
found poetry.

I could not have written those words the summer before. In
the interim, a former student of mine "found" and wrote one of the
most exemplary poems I had ever seen. I knew it would be the best
way to end the article. I wrote, "I believe Julius Lester would enjoy
the following result," and I concluded with only one sample of student
work, Geoff's found poem, "Veteran."

When I was finished, I knew it was practical. The cutting, however
severe, was necessary, refocusing the article from a reader-response
thesis to a genre approach. My only regret was my discarded introduction. I was particularly fond of the way I had introduced the issues
of response. It was then that my thoughts turned to the manuscript
I was still writing for the Committee on Classroom Practices. Why
not use the "discarded" introduction? It would be an ideal way to
begin a discussion of how to engage students with poetry. By August
1, I mailed both manuscripts and waited. This time I didn't wait long.
In a few weeks *EJ* accepted my revised article on found poetry (Gorrell,
1989a), and I received my first consent-to-publish form.

I was more than renewed. I felt transformed. Professional publication
confirmed what I had already begun to discover in myself. There *was*
a writer inside of me waiting to be heard, and I began to write for
myself in a way that I never had before. I was able to tap into the
inner voice I was hearing, and the poetry that used to be so hard
in coming seemed to flow. I remember one morning in particular. I
awoke to an inner voice, and it said, "It was blueberry pie." From
there came a stream of memories about baking with my grandmother,
part real, part subliminal, and I began to write with an ease I can
only compare to riding on the high crest of a wave.

When it was over, I knew it was right. It came as a rare gift
and spoke in a voice. I reveled in the joy of it and the hope that
"it" would happen again. The revisions were minimal. I knew I had
to somehow structure the prose poem, and I went with the pulse of
that inner voice.

Blueberry Pie

It was blueberry pie
and the crust was rolled
and folded and flaked and baked
and the heat of the summer day
blended with the heat of the oven
and grandma as pink as a sunset
kissed my cheek with her soft wet
cheeks and the pie splattered blue ooze
on the oven floor and there was only
blueberry air and she peeked in the oven
and it was cooking and grandma said "good"
"it will be ready soon" and she took a spoon
in one hand and me in the other and we opened
the oven door once more and the hot winds slapped
my face and grandma scraped the viscous blue and handed
me the spoon and the burning blue kissed my lips
and we smiled blue all day.

That winter, with renewed inspiration, I continued writing more poetry. I looked forward to my creative writing classes so I could write during my own poetry lessons. At the time, we were working on early childhood memories. I suggested students close their eyes and picture a place where they learned something for the first time. I said: "See that place, hear it, and feel it. Now open your eyes. Describe what happened, step by step." I found myself remembering painting in kindergarten and the reaction of a particularly harsh teacher. I wrote: "The mountainous easel stood before me, a vast matted grey sky." Recalling the awe and fear, I continued, trying to describe how the jars of paint looked to me at that moment: "Below, mouths of mayonnaise jars beckoned cavernous reds and bubbling blue whirlpools." As I wrote, the idea of creation came to me, and I knew then I had started a poem which I would finish. I called it "Kindergarten Creation," and I completed it that evening at home:

Kindergarten Creation

The mountainous easel
stood before me
a vast matted-grey sky.
Below,
mouths of mayonnaise jars
beckoned cavernous reds

and bubbling blue whirlpools.
Deep within,
forests of black timber
sprouted tall peaks,
dug roots in the red/blue
brushed heavy and expectant.

"Now" said a cloudless voice,
and my hands knew
and flew with full
expanse of wings
and landed nearly
wounded on the peaks
of each black shaft.
And one hand gripped
the viscous red
and the other
clung for life
to the blue of possibility
and the earth quaked
and the white world
was no more.

And it was good
(or so I thought)
But the teacher,
shards of glass
in her voice
spoke "No!"
And the floor
quicksand sinking
leaden feet,
and my heart
rushing a thousand beats,
and the easel
rivers of red/blue
dripped, dropped—
And I wondered,
how long
I could live
on the precipice of purple.

The following week, when we shared our memory poems in
an anonymous feedback session, I placed "Kindergarten Creation" on
the desk with the others. None of my students knew it was mine,

---

and I was as excited as they were to receive the "objective" comments. I was pleased when a student I particularly admired wrote, "Wow! This is really different; truly captured the meaning of kindergarten. I love 'and the earth quaked/and the white world/was no more.' This is incredible." At the end of class, I shared my poem with my students. I could see how much they appreciated my struggle as a working poet. (I had yet to feel comfortable calling myself a poet, but I knew I was getting there.) The more I discovered the writer inside myself, the more I felt personally and professionally renewed. I had found work meaningful to my life.

When the February 1989 issue of *EJ* arrived in my office, I was greeted by a surprise breakfast party and balloons which said "Write On!" from my students. But I was in no way prepared for the many notes I received from colleagues outside my department. One math teacher wrote, "Bravo! Can I be a student of yours?" Teachers were coming to me to express their personal feelings and experiences learning about poetry. Just as I was enjoying the growing sense of camaraderie and support among my colleagues, I received a letter from a professor at Gardner-Webb College.

> I enjoyed and was intrigued by your article on found poetry and I decided to use the Lester poem and your ideas with a large group of freshmen and sophomores. Hope you enjoy the enclosed two responses. Thanks for your article. This has been a pleasure.

It was then that I truly felt what it means to reach an audience. I had written well, that I knew, but I had not envisioned teachers nationwide using my ideas and enjoying them. I felt more than a sense of personal satisfaction and professional pride. I felt a growing sense of connection with my colleagues.

And then I received a phone call from Patricia Phelan, chair of the Committee on Classroom Practices. She called to say how impressed she was with my manuscript, and that she was recommending it for publication to the NCTE Editorial Board. If all went well, it would be published in a book within the following year. She indicated she liked the lesson so much that she was going to try it with her own classes. The timing of the phone call couldn't have been more fortuitous. I had just been brainstorming with my classes about a possible follow-up program to the unit. One class had enjoyed poetry so much they asked, "Why does it have to end?" It was then that I began to think of ways to engage students' interest in poetry as an ongoing process. One thought that came to mind was students exchanging favorite poems with a pen pal. I mentioned to Pat that my follow-up plan involved students writing to each other about poetry. She was intrigued by "Poem Pals" and agreed to pilot the program with me that spring.

Shortly thereafter—on February 28, to be exact—I received a letter from Duquesne University:

> I am an editorial consultant for a textbook to be published by Allyn and Bacon. I have been reviewing the literature on teaching in order to discover examples of innovative instructional practice. Recently, I became aware of your educational work. In view of your accomplishments, I feel a contribution from you would be a valuable addition to our research.

Apparently, my *EJ* article had placed me on a mailing list. Although I knew this was a form letter, I was still enticed by the prospect of writing for a book. The proposal was for a case study in educational psychology. The editor was looking for teachers to describe experiments in the classroom in terms of specific goals and outcomes. I was about to teach *Death of a Salesman* to my English classes. Why not experiment with improving students' appreciation through the technique of improvisation?

I devised an improvisation scenario to parallel a critical scene in the play and used the scenario as an anticipatory set. Then I taught the rest of the unit as I had done in the past. My students read the play aloud and acted out important scenes. At the conclusion, I asked my students for a written evaluation of how the improvisation affected their appreciation and understanding of the play. The results were enlightening. One student wrote, "We actually lived an aspect of what happened." Another commented, "We were able to feel Willy's desperation for ourselves." My experiment with improvisation seemed successful enough to write up, and during spring break I drafted and submitted a case study entitled, "Improvisation Technique as an Envoy to Aesthetic Appreciation."

That spring, as students from Morristown, New Jersey, exchanged poetry with their peers from San Diego, California, in the pilot "Poem Pals" project, I felt the end to my isolation as a classroom teacher. I was becoming part of a larger community of teacher writers and researchers.

It was not until the arrival of the September 1989 issue of *EJ* that I experienced the full impact of this collegial community. I remember sitting at the kitchen table, skimming the table of contents, when I noticed an article entitled, "Let Found Poetry Help Your Students Study Literature." I remember my sudden confusion. What could this be?

Someone was using my title. It never occurred to me that this was an article in response to mine. When I read Don Phillips's first paragraph, I was astonished: "Among the many articles in recent issues of the *English Journal* which have tempted me to try something new, Nancy Gorrell's 'Let Found Poetry Help Your Students Find Poetry' proved irresistible." Don Phillips, an instructor from Lambton Vocational Institute, Ontario, Canada, had adapted the concept of found poetry to literature. He mailed me a note of thanks: "Until I read your article, I was really not aware of it [found poetry] as a genre," along with more samples of his students' found poems.

I do not think my evolution as teacher writer is in any way remarkable. There are vast numbers of teachers doing fine work in the solitude of their classrooms year after year as I was. They just need a Mary to say, "Why don't you write it up?" Thanks to many colleagues who have lent me support, I am now starting to take the rest of my writing out of the closet. I joined a women's writers' guild, acquired a computer, and I write daily, like eating, drinking, and breathing. I recently participated in my first public poetry reading at the Newark Public Library.

I have submitted my poems to literary journals and several, including "Kindergarten Creation" and "Blueberry Pie," have been accepted for publication (Gorrell, 1989b, 1990a). "No-Fail Poetry Unit Strategy" was published in *Literature and Life* under a new title, "Poetry to Engage the Person" (Gorrell, 1990b). It was the only change the editors suggested. Since I heard nothing for a long time from Duquesne, I assumed my article had been rejected. Nearly two years after I submitted "Improvisation Technique," I was notified that my article would appear in an educational psychology textbook (Gorrell, 1992). Becoming a writer has been a journey of constant self-discovery, renewal, and surprise. Perhaps my story will encourage other teachers in their personal journeys.

References

Gorrell, N. (1989a). Let found poetry help your students find poetry. *English Journal, 78*(2), 30–34.

Gorrell, N. (1989b). Kindergarten creation. *The Rockford Review, 8,* 62.

Gorrell, N. (1990a). Blueberry pie. *English Journal, 79*(8), 88.

Gorrell, N. (1990b). Poetry to engage the person. In P. Phelan (Ed.), *Literature and life: Making connections in the classroom* (pp. 35–43). Urbana, IL: National Council of Teachers of English.

Gorrell, N. (1992). Improvisation technique: Envoy to aesthetic appreciation. In R.R. McCown & P. Roop (Eds.), *Educational psychology and classroom practice: A partnership*. Needham Heights, MA: Allyn and Bacon.

4 Writing Groups: A Personal Source of Support

Betty Van Ryder
Advanced Learning Centers, Yakima Public Schools, Washington

I have an office where I have told my husband not to disturb me if the door is closed. One day when the office door was closed while I was out in the kitchen, he came up to me and said, "Your office door is closed. Does that mean I shouldn't disturb you?" Despite his teasing, it has worked to have an office and that rule. Quiet, secluded spots without interruption are necessary for many of us in the initial stages of our writing.

But when my first draft, or even the second or third one, is completed, when I have read my writing out loud to myself and made all the changes I can think of, then I want to go to my writing group to get its opinions—and there will be several. Sometimes I'm quite sure about my writing; the pieces go together and it sounds right. Then I want validation, but other times I know it's not working and I want some feedback. My writing group is supportive, whether it is for confirmation or suggestions. Since one of the purposes of writing is to communicate, it is helpful to use a group of other writers as a sounding board.

My writing group is diverse. Many of the writers are part of the business community, some are retired, some do not work outside the home, and a few are teachers. We are all serious writers. Some have had articles and poetry published. Some have manuscripts that are likely to be published and work with agents and editors.

Our writing group was formed about seven years ago by Pat, who had recently moved to Yakima from San Diego. She had been in a writers' group where the members made a living from their writing. In a newsletter circulated by the local arts organization, Pat advertised two meetings at the Warehouse Theater; each meeting was attended by more than twenty people. Pat explained that the primary purpose of the group would be offering support and suggestions to each other.

From that beginning a nucleus of ten writers met regularly and critiqued the writing presented. One disgruntled charter member dropped the group because she thought we sounded too much like English teachers, although at the time I was the only English teacher in the group. This member was writing romances, and our response was that because she was such a good writer, we had loftier goals for her. But if making money were her goal, we probably gave her poor advice. She is now an established, successful romance writer, and the rest of us have not the luxury of abandoning our present job for a writing career.

We meet every other week in members' homes. People are informed of the meetings only if they did not attend the last one. We come when we can; we don't need to let the group know if we can't attend. Sometimes someone doesn't attend for several weeks or even months; others seldom miss a meeting. Of the seventeen people on our roster, three are from the original ten and seven are fairly new. With so many new people, we have had some difficulty reestablishing our pattern, but based on past experiences, we will settle back into a workable eight or ten regular members. This constant change brings fresh perspectives, but having a more stable group might allow us to move to more sophisticated issues.

New people may come one time without bringing their own writing to read, but we stress that we do not encourage spectators. We are active writers whose purpose is to help each other. Only once have we had to drop a person from the group. Because this individual had so little basic writing skill and no idea how to critique, our leader suggested that writing classes at the local community college would be more appropriate.

Structure of Writing-Group Meetings

We begin promptly at 7:30 by finding out what and how much each of us has to read. If it looks as though the reading will exceed our meeting time, someone is apt to say, "I read the last two times. Put me last in case there isn't time for all of us." The leader then determines the order and limits us to fifteen minutes each. Since not everyone needs fifteen minutes to read, we generally have time for all manuscripts. We usually take a break two-thirds of the way through and finish close to 11:00. (I'd like it if we ended at 10:30, since it is hard to concentrate beyond that time and the last person usually gets shortchanged.)

We try to adhere to the fifteen-minute limit because responding to the writing takes quite a while, especially if more than eight people are there. Before writers read, they give only necessary explanations, since we feel the writing should stand on its own merit. We do not bring copies of our manuscripts to pass out to the group. We have talked about that practice, but many of our manuscripts are handwritten and often composed during the day of the meeting. Some writers do not have easy access to a copy machine. Because we do not have a copy in front of us, we have learned to be careful listeners. People new to our group are amazed at our ability to listen and make notes. With poetry, however, writers will occasionally bring copies or the original poem will be passed around, and poetry is read twice.

During the reading we jot down notes. Then each person responds orally to the writing and also gives the writer his or her notes. Readers don't respond to the critiques, although if the speaker asks a question, sometimes it is appropriate to explain. Some people have a tendency to rebut what has been said. Writers may disagree or wish to disregard what is said, but they should let the response go unchallenged. Responses are generally brief, and we try not to repeat the information already covered, but try to add new ideas. Grammatical and usage errors can adequately be handled through the notes and are not presented orally, since we do not want to embarrass the writer. Occasionally, we do discuss an error several of us make. We also are more apt to discuss things like changing points of view or inconsistency in tenses, but we try to keep that to a minimum. Whether we as responders agree with the content or the philosophy stated in the writing is irrelevant. Our purpose is to react to how effectively the piece is written.

Personal Growth as Writers

All of us have grown as writers, listeners, and critics. Jim joined our group after going to the community college to get help on writing his story about recovering from his Vietnam experience. The help he was getting there was diluting his powerful story and submerging his voice. As he has participated in our group, his writing has become stronger. He has learned how to get in and out of flashbacks, where dialogue will enhance a scene, what details should be eliminated, how to add sensory imagery, and how to incorporate his own feelings into the writing. He already had a strong theme and an effective understated tone. Jim has not been the only one to benefit from sharing his writing. All of us feel privileged that he has wanted to read his story to us and has wanted us to respond to it.

Although she died recently, Mabel still seems to be part of our group. Her storytelling had characteristics not often found in contemporary writing, but they still hold universal appeal. She was one of our charter members whose writing included family history, drawn from four generations of letters saved and passed on to Mabel. Her gentle humor and sharp wit added much to our sessions.

Bob was another member who added a different flavor. He was writing a textbook on economics that he hoped would appeal to laypeople. His warm, natural, and humorous oral explanations were always needed, because his writing was so formal and full of language peculiar to his discipline. We finally convinced him to write in that more informal style, and each chapter got better and better. We learned from the content of his writing, and often, when the critiquing ended, we would have discussions based on his information.

Rod, an attorney, was considering dropping his law practice to write full-time, but decided on the more lucrative career. He wrote contemporary fiction reminiscent of Hemingway, but often questioned the necessity of lengthy descriptions. Aside from his valuable comments and outstanding writing, Rod contributed youthful enthusiasm that sparked the group.

Whether writing a mystery or an article about her trip to France, Nancy sprinkled humor throughout her writing in generous spoonfuls. She made us part of the scenes she wrote about.

Initially, I shared poetry in the writing group, and later childhood reminiscences that evolved from my work in elementary classrooms. Pat, who is a novelist, convinced me to develop my collection of childhood memories into a novel. I have written many chapters, some of which I have shared, but the idea is on hold since I have become involved in writing articles for journals and for my own school district. I also have to admit this venture into fiction has not been very successful.

Because we are such a diverse group of writers, I receive valuable feedback. In my writing for journals, the group is particularly helpful in reminding me to limit the use of educationese and long, involved sentences. Because some of us have been in this same group for more than five years, we are comfortable with each other and know what kinds of comments to expect. For example, Wendy likes dialogue, knows how to write it, and gives advice regarding the authenticity of the dialogue we write. Pat writes strong sensory images and points out when our writing is quiet, colorless, and odorless. Jan wants the hook early in the writing and tells us what to pare away to get the story rolling. Donna, the most versatile writer in our group, identifies rough spots and suggests subtle language changes. Because of Clyde's ability to use humor effectively, he helps us interject humor appropriately.

We laugh and say we don't need to meet. We can just read our papers at home to ourselves and pretend we all are there and imagine the comments each person would make. I think sometimes I do that unconsciously when I read my work at home.

Case History of a Manuscript

In the fall of 1984 I was asked to contribute to an article for the *Washington English Journal*. I was to focus on how the Language Arts/ English State Guidelines, which I helped write, might be used. My writing group addressed two problems regarding my article. The first issue was in the choice of language. In an early draft, I wrote:

> Traditionally, in our teaching, most of us have not made connections among the four communication modes. We are apt to have students read and discuss, read and write, speak and listen. The way this document was conceived and designed lends itself to an integrated way to look at and teach the total of language arts. By highlighting all four modes as well as literature, language, and cultural values, we are showing the importance of each.

The group's general response to the article was to be less wordy, cut some of the sentences in half, and think of some way to make it more interesting. Pat specifically responded, "Too many words. Leave out phrases like, 'We are apt to have' and 'The way'." I made some notes on my manuscript and collected the suggestions members had written. When I revised, I looked over their comments and made the following changes:

> Traditionally, in our teaching, most of us have not made connections among the four communication modes. Students read and discuss, read and write, speak and listen. This document was conceived and designed for teaching language arts integrating listening, speaking, reading, and writing as well as literature, language, and cultural values.

The published version was further revised by Julie Neff, the editor, to read:

Traditionally, in our teaching, most of us have not made connections among the four communication modes. The new curriculum guidelines integrate the teaching of the language arts— reading, listening, speaking, and writing as well as literature, language, and cultural values.

Writing-group members talked about the sentence structure and word choice, but they also were concerned with the article's tone. They thought it was boring. No specific suggestions were given, just the recommendation to "make it more interesting." Our writing group doesn't necessarily provide a solution, but presents the problem. Members don't take the ownership of the writing away, but give the author a problem to grapple with. Whether the writing is an article, short story, or novel, Jan insists that there be something to grab the reader, and clearly my article did not grab anyone. During the next two weeks I thought of several ideas and finally came up with four scenarios that showed how various individuals in a school district might respond to the document. For example:

> In a small middle school Teacher Jones receives a copy of this document. He reads the publication. He thinks, "Where are my SLO's (Student Learning Objectives)? This isn't anything like the way I teach. Why should I change? My kids get along, and I don't have to prepare materials; it's all in the textbooks and workbooks." Since he is the only language arts/English teacher in his building, he does not talk to any other teachers. He does not belong to any professional organizations. His principal is not concerned with curriculum planning; he is wondering if they will have enough paper to run off all the workbook materials his staff uses. Teacher Jones puts the guide for developing curriculum on a high shelf with the other guides he has received during his twenty years in the same classroom. He sits at his desk with a green blotter and carefully stacked texts for spelling, grammar, literature, and reading, and the six workbooks that he has collected at book fairs, takes a sip of cold coffee from a stained mug and plans tomorrow's assignments.

At our next meeting, I read the new version with four scenes ranging from the above scenario to ones in which the teachers find the guidelines helpful. Jan approved of the attention-getter. Mabel enjoyed the humor. Pat had one further suggestion. I had alternated unacceptable with acceptable scenes, and she thought it would be clearer and have more impact if I started with the worst scene and ended with the ideal.

With the revisions complete, I considered which version to send to the editor. I had not worked with this editor before, so I wasn't sure whether she would prefer the concise version or the colorful one. I sent both, with the following explanation:

> After writing and rewriting this paper, I was not satisfied with what I came up with so I tried a completely different approach using the four scenes.
> I read it to my writing group. They thought this second approach would catch the reader's attention. . . . I decided to send you the first version as well, thinking . . . there may be some usable parts.

Editor Julie Neff responded:

> Thank you for both versions of your piece of the article. I will try to use as much of both as possible. I felt each addressed a different need or set of questions.

The moral of this story, I guess, is that writing groups can offer advice, but editors might not entirely agree. However, I wouldn't have written the second version if my group had been satisfied with the first one. My writing-group partners inspired me to be more creative in writing about a pretty traditional topic.

Even though I write for journals and generally write more nonfiction than most of our members, I advocate having a writing support group that is not limited to writers for journals. Belonging to a group whose members write in a variety of genres has enabled me to develop my listening ability and my critiquing skills. When I write, I remember comments from my writing group and often carry on a dialogue with the members. These voices mingle with the voices of Graves, Macrorie, Murray, and Elbow and become editors perched on my computer keyboard and screen, offering me advice.

When our writing group first started, most of us were not serious about writing for publication, but with the encouragement of the group we have all worked toward that goal. Jan had a travel article about Vancouver's Expo in the local newspaper, Donna has had humorous seasonal pieces published in *Woman's World* and a local newsletter, Wendy has had biographical sketches featured in *Northwest Runner*. I have had poetry published in various small publications and articles published in the *Washington English Journal*.

Two members of our group received awards for manuscripts at the Pacific Northwest Writers Conference last year: Pat for a young adult novel and Jan for a travel book. The continuing encouragement and faith we have in our own and each other's abilities have kept this group going.

Knowing that the group is meeting next week has given me the momentum I need to finish this draft of this chapter. The writing group will give me suggestions to help me make it a better piece of writing. Jan will tell me to get the hook in sooner; Donna will pick out a passage that needs smoothing out. Wendy will tell me where the ideas might not be clear. And Pat may tell me she can see the possibility of a novel (who knows—maybe my writing group will become characters in a novel). Support and help are what we give and receive in our writing group, and I heartily recommend that teachers form one of their own to help them in writing for publication.

Guidelines for Writing-Group Members

When the group in which I am presently active first met, Pat gave us some general advice about the purpose of a writing support group. Over the years we have developed our own informal set of rules. When a new person joins, we share this information, which also serves as a reminder to all of us.

As an Organizer

If people who are not writing want to join the group, tell them that is acceptable to begin with and that the writing group will probably motivate them to write. But once the group gathers momentum everyone is a writer.

Set up regular meeting times and places. We meet every other week in members' homes.

With smoking such an issue, decide on the policy before you get organized.

Decide if you want to set a size for your group. Seven or eight regular members works best for us. We have an open membership that grows almost monthly, which is somewhat of a problem, but the new members have been a welcome addition.

As a Leader

Start on time. Our sessions usually last from 7:00 or 7:30 to 10:30 or 11:00. It's hard to concentrate much beyond three hours.

Ask writers what and how much they have brought to read, prior to starting. A typical response would be eight pages of a chapter, three poems, or a four-page essay.

Determine if everyone will have time to read. If not, usually someone doesn't mind waiting until next time.

Limit each person to fifteen minutes of reading time. In our group most manuscripts can be read in that time.

Decide on the order the writers will read. Try to have a different order each time. Alternate types of writing.

Discourage readers from responding to each critique.

Take a break about two-thirds of the way through. We serve refreshments at that time and converse about our nonwriting lives.

As a Reader

Do not give a lengthy explanation of how you came to write this piece. If you need to explain that much, then the information should be in the paper.

If, however, the paper is not the beginning of the writing, a brief explanation is helpful.

Do not explain why it is so rough. If you need to say that, it's not ready to read.

A comment as to the purpose and audience is appropriate.

Apologies for being a poor writer are not appropriate. If you really are, your listeners will soon know.

Read slowly. If you have a long chapter that will take more than fifteen minutes to read, read part of it; don't try to rush through it.

Don't add asides. If they are worth saying, maybe they should be in the writing.

Read poetry twice and more slowly than you think you should.

As a Listener

Listen carefully.

Jot down enough notes to be able to respond to the writer.

Writing the reader's name and chapter number or date on your notes is helpful. I also put my name on the notes, although by now everyone knows the kind of paper I use and my handwriting.

Be an attentive listener even though you may not be interested in the topic.

As a Responder

First talk about what works.

Discuss the bigger issues, which might include point of view, tense inconsistency, tone, pace, clarity.

Write minor grammatical problems on paper, generally without giving oral comments.

If others have discussed the same points, just say you agree and don't rehash the same problem. If you can add a fresh perspective, however, that is helpful. If you don't agree with other comments, that's important, too. Often in our group we have differences of opinion. If we have time after everyone has critiqued the writing, we often discuss the options.

Don't argue about content. The discussion is on how it is written, not what is written.

Don't talk so long that you have taken more time than the reader.

Don't overdo the praise. You don't have to be overly critical, but gushy praise does not assist a writer.

Ask questions sparingly. The writer is apt to give you more information than you need.

As I developed this list, I thought presenting it to prospective writers would scare them away. But this is the way we have evolved into an effective, efficient, friendly writing group. Occasionally, friction results when a member insists on reading for more than fifteen minutes, or argues a philosophical issue that a paper precipitated, or says, "I don't know anything about poetry," but those minor detractions are clearly offset by the benefits derived from belonging to such a group.

Members of my writing group are among my best friends. While our families may consider our writing a hobby, the writing group takes it seriously. We share the rejection notices, the awards and acceptances, and are looking forward to editors knowing what we know about our writing group. Our lives have become richer.

5 Teacher Research: Catalyst for Writing

Cora Lee Five
Edgewood School, Scarsdale, New York

I have never thought of myself as a writer, but it seems I have always thought of myself as a teacher. Not surprisingly, it was through teaching that I began to write. Now I feel that I couldn't write if I didn't teach, because I write when I have something to say, something that is important to me. That something is usually what is happening in my classroom.

Exciting things began to happen in my fifth-grade classroom once I became involved in the process approach to teaching writing. Nine years ago Nancie Atwell taught me about the writing process. More important, she introduced me to teacher research, because she linked the study of writing to classroom research. Atwell stressed the importance of teachers keeping journals of what they observed, and these journals provided opportunities for me to reflect on my teaching. I began to observe children, to learn with and from them, and to take risks. It seemed I was filled with questions and what Bissex and Bullock (1987) describe "a 'wondering' to pursue." Both teaching and learning became areas for investigation.

As a teacher researcher, I became interested in looking closely at what children actually can do and how they do it. My research led me in two directions: the study of individual children and the study of new approaches to teaching. As a result, the classroom became an exciting place to be and a vital place to learn and improve as a teacher. Suddenly, it seemed I had information I wanted to share. As a result of my classroom research, I began to write about my experiences. My studies of children with special needs became chapters for a book I wrote (Five, 1992). New approaches to teaching were not only learning experiences for me but topics for journal articles and chapters in books.

Portions of this chapter first appeared in *Harvard Educational Review:* Five, C. L. (1986). Fifth graders respond to a changed reading program. *Harvard Educational Review, 56,* 395–405.

One such experience, trying a new approach to reading, became an occasion for writing that eventually led to publication. The occasion was the creation of a reading program that gave children time to read and time to make meaning through writing and talking about books. I gave up a traditional program, one that included the teaching of isolated skills, and set up a reading program based primarily on Atwell's (1987) approach, where children select their own books, have time for reading, and respond to them in reading journals and letters to friends. I added mapping, sketching, and graphing to increase the variety of response. I hoped my students would turn into readers who loved reading, and I hoped research would help me recognize how that happened.

My first year using a reading workshop was a fascinating one. I was caught up in everything that was happening in my classroom. As a teacher researcher, I began to observe and listen very carefully to my students. I became involved in their conversations. I collected samples of written work from their reading journals and from their writing folders, and I had periodic conferences with individual children concerning their perceptions of progress.

All of these data, as well as my interpretations, responses, and reactions, were recorded in my own journal. I carefully dated and stapled into my journal quotes from children as they discussed their books. I jotted down little notes for myself regarding theories I had and the discoveries and frustrations I experienced.

In the winter I realized that something exciting was happening in reading, and by the spring I wanted to share it with others. At the same time I became aware of a call for manuscripts from the *Harvard Educational Review*, which was doing a special issue on teachers and teaching. The combination of the two events—the success I had with reading and the call for manuscripts—prompted me to write. I began by going through my folders of samples and the notes from my journal, selecting and marking those items that would show the kinds of things children were doing and my thoughts about them. I had no particular format in mind; I just knew that I wanted to describe the effects this approach to reading had on my fifth graders and on me.

Once I made the decision to write, I experienced my own excitement, a feeling that seems to accompany most writing commitments I make to myself. I have discovered that I tend to follow a similar pattern each time I decide to write. My mind begins to race with ideas. Various possibilities abound, and at first it feels confusing. However, after studying myself as a learner (Five, 1986b), I have allowed myself to live with uncertainty, to let the focus remain unclear, and to permit questions to go unanswered. I know my mind needs time to make order, to allow ideas to merge, to rehearse, to let things happen in my head. So I live with confusion, with no clear-cut plan, confident that some organization will emerge. My mind seems to sift and make meaning while I go on with my daily life.

It is during this phase of my writing process that I know I need time, time to think and reflect. Running provides the solitude I need, the time. Just as I believe I can't write without teaching, I feel I can't write without running. During this uninterrupted time ideas come from my unconscious, often in a rush. I run with a paper and pencil in my jacket and stop often to jot down phrases, leads, and endings, or a plan of organization. I save these wrinkled, often soggy, "ideas" and keep them in a pile or staple the scraps of paper into my journal.

I usually wait until the weekends or a school vacation to write. My mind seems too cluttered with schoolwork, meetings, and other activities to try to write during the week. I plan uninterrupted days. I need to know I have a whole day to write; a two-hour period of time will not do. Whatever the reality, I need to feel there is enough time. Otherwise I cannot begin; I feel too pressured if I know an end is imposed on me by an appointment or another interruption.

The beginning of my first writing session is usually the same and has become a procedure I can now accept and often find amusing. I call it my "circling the computer" stage. I walk around the room, approach the computer, walk away, decide to water the plants, set up the computer, visit the kitchen a few times (unfortunately), arrange my mail, look for empty disks, and do many other small tasks that have nothing to do with writing. Strange as it may seem, however, I am usually unaware of my activities because I'm involved in thinking. This prewriting seems to be very similar to what my students do. Their walking around the classroom, sharpening pencils, getting paper, and clearing desks seem to parallel my own behavior, although I know because of the setting they don't engage in my wide range of activities.

Finally, after my period of pacing or "messing around," I become settled and am ready to write. Then I sit down for two to three hours at a time and tell the story of what happened in my classroom and how it happened. I try to be very honest so the reader will know exactly where I am coming from and what feelings I had about trying something new. In the piece about my reading workshop that appeared in *Harvard Educational Review* (Five, 1986a), I wanted other teachers to know of my fears about abandoning the traditional reading program and the teaching of isolated skills. I wrote, "The first thing I did was the most difficult: with much trepidation, I gave up reading workbooks."

When I wrote a chapter for another publication about using poetry in the classroom, I wanted teachers to know my previous background and feelings about poetry. If they had similar feelings, I thought they might be tempted to try poetry despite their insecurity. I wrote in the beginning of the chapter:

> In my first eight years as a teacher of writing, my students did not write poetry because I was afraid to teach it. I remembered struggling through high school and college literature courses, analyzing poems and writing papers that compared the works of major poets born hundreds of years ago. This past year, despite my insecurity, I finally decided to expose my fifth graders to poetry and see what happened. (Five, 1989)

The time goes very fast once I start writing. Often I look out the window near my desk and gaze at the trees or the woman who sunbathes regularly on her patio, but I don't really see them because I'm involved with my mind. I realize that my students also look out the window or sit at their desks staring into space, a behavior that I formerly thought was unproductive. Now I know they, too, are thinking.

After two or three hours of writing, I stop for a break. I print a copy of what I have written and take it to another room to read. I usually feel happy and productive—at least I have a pile of pages in my hand. I make revisions in pen and usually head for the kitchen, hopefully for nothing more than water. Then I begin writing at the computer again. I include my revisions first, often word changes or changes in the order of sentences. I usually work for another two or three hours. Most of this time is spent continuing the piece. Frequently I jump up to select samples of children's work and pages from my journal. They are usually scattered all over my desk and nearby floor. I read them over and decide whether and where to put them.

For the reading article (Five, 1986a), I decided to show the progress of several students. I selected Danny, who did not like reading at the beginning of the year. I included a letter he had written to me describing his experience of learning to read. I then showed a letter he had written two months after school began. The letter revealed his increasing involvement with books. I decided to end my section about Danny with a letter written four months later about a book he loved. I had noted in my journal that Danny had written to the author of the book after he finished it. I realized, when I looked through his folder, that he had read all of the books written by that particular author. Then I came across a quote from Danny that I had jotted on a piece of paper and stapled into my journal. All of this information helped me select Danny and relate his story in the article:

Four months later Danny loved to read and write and developed an interest in the authors of the books he was reading. He discovered the writer Byars through *Good-bye, Chicken Little* (1979) and began to wonder about the basis for her story. He wrote:

> . . . I thought that this book was so true and this may have happened to a kid. I think I might send a letter to Betsy Byars to see if this book was based on experience. I thought his biggest mistake was fighting with conrad. this book was so good I wish I could read it forever.

That discovery was important to Danny in several ways. He wrote to Byars and treasured the letter he received in return, stapling it into his literature journal. He read all the rest of her books. He also decided to write in his personal journal every night because, as he explained it, "In case I really do become an author, I want to remember all my experiences so I can put them in books for kids my age."

As my students and I became more involved in a reading workshop approach, I realized that many children began to experiment with interpreting the ideas in the books they read. Their letters revealed their continuing attempts to search for greater depth. Because I wanted to show samples from a variety of readers, I included letters from good readers as well as less able readers.

Josh described the character Jess in Paterson's (1977) *Bridge to Terabithia*.

> Dear Miss Five,
> Jess has so many feelings its hard to describe him. Let's say he had three stages. First, a normal, hardworking stage at the beginning, and feelings, if he had any, would never be shared with anyone else. The second stage, when Leslie came into his life, turned into a kind of magical stage in a way for him. The third stage, when Leslie died, he began to relate to adults. These three stages make him real.
> Sincerly,
> Josh

John, a less able reader, responded to the same character.

Dear Miss Five,
   I think that Jess is changing on the inside because of lesslys death. He is starting to understand not only his father but all gronups and I think that he likes his sister better.

In the process of rereading my students' letters to me and writing about them, I began to think again about what was happening in my classroom. I decided to include my observations and theories at various places in the article.

> The letters my students wrote to me and to each other also made me think about the classroom context needed to support their reading. I realized that they read with greater depth when they selected their own books, ones that appealed to them rather than those that I thought they "should" read. I also realized that they probably took risks to find ways to express themselves because I did not label their comments as "correct" or "incorrect." A classroom environment that accepted and respected what children said about books was necessary for these journal entries and their increased interest in reading. (Five, 1986a, p. 401)

The reading article, like others I have written, followed a familiar pattern of revision. After spending the weekend writing, I spend the weekdays reflecting and revising. I think about the piece when I am running and am often awakened by it during the middle of the night. I again jot down ideas and plans for revision on scraps of paper. I read and reread my draft, add my running and midnight ideas, and continue to make changes in pen. I save the actual writing on the computer for the following weekend. Once I am involved in writing a piece, my prewriting behavior disappears and I start each weekend writing session by rereading my last draft. Once again I use thoughts from my Saturday morning runs to make changes before I begin writing.

Frequently when I'm revising or completing a piece, I read it aloud to myself and try to listen to it. I am reminded of my fifth graders, who often read their pieces aloud to themselves or a friend, making changes as they read. As I read my draft in the solitude of my apartment, I am aware that what I really need is what my students need, too: response. I had realized the importance of response when I first started teaching writing through the process approach. I saw how it helped my students, and once I began writing, I understood its value for me.

When I first started to write, I gave my sister copies of my manuscripts and let her read them, waiting for feedback. In the past several years I discovered another teacher researcher who lives nearby and writes. Now I call her often to confer. I either read parts of my writing to her, or I discuss my ideas for a piece and ask for advice. Sometimes I send her copies of chapters and we meet to confer. Often we laugh over our individual writing processes, which at times are quite similar. Like my students, I realize the need for response and the benefits of conferences. I value the suggestions my friend gives me, but more important, I value the support and encouragement she provides.

In most of my articles I want to convey my excitement about trying something new. I hope my enthusiasm will encourage other teachers to experiment. I usually include my feelings and what I have learned toward the end of my manuscript. For the reading article I described the effect that the reading program had on both my students and me:

> And the new approach had an effect on me. My students and I began to talk books before school, at recess, and at lunchtime; their reading period never seemed to end at twelve, even though the bell had rung. Their enthusiasm was infectious. I was constantly drawn into their discussions and especially their thinking, as I became more and more involved in their reading and their responses. This approach and my researcher's role helped me continue to learn more about these students, their reading processes, and their attitudes. Again and again, I saw the importance of giving them freedom to read and opportunities to experiment with and to explore their own ideas. (Five, 1986a, p. 404)

I am excited when I feel I'm close to the end. My mind is racing again, with phrases, words, endings, but more important, insights. My discoveries as a teacher researcher become clear. It seems that I'm not really sure what I've learned in my classroom until I write about it. Again I'm aware that my writing process parallels that of my students. They, too, need to write in their various journals before they are truly aware of their own thinking and discoveries, their own learning. Writing the article about my reading program was cause for reflection. Eventually, it led to new questions for me and my teaching. I decided to include some of these reactions at the end of the article:

> By collecting, sorting, reading and rereading their letters, maps, and sketches, I found for myself a much closer view of how children struggle and then succeed to find meaning in books. The process also kept me engaged in learning because it led me

to new questions. What do children learn from my mini-lessons? In what situations will children take more risks with interpreting what they read? (Five, 1986a, p. 405)

Other articles and chapters have also come from questions, observations, and "wonderings." For me, writing has become a natural outgrowth of teacher research.

In the very writing of this chapter I continued to learn by examining myself as a writer. It seems I engage in teacher research even when it comes to studying and writing about myself. The data I discovered about my own writing process were cause for further reflection. It became apparent that my writing process parallels that of my students, and I realized that Giacobbe's (1986) three basics—time, ownership, and response—seem to be essential elements not only for my students but for me. Time is mine through the uninterrupted periods I spend running and thinking and the uninterrupted time I schedule for writing. Ownership comes from choosing to write about topics that are important and meaningful to me. I receive response through discussions and conferences with colleagues who understand. More important, as I looked at myself as a writer, it became clear to me that teacher research is the catalyst for my writing, and my writing becomes an extension of my own learning which I can then share with others.

References

Atwell, N. (1987). *In the middle*. Portsmouth, NH: Heinemann.

Bissex, G., & Bullock, R. (1987). *Seeing for ourselves*. Portsmouth, NH: Heinemann.

Byars, B. (1979). *Good-bye, chicken little*. New York: Harper & Row.

Five, C.L. (1986a). Fifth graders respond to a changed reading program. *Harvard Educational Review, 56,* 395–405.

Five, C.L. (1986b). Joy in learning: A teacher investigates her own learning process. *Language Arts, 63,* 710–715.

Five, C.L. (1989). A garden of poets. In N. Atwell (Ed.), *Workshop I: Writing and literature* (pp. 61–71). Portsmouth, NH: Heinemann.

Five, C.L. (1992). *Special voices*. Portsmouth, NH: Heinemann.

Giacobbe, M.E. (1986). Learning to write and writing to learn in the elementary school. In A. Petrosky & D. Bartholomae (Eds.), *The teaching of writing* (pp. 131–147). Chicago: University of Chicago Press.

Paterson, K. (1977). *Bridge to Terabithia*. New York: Crowell.

6 Students Teach Me What to Write

Jay Simmons
Moharimet School, Madbury, New Hampshire

I continued to teach high school English as I pursued my doctorate in reading and writing instruction at the University of New Hampshire. In fact, several springs ago I was teaching newswriting again, after a five-year hiatus, and hating every minute of it. Students, it seemed, were unwilling to interview indepth, get work in on time, or edit with any accuracy, in the manner I had been taught by my own tough city editor.

That spring when I was again teaching newswriting, I was also enrolled in two graduate courses. In one I was reading composition and cognitive development theory. For the other I needed to devise a group learning experience and write a paper about it.

I wrote all major course papers at UNH as if they were for publication. Writing being as painful as it is, I now insist it be useful to more than two people. In designing, researching, and writing the article I recently submitted to *English Education* (Simmons, 1991), I had to recapture my own beginnings as a journalist and teacher, reassessing what still works and what doesn't. I wove human stories around the statistical frame of my doctoral research, changed the way I use journals and literacy groups, and have become convinced that teachers who research in and write about their classrooms become better teachers and more prolific writers. This chapter recounts the interplay of my work as a teacher, doctoral student, and writer, and presents the evolution of some of my recent writing.

Literary Scholar Turns Reporter

A freshly graduated literature student, in 1969 I became superior court reporter for *The Springfield* (Mass.) *Union*. My city editor, Jane Maroney, told me, "Kid, you graduated from college; congratulations. I'm going to teach you to write." Which she did, in no uncertain terms, few of them the queen's English. I recall retrieving from my mailbox my first bylined article, bleeding badly from felt-tip pen, after Jane had finished the job the copyeditors had timidly begun. I got the message: this was her paper, and she cared what got printed.

Jane's attitude helped me teach newswriting at UNH eight years later, and I brought it with me to my first high school journalism course as well. Soon students were retrieving their own bleeding copy from my out basket, but we were printing gritty news pieces in photo-offset.

Unfortunately, however, Don Graves had come to UNH, and local elementary school teachers began heeding Graves's call to follow students as they find their own territories and develop as writers. By the time I returned to the high school newsroom in 1989, their first crop of fifth graders had developed into sophomores. These student writers were shocked to hear that some writing followed a formula, and some editors dared change the writer's hallowed prose.

Don Graves had gotten me into this mess, so it was only fitting that he should help me dig myself out. As part of his seminar in reading and writing research, I had been learning about the development of thinking through Vera John-Steiner's *Notebooks of the Mind* (1985). Her writing taught me that our best and brightest develop their professional thinking abilities in the company of others—peers, friends, family, and mentors—with whom they can share their thoughts and feelings, hopes and fears, as they develop the invisible tools of thought.

The articles I read by Kenneth Bruffee (1988) and Mike Rose (1989) taught me that all learners who are changing cultural affiliations—be they open-enrollment students in New York, nontraditional learners at UCLA, or my own fledgling journalists in Durham, New Hampshire—need support groups.

My UNH doctoral program had but two required courses—the seminar in which I was enrolled that spring and one education course of our choice outside the reading and writing domain. Since I codirect a dropout prevention group at my high school, I had selected group counseling to satisfy this requirement.

There I was learning that the human potential movement has developed methods for fostering and assessing change in human beings through group activities. As part of this course I had to design and lead a group, then write a paper discussing the process.

I asked my two dozen high school newswriters to keep journals each week about their reading and writing of news. These they shared in weekly group meetings, later reporting their concerns, emotions, and realizations to the entire class. Each week they also wrote one piece from canned information and another from independent interviewing. At the end of the quarter students constructed portfolios to demonstrate their growth as readers and writers of news. Some included clippings or bleeding copy; most used excerpts from journals; all wrote the required "Dear Jay" letter, evaluating their development.

Counseling Theory to Writing Practice

As soon as Dwight Webb, my counseling professor, approved the writing-group idea, I began to read his course assignments with an eye to finding suggestions for the planning, facilitation, and evaluation of human potential groups (Corey & Corey, 1987) as they applied to my classroom. In my written responses to the readings, I attempted to explain the connection between collaborative writing groups in practice and counseling theory.

The article by Corey and Corey (1987) caught my attention quickly by asserting that statistical measures are generally ineffective in assessing the kinds of growth fostered by human potential groups. I shared their concern that such discrete measures focused on concrete products, not on the more elusive changes in attitude, feeling, and ability sought in writing classes. I began to realize that writers, too, change their selfhood as they learn to write; therefore, they might also need the trust, security, and cohesiveness offered by carefully run collaborative groups. Much growth in counseling groups develops in response to feedback given and received by members, a clear connection to group and individual conferences in the writing classroom. Finally, Corey and Corey described a necessary reflective process that echoed the work of writing portfolio projects. Human growth is facilitated and retained, they said, when members set specific, personal goals for themselves and keep records of their own process for later assessment.

These insights were useful in both my doctoral work and my teaching. They also helped me develop an article on the thinking processes of my students.

Learning Theory to Counseling Practice

The University of New Hampshire's education department created a new genre—the One-Pager, its version of the Hewlett-Packard one-page memo. In my one-pagers for Don Graves I attempted to connect composition theory to group counseling practice. Again, I drew on my reading for insights. Vera John-Steiner had studied the journals and letters of noted artists, scientists, and writers to trace the development of their thinking, much as Corey and Corey suggested I do to find the growth in my writing groups. John-Steiner (1985) poignantly described the need of talented novices for emotional support from friends, mentors, and family during their formative years. Other writers described classrooms where students needed the same security offered by counseling groups. Bruffee (1988) stressed the need for well-tailored tasks to facilitate feedback that would teach students to talk to themselves in new ways. Rose (1989) complained that American education has excluded our weakest students from the sort of collaborative, peer-group support that allows the best and brightest to reflect on the method of inquiry of a given discipline.

From this reading and writing, I discovered that the two bodies of learning theory converged at emotion and social interaction. That is, human growth, be it the development of writing abilities or recovery from the trauma of incest, means coming to grips with difficult emotions, carried over from the past or arising in the present. And growth takes place through interaction with other human beings.

My article, it was becoming clear, would necessarily explain these learning theories and demonstrate their applications in a high school writing class. Corey and Corey had listed six areas of learning in groups, and I would need space to excerpt student journals, conversations, and letters as examples of those areas.

Originally I thought of *English Journal* as a market for the piece, but its guideline of ten to twelve pages would be too short for the task as it was developing. I felt *English Education*, which is dedicated to the development of English teachers and their training programs, publishes longer, more theoretical pieces aimed at college scholars as well as English practitioners. It is also a refereed journal, and although intimidated by the thought of seeking the approval of three expert referees, I decided *EE* was an appropriate choice and began my work with new energy.

Knowing I would be writing to an audience of teacher educators, I began to collect data that they would find convincing—data from weekly sessions in my journalism class. I took desperate notes as the groups reported their concerns during weekly journal shares. I photocopied journal entries, and later, portfolio letters. These showed how the process worked and what the writers had learned about themselves.

My students seemed a little bemused when I consulted with them about what they had to teach me, or when I asked permission to quote their work. I learned to see my students more clearly. A counselor friend of mine tells the story of having marjoram crushed under his nose while he was blindfolded. The aroma exploded in his head as if for the first time, he said, despite the fact that he'd smelled marjoram hundreds of times while cooking. "What had been missing all that time," he asked, "me or the marjoram?"

In my quest for perfect papers, I had missed the marjoram my students were presenting me. As I wrote for publication, truly "blind" during the composing process, I finally let my recalcitrant journalists teach me that the theorists were right: developing writers need the support of their peers at least as much as they need the dictates of teachers. But they need this support to develop their thinking, not merely to produce neatly inverted pyramids and short, active sentences. I began to write about these insights and about the convergences I observed (Simmons, 1991). As my doctoral program progressed, I explored other topics and issues related to writing and teaching.

Lost in the Statistical Wasteland

Although research for the writing-group article drew me closer to students, my dissertation seemed to isolate me in a desert of numbers. Several years ago, during a sabbatical dedicated to full-time coursework, my sadistic adviser insisted I take a year-long statistics and research methodology course from the psychology department. I dusted off my twenty-year-old knowledge of calculus and slipped in fearfully among the recent psychology graduates who were furiously taking down pages of equations, deriving formulas, and calculating p-values.

At the same time, I wrote a long review of the writing assessment literature, trying to discover if anyone else allowed for level of difficulty when rating papers. The year I taught writing with him, Tom Carnicelli of the UNH English department sold me on his "Greg Louganis" method. Argumentative prose, Carnicelli holds, is more difficult than mere description and should be graded differently. I discovered that most writing assessments skirted the issue by dictating the subject of the sample essay. I worried that many students would be denied the chance to do their best work on tests that made such choices for them.

Don Graves again offered a deceivingly simple alternative: how would I like to construct a new, large-scale assessment, say with portfolios, that used statistics and kept track of the types of discourse children chose to write?

Three years later, I had become the doctoral program's "quantoid," the lone sufferer in the statistical wasteland. While my ethnographic colleagues merrily followed children, collecting snuggly data in notebooks and on audio- and videotapes, I was buried in significance levels and non-parametric statistics, disconsolately looking for flesh for these computerized bones.

After my first year of research, I wrote an article (Simmons, 1990a) reporting that teachers seldom listed the emotional components of writing (either the flavor or the writer's experience) as strengths of students' pieces, while fifth-grade writers frequently did. I also wrote that students who mentioned teacher-favored qualities (ideas and organization), but left the emotional aspects off their lists of criteria, got the highest scores. But I had also heard teachers talk about their emotional reactions to papers as they scored them.

After my second year of study, I wrote (Simmons, 1990b) that eighth graders and their teachers overwhelmingly agreed more on the strengths of papers than did the fifth- or eleventh-grade teachers and students. Moreover, the emotional qualities accounted for the difference. The eighth-grade raters also handed out the most high scores and the fewest low ones in any of the scoring groups. If the scores were any reflection, somehow writing abilities seemed to develop best when teachers and students understood and valued each other's emotions.

Students' Self-Assessments Teach the Teacher

Yet numbers could teach me only so much. They, like Corey and Corey, had taught me to look at students' references to emotions in their reflective essays and journals. As I continued to write by sifting through those journalism portfolios, I heard the voices behind the theories and numbers. At last, I, too, was collecting cuddly data.

One student, Laurie, voiced her frustrations with the negative slant to news, then expanded her range and depth of information. "I was becoming more worldly," she noticed. "I was soon to become among the most knowledgeable in the school."

Another young woman, Molly, who went on to edit a school paper, used her dislike of negative news as an opportunity for self-examination: "I HATE reading the newspaper!!! . . . In short, the news is depressing. . . . It creates a sort of hopelessness that is discouraging to deal with as a sixteen-year-old." Thanks to Molly, I understood more about why my students didn't read the newspaper: it offended their idealism, a quality that I value in myself but had overlooked in them.

Melissa was frustrated by newswriting more than by news itself. "To me journalism is like math or science and therefore I find it quite a challenge," she wrote tactfully. "Art and English have not forced me to follow rules that inhibit me, but journalism . . . has guidelines . . . personal opinions . . . are exempt." Melissa explained that she thinks in different ways, "I tend to think more in color and shape than when, where, why, and who."

I, too, had been having trouble pursuing both teaching and poetry at the same time and had developed a plan to manage it— teaching and studying during the school year and writing poetry in the summer. My writing plan was working; in the last year before graduate school I had published three poems. But much of my writing consisted of reworking "failed" or "resting" drafts. I was generating fewer and fewer new pieces and seemed trapped inside the same few themes—death, the mysteries of nature, isolation—and what Don Murray calls a "constipated" style—three-word lines, three-line stanzas. In 1989, for instance, I published this poem:

translation

solitary fireflies incandesce
like stars translating
earth to light

Like my students Laurie and Molly, I had to change my negative thinking and give fuller voice to the idealism trapped in "Translation."

Melissa's final portfolio showed me she had found a vantage point from which to begin her integration. Her writing experience had helped her to see the more rigorous aspects of art. "In journalism," she concluded, ". . . greatness is based on clearness, facts, and being to the point. In itself journalism is an art, an art of control and perfection." I had learned that she was learning. Now I needed a place from which I could begin to connect my poet self to myself as journalist.

Students Teach Me to Join a Peer Group

In their discussions and portfolios, students praised peer-editing groups, calling the atmosphere "laid-back" and the group "a family." One boy, Chris, had trouble with *family* and offered *team* as an alternative.

"Translation" by Jay Simmons first appeared in the Winter 1988–89 issue of *Folio.*

"But," Kevin explained, "you don't compete. People can loosen up more when we are workshopping articles." Another group agreed: "The group helped out with writing and reporting," they said.

One student, Mark, explained that specific, cognitive learning takes place in this supportive group:

> I do in fact learn many things from these group working times. I have learned about format and a great deal of editing and punctuating thanks to Brad. I believed he is a great influence on our group due to his achievements as a reporter and his effort as a student.

As the teacher, I admit to feeling a little like chopped liver, since I had been giving the group lots of help with news format, editing, and punctuating. Yet I was reminded of the peer-counseling dictum that anything heard from a peer will be more effective than that which comes from a teacher.

As a writer, I needed to learn from my peers as well. I joined a writer's group similar to what I had provided for my students. One night I brought a story poem, a scene I had witnessed as a nine-year-old, of a woman beheading a chicken. I heard the voices of Don Graves, Don Murray, Mekeel McBride, Andy Merton, Mimi White, and others challenging me to tell more stories.

Students Show Me How to Set Goals that Work

I had been miserable returning to the high school newsroom after my sabbatical, especially because my writers were not responding to *my* challenges. I dared them, as I had dared myself as an undergraduate at Bowdoin writing for Herbert Ross Brown, senior member of the English department and editor of *The New England Quarterly*, to get at least one page of copy back without a red mark. I had forgotten Don Murray's advice to wait to grade until I was ready for work to stop.

While collecting data for my article, I saw that Laurie was setting interviewing goals for herself. Next, I looked back at her letter and found a reading goal: "As a result of my frustration with newspapers and their content, I began to look at just how the newspapers were laid out." Laurie extended this interest to work on layout of the school paper, and eventually her college paper.

Today I ask all my students, at-risk counselees, developing readers, or reluctant researchers to set goals for themselves, as researching my own writing assignment taught me they can. I ask my potential dropouts to set for themselves personal and academic challenges to work on in the reading and writing that follow each day's group counseling session. I have learned there is no clear line between the personal and the academic, as far as students are concerned. While some group members dealing with alcoholic parents have taken my suggestions to read some of the self-help literature, others have on their own used their journals to manage personal crises—breakups with boyfriends, anger at another student, or sexual abuse. These teenagers teach me what reading and writing can be for.

I, too, have gained an expanded sense of the uses of writing. In my roles as teacher, doctoral student, and writer I wrote two chapters, five articles, and two speeches in one year alone. I have consulted and presented workshops in three states, all the while teaching, passing my qualifying exams, and beginning my dissertation. And, most pleasing of all, I have written twenty-three pages of poetry, largely built on stories from my childhood.

References

Bruffee, K.A. (1988). On not listening in order to hear: Collaborative learning and the rewards of classroom research. *Journal of Basic Writing, 7,* 3–12.

Corey, M.S., & Corey, G. (1987). *Groups: Processes and practice* (3rd ed.). Pacific Grove, CA: Brooks/Cole Publishing.

John-Steiner, V. (1985). *Notebooks of the mind.* New York: Harper and Row.

Rose, M. (1989). *Lives on the boundary.* New York: Free Press.

Simmons, J. (1990a). Portfolios as large-scale assessment. *Language Arts, 67,* 262–268.

Simmons, J. (1990b, May). *Seacoast Educational Services 1989–90 writing sample portfolio assessment grades 5, 8, and 11.* Report presented to Seacoast Educational Services, Somersworth, NH.

Simmons, J. (1991). *Thinking under construction: Groups, journals, and portfolios in writing class.* Manuscript submitted for publication.

7 Reflections of a Teacher Writer

Vera E. Milz
Conant Elementary School, Bloomfield Hills, Michigan

Entering my classroom, you will see children with pencils, markers, and crayons—many engaging in the act of writing. Derek is curled up with pencil and paper while he writes what he knows about Martin Luther King, Jr. After a class meeting to discuss why King is honored with a January holiday, Derek became interested in learning more about this great man. He has read several books and checked the encyclopedia, and eventually he will report to his classmates on what he has learned. Amy and Erin are busy writing in their journals—talking as they write about everything from their stuffed animals to the books they have just finished. Erik is drawing a poster to tell the class about a book by Bill Peet that they should be sure to read. These are only a few of the many acts of writing in which my students are participating. The children write very easily and with lots of self-confidence. They have stories to tell to their classmates and to themselves.

It wasn't as easy for me to write! I grew up in an era where writing was not a valued part of the classroom. I wrote to please my teachers, on topics that they assigned. Yet as a teacher of children who have shared their writing with me, I have discovered that I also have stories to tell about their writing. It is through this writing that other teachers have entered my classroom to discover what is happening there. Since the early 1980s, I have published many articles for teachers in various monographs and books.

Reflections on Why I Write

My writing has been something that has evolved, a natural outcome of a lifelong search to meet the needs of the children in my care and to understand how children learn to write. Initially, all the writing I did was to fulfill the requirements of graduate classes at the universities I attended in Michigan and Arizona. As the years and credits began to add up, I reached the point of choosing a topic for dissertation research. With little confidence of ever finishing, I began to decide what I wanted to do. Instinctively, I turned to my classroom and the children. Within its walls, I knew there was a story to be told.

Over the years, my students had written prolifically—long before the "writing process" work of Donald Graves became popular. After a trip to England in the early seventies, I gave my children notebooks and then watched as they kept daily journals. I had boxes of notes and stories given to me by many children. It was easy to decide that I wanted to collect my students' writing over a school year and describe how they grew and changed as writers. The hard part, which I didn't know then, was that over the next seven years I would copy more than 7,000 pieces written by these students, all of which needed to be sorted, honed, organized, and analyzed. Yet it was from this enormous project (1984) that I found I could write, that I had something important to say to teachers. As I reflect on the process of writing a piece today, I realize that I learned some important things from that study. I would like to share those insights with teachers who would like to write professionally.

Getting Started

Watching children write was of special interest to me, but I would like to suggest that we each begin with reflecting on our own classrooms. What interesting or unusual patterns do you observe? Is there a child with special needs? What most excites you in your classroom? Is there a new technique or method you want to try? What questions do teachers ask you if they visit?

When Regie Routman wanted to use children's literature instead of a basal reader in her reading program, she gradually tried many new techniques in her classroom. Her books, *Transitions: From Literature to Literacy* (Routman, 1988) and *Invitations: Changing as Teachers and Learners K–12* (Routman, 1991) document her discoveries. When teachers asked me, "How do you get started on the first day of school," I used this question as a focus for a chapter I was writing for *Portraits of Whole Language Classrooms* (Milz, 1990). Whether it is an article or a book, what we are doing in classrooms is important. We are with children every day, sharing their interests and supporting their learning. Believing in the importance of what we and the children are doing is the first step that we all must take.

Next, we must want to share what we observe and know, and what we are learning. As I think back to some of the most important influences upon me as a teacher wanting to help children write, I remember an article by Rhea Paul (1976). In it, she told how her kindergarten students were categorizing speech sounds in their writing. As they wrote, she discovered patterns in their writing, which were similar to those used by children in my own first grade. Carol Avery, another classroom teacher, has written many pieces describing her classroom and the learning within it. She very poignantly describes Laura, a child who died in a fire, and how she and her students knew Laura through Laura's writing (Avery, 1988). I'm glad that Avery found the time to help me to know Laura, and to confirm the importance of whole writing instead of the traditional worksheets and assignments given in many classrooms.

In Process

Once you decide to begin an article, it helps to look back through the materials you have collected. Often, many of my samples are from the folders I keep on each child for evaluation purposes during the year. Self-stick note pads help me keep anecdotal records to communicate with parents, and they also help me retain information for professional articles. If I am working on an article, I do talk to parents about copying these materials, and never once have I been turned down. In fact, parents are usually anxious to see the final article in print and often ask for progress reports on my piece.

While children in my classrooms have provided the insights for articles I have written, I read other articles and reports to look for confirmation of the conclusions that I reach. As I describe the children's learning within the environment in which I teach, I find that I am analyzing and questioning its elements. Guba (1978) uses the term *triangulation* to describe the accumulation of evidence. He concludes, "When a series of bits of evidence all tend in some direction, that direction assumes far greater believability" (p. 64).

When I first began to understand that children did not write randomly, but made definite decisions to spell words they needed, Read's work (1975) provided the first information. It was comforting to find that other children had responded in similar ways. I believe it is because so many teachers have reported similar findings that Read's innovative work on invented spelling is widely accepted and has become part of today's classroom expectations.

Problems

Once I sit down at my computer, I find it easy to write. Yet one problem I constantly fight is finding a block of time that allows me to think about what I want to say. There are times in a classroom teacher's schedule when it becomes so hectic that just surviving seems impossible. Conferences and report card periods, school paperwork, producing a class play, making arrangements for a special trip or project all seem to take hours beyond the usual school day. It also doesn't allow for a case of the flu, an abscessed tooth, or other emergencies that seem to crop up in anyone's life. Yet a week's interruption while working on an article means it will probably take two weeks to catch up, regroup, and begin to make progress again. I really don't know the answer to this problem, except to go back to the purpose for which I write—to share my learning with my colleagues and to help create a better educational world for my students—and try a little harder!

Another problem that I must deal with is finding some natural stopping points. Each time I turn on my computer I reread and revise the article I am working on. Unfortunately, I can get bogged down and begin to feel that an article is hopeless. I find that having a colleague read and respond is often what gets me moving again. Writing is a solitary pursuit, but the more I talk about what I am working on, the more progress I seem to make.

A Plea for Action

Classroom teachers lead hectic lives, and it is not easy to fit professional writing into our schedules. Yet we are the ones who can document what is happening in our classrooms, and we can provide the insights upon which educational methodology and techniques are based. In a talk at the Oakland County Reading Council's January 1991 brunch, Kenneth Goodman stated, "What teachers implement and reflect on in their classrooms is important research for our profession." The importance of the teacher writer is being recognized. The National Council of Teachers of English honored Nancie Atwell for her book, *In the Middle* (1987), with the prestigious 1990 David H. Russell Award for research in the teaching of English.

It is a most rewarding feeling when a colleague stops you to say, "I liked what you wrote. It was really helpful to me." I recently received an autographed book from Mem Fox, a respected children's author and teacher educator from Australia. She wrote, "For Vera, whose writings I have admired for years!" As I looked at that autograph, I realized how powerful the written word can be. For my words to travel from my classroom around the world to Australia is miraculous to me. I hope in the months to come that you will share your insights with colleagues and with me. Together, we can make our classrooms better places for all children.

References

Atwell, N. (1987). *In the middle: Writing, reading, and learning with adolescents.* Portsmouth, NH: Boynton/Cook.

Avery, C.S. (1988). Laura's legacy. *Language Arts, 65,* 110–111.

Guba, E. (1978). *Toward a methodology of naturalistic inquiry in educational evaluation* (CSE Monograph Series in Evaluation, No. 8). Los Angeles: University of California, Center for the Study of Evaluation.

Milz, V.E. (1984). A psycholinguistic description of the development of writing in selected first grade students (Doctoral dissertation, University of Arizona, 1983). *Dissertation Abstracts International, 44,* 3279A.

Milz, V.E. (1990). Supporting literacy development: On the first day in first grade and throughout the year. In H. Mills & J.A. Clyde (Eds.), *Portraits of whole language classrooms* (pp. 96–106). Portsmouth, NH: Heinemann.

Paul, R. (1976). Invented spelling in kindergarten. *Young Children, 31*(3), 195–200.

Read, C. (1975). *Children's categorization of speech sounds in English* (NCTE Research Report 17). Urbana, IL: National Council of Teachers of English.

Routman, R. (1988). *Transitions: From literature to literacy.* Portsmouth, NH: Heinemann.

Routman, R. (1991). *Invitations: Changing as teachers and learners K–12.* Portsmouth, NH: Heinemann.

II Thinking Like a Writer

8 Getting It Down and Sending It Out

Rick Monroe
Woodinville High School, Washington

I write because I need to understand myself and others, because I want to be a part of, even help shape, the printed professional conversation. We all have a story, and perhaps mine will encourage you to tell yours.

Because teachers are isolated, activities such as presenting at conferences, taking on a student teacher, and publishing are ways to create relationships with colleagues that reach beyond the walls of our respective classrooms. And it seems to me that taking part in that dialogue is important, because each story might spark change or confirm what others believe or do. Furthermore, writing for publication puts us in the role of student learner, something easily forgotten after a few years in front of the class. Whatever the motive, writing for publication extends what it means to belong to our profession. My own professional history and the writing that was part of it provide a case in point.

My first teaching job was in a small school. I was the only English major in the school, and I was responsible for the eighth-grade language arts curriculum. What I lacked in experience I made up for in bravado. I remember being overworked that year. I remember being lonely. I didn't realize and couldn't articulate what I needed, but instinctively I sought mentors. I read the state affiliate's journal, the national *English Journal,* and I called my supervising teacher. I was searching for advice and confirmation. I was trying to get connected with my colleagues.

The next year I taught in a large, four-year high school in Vancouver, Washington. There I was part of a department of eight English teachers. I didn't feel much better because, except for the department head, my colleagues remained guarded. I still felt isolated, except then it was worse because I wasn't the only English teacher in the school.

Weary of being a stranger, of feeling like an outsider, I moved back to Seattle. My wife and I took an apartment in a familiar neighborhood, and while starting graduate school, I took a job teaching eighth grade in another small school. It felt good to be recognized by friends, professors, and neighbors again. I stayed very busy that year. I attended conferences sponsored by the state's English council. At the university, I made contact with other English teachers. When one of our state's National Writing Project sites offered a workshop, I attended, taking intellectual nourishment whenever I could find it.

Being a bit brash, I wrote an article that year and sent it to the editor of the state English council's journal. I wasn't sure if anyone cared, but I wasn't about to be left out. And that's my advice to you: don't wait to be invited.

An amazing thing happened. I received a detailed response from the editor. The letter began:

> Our reviewers liked your article "Computers and Composition: A Warning." They have recommended that we publish it in the fall computer issue provided that you think about the following suggestions. . . . We'll be looking forward to hearing from you by September 6th if possible. Please call if you have any questions.

The letter was written on official letterhead and closed with *Cordially*. The editor provided her work and home phone numbers. When I reviewed my manuscript and the suggestions, I saw the editorial board was right. I made the necessary revisions and was published the following fall (Monroe, 1984).

When I look back on this first experience, I appreciate how helpful the editorial board was and how easy it made getting published. I have since served as president of the Washington State Council of Teachers of English and from an insider's point of view, I see that affiliate journals are begging for good pieces written by teachers working in the field. I didn't know then that the editor was coaxing me along because she needed submissions. I thought then that I had hit the big time! Actually, what I had done, like many before me, was join the professional conversation.

There are more than one hundred affiliate journals in need of good articles written for and by practicing teachers. All I did was pay attention to issues in the profession, write something I felt was important, and send it off. Of course, I did my homework. I read the journal and looked closely at what was published. But the most important step I took was to submit the manuscript. I cared about what I was doing and hoped someone else would want to hear what I had to say. My article, grounded in theory, came out of my classroom experience. It was anecdotal in nature and expressed honestly what I felt. Had I to do it over, I might have avoided some jargon, and I would have been less pedantic. But because I wrote out of my experience, because I expressed something important to me, I can still look back on that article and feel proud. That first publication gave me the confidence of an insider.

In the same year, I linked up with the parent of one of my students. Colleen's mother taught at a new, suburban high school; in fact, she was the department head. More important, Mary Kollar was (and still is) a committed teacher, someone helping to shape the teaching of English in our state. Both of us were trying to help our students gain a sense of audience. During the October parent-teacher conference, Mary and I talked about the frustration of getting students beyond writing for the teacher. Near the end of the conference, she suggested a writing exchange between her seniors and my eighth graders.

The exchange lasted six months, and toward the end, we wondered if others might be interested in what we were doing. We started drafting an article that spring. Neither of us had written collaboratively before, and we weren't sure how to begin. Mary suggested that we each write our own versions, talking about what our students learned and what we thought was valuable about the exchange. A few weeks later, we had two separate drafts. The interesting part was that both essays, with a bit of rewriting for unity, blended nicely. There was enough of a common theme between what our students had learned and what we thought was worthwhile to make an article. Over several long sessions of talking and drafting, we reworked our separate pieces into one manuscript. Both of us were extending our definition of what it meant to be part of the professional conversation. By February of the next year, "Our Audience Is Real" was published in *English Journal* (Kollar & Monroe, 1984).

Seven months later, I was struggling again in another new situation, making my way this time in an established, tight-knit high school English department. That fall Donald Murray spoke at the Puget Sound Writing Program's reunion. I listened to his commonsense advice about teaching writing and realized I had been doing what he advocated. That workshop, combined with a coincidental conversation I had with a colleague two days later, led to another period of writing and a new publication.

My colleague and I chatted briefly outside the library. He asked how I liked Murray's workshop, and I said it felt good. He announced his disappointment in the workshop because Murray hadn't presented anything new. He had expected Murray to break new ground.

After that unnerving conversation, something started gnawing away at me, so I started writing. My colleague was right; Murray hadn't said anything new, but I had gained from his presentation. I needed to hear something old, something familiar and affirming. Unlike my colleague, who was well-established in his position, I was getting used to new faces, a new curriculum, and a new environment. I was adjusting to high school students, getting used to the differences between them and the inner-city eighth graders I had taught during the last four years. In attending Murray's workshop I was looking for something familiar, something that would give me a settled feeling, and Murray's comments were reassuring. I wasn't looking for something new, because I was already overwhelmed by newness.

But that wasn't all. I was having difficulty adjusting. I expected something new of my teaching. Somehow, because I was in a new position, I thought I should have something fresh to offer my students, that somehow what I had been doing wasn't good enough. My colleague's comment had raised the bigger issue: I decided I didn't like the assumption that new was somehow better.

Writing to explore this notion, I was able to discover why I had found the Murray workshop so comforting. I wasn't trying to write an article, but after several pages I wondered if other teachers had the same thought. I worked on the essay and then sent the finished piece entitled "Nothing New" to *English Journal*. A month after the article was published (Monroe, 1986), I received a note from Donald Murray.

> Dear Mr. Monroe:
> Imagine my surprise as I read through the *English Journal* and got into your article before I met myself staring back from the page. I think the point you made is very important. I often feel uncomfortable as I talk as though I were inventing the wheel, but I have to keep relearning what I know, and so does everyone else.

Originally, as a writer and a teacher, I had hoped to join the ongoing conversation my colleagues kept alive in print, and Murray's letter made me feel included. Here was a man who, much like the editor of my first published article, took time to respond to colleagues.

Looking back, I realize that most of my articles began as a kind of gnawing, nagging feeling. Rarely have I actually sat down determined to write this or that. Instead, what I do is try to make sense of my profession, hoping that what I discover will inform my classroom practice. Writing helps me make that sense. Writing also helps me get a grip on my own confusion, helps me think clearer about myself and my work.

As a result of my professional participation, I am an insider now. As an affiliate leader and NCTE committee member, I am keeping the conversation alive, nudging colleagues to present at conferences, to write reviews for our affiliate newsletter and journal. Like Murray and my colleague Mary, I try to be inclusive. As part of a writing group, I am continuing the conversation with my colleagues, working at writing, getting it down and sending it out.

Practical Suggestions about Writing for Publication

These experiences over the past eight years suggest some practical pointers for myself and others.

Read the affiliate and national journals. I have found confirmation in print. It is always heartening to read what others care about.

Pay attention to issues in the profession and themes announced in the affiliate and national journals. It takes time to put out a journal and even more time to collect articles centered on a theme. Ignoring the theme tells the journal editor you aren't paying attention and is not a good way to begin a conversation.

Write the editor(s) of the state journal and ask for help. I have written to three different editors of our state journal, and all of them have been willing to help me shape my manuscripts. This is also true for the national journals. Although pressed for time, the editors often will take time to give advice.

Write about what people like to read. I like reading articles that are anecdotal, grounded in theory (but not pedantic), honest, and voiced. I don't want to read jargon and educationese. Lately, I am getting weary of *empower* and the current use of *impact* as a verb.

Write out of your own experience. I am always amazed when topics important to me are also of interest to my colleagues. I have learned not to discount what I do and what happens to me in or out of my classroom.

Finally, I have learned in these eight years to be brave and send out my ideas. Like most worthwhile relationships, a little risk is necessary. I have also learned to be tolerant of my own work and my progress as a writer. I think it is important to participate in the professional conversation. I am not concerned with being brilliant, just being included.

References

Kollar, M., & Monroe, R. (1984). Our audience is real. *English Journal, 73*(2), 75–79.

Monroe, R. (1984). Computers and composition: A warning. *Washington English Journal, 7*(1), 30–32.

Monroe, R. (1986). Nothing new. *English Journal, 75*(7), 43–45.

9 Why Write for Publication?

Chris Crowe
Brigham Young University, Laie, Hawaii

Elementary and secondary school teachers, unlike their university colleagues, rarely have the time or the institutional support necessary to encourage them to write for publication. Secondary school teacher Patricia A. Gazda-Grace (Donlan, 1987) described some typical impediments to writing for publication:

> Something always seems to come up—grading five sets of essays, making up study guides and tests, running off dittoes, conferring with students and parents, running a household, etc. Teachers know the details all too well. (p. 1)

Donlan (1987) gave additional reasons—from his own experience—why teachers don't write. He admitted that in his twelve years as a high school English teacher, despite his regular reading of other classroom teachers' experiences in *English Journal*, he never wrote an article for a professional journal. His reasons?

> I felt I had nothing of interest to communicate. I feared rejection. I was being evaluated for teaching students, not for writing articles. But probably the most significant reason was lack of time. (p. 1)

In addition to the lack of time, teachers sometimes are reluctant to display their writing in public, where their colleagues—and their students—are free to scrutinize their work. Such scrutiny was intimidating to high school teacher Borstein (1989). "What if they found it lacking, or worse, shallow and boring? There goes my credibility!" (p. 60). Borstein pointed out another concern: "Most other teachers were not writing . . . probably for the same reasons as I had. Why should I?" (p. 60).

These are all valid and real reasons why more teachers don't write for publication. Nevertheless, many teachers do want to write and are quite capable of writing publishable articles; what they lack is an answer to the nagging question, "Why write," an answer solid enough to motivate them to find the time and overcome their inhibitions about writing for educational journals.

Here, then, are some answers designed to encourage teachers to write and submit articles for publication.

Writing for Publication Improves Teachers

To teach writing effectively, teachers should understand all that writing is. And the best way to really understand writing is to write. As one experienced writer put it, "Expertise in another field, even in one requiring advanced degrees, does not mean expertise in writing" (von Schussler-Schell, 1988, p. 6). Just because a person is a writing teacher, one with a diploma, or several diplomas, doesn't mean that person fully appreciates the art and skill of writing. That understanding only comes through apprenticeship.

Thus, the more involved teachers are in producing their own writing, the better they'll be able to understand the problems writers have. Composition teacher writer Mem Fox (1988) described that understanding this way:

> Teachers of writing who have been soldiers themselves, engaged in a writing battle, *must* be able to empathize more closely with the comrades in their classrooms than teachers who are merely war correspondents at the hotel bar, as it were, watching the battle from a safe distance, declining to get in there and write themselves. (p. 118)

Others (Johnson, 1987; Nash, 1987) have found that writing for publication has helped them become more effective teachers. When teachers are writing for publication, they have some built-in materials to use in their writing classes. They can show students their written drafts, and they can talk about the obstacles they've encountered and how they've overcome them. Teachers who are writing for publication can even ask for student suggestions on how to improve an article that they're working on.

Borstein (1989) reported that sharing her writing in class helped her students understand that writing is a real process done by real people. This kind of classroom practice helps students see that writing is a messy and difficult process, one that is not easy, not even for teachers (Johnson, 1987). And, of course, when students see that their teachers are also engaged in the writing battle, it certainly helps improve the teachers' credibility. They know their teachers have been there. They know their teachers understand.

Writing for Publication Develops Credibility

Credibility is scarce in many schools today. Students, parents, voters, and critics of education have all, at one time or another, taken their potshots at inept, unskilled teachers. And, in a way, they cannot be blamed for negative views of the teaching profession. Beyond personal knowledge of students, the only way the public has to gauge teacher effectiveness or ineffectiveness is through standardized test results (taken by students), Education Task Force reports (written by bureaucrats and academics), and news articles (written by journalists).

It only takes one hastily scrawled memo, one typo-filled article, or one illegible (or unintelligible) note to a parent to provide critics with enough evidence to lump the entire profession under the condemnation that "teachers can't write." Teachers can help undo some of that damage by writing, and writing well, for publication. As Donelson (1988) recommended, writing for publication is a very effective way for teachers to demonstrate their literacy to the public.

Writing for Publication Broadens Understanding

Of course, it's long been known that writing can help people refine their knowledge of a subject (McCrimmon, 1984; Tchudi, 1987). Writing for publication also provides an opportunity for introspection, a chance for teachers to do some soul-searching by thinking about their profession, their job, and how they feel about it. Novelist Lawrence Block (1988) wrote, "Every teacher is still learning . . . The writer is a teacher, seeking to instruct himself at least as much as to impart his message to others" (p. 70). Bartholomy (1983) considered increased self-awareness and awareness of the world around us as a fringe benefit of writing.

When teachers write for publication, they have to think beyond their classrooms to the broader world outside, to other teachers who also have students to teach, papers to grade, critics to contend with, and daily obstacles to face. When teachers are involved in writing projects, their horizons expand. They realize that education is more than just what goes on inside the four walls of a classroom; it goes beyond the classroom and into everyday life. Writing for publication helps teachers interact with the profession more broadly.

Further, teachers who are writing for publication are also reading. If they are serious about getting published, they will read the journals in which they hope to be published, and will probably do additional background reading on the subjects they're considering. The result of such reading and researching is personal and professional growth, as well as fine writing.

Writing for Publication Is a Professional Obligation

Teachers' responsibilities are not limited to their classrooms. As members of the teaching profession, they should also be involved in improving and supporting the profession as a whole. They can do that by joining professional organizations, attending professional conferences and meetings, and being involved in the development and planning of curriculum in their own schools or districts. Moreover, they can improve and support the profession by writing for publication.

As teachers, we depend on each other for support, advice, and information, and much of that comes through the professional journals we read. In fact, teachers who responded to a survey reported that "reading professional journals was the single most helpful kind of preparation" for their work in the classroom (Pickett, 1988, p. 3).

Editors of journals are hungry for articles about research, classroom experiences, and ideas that will help other members of the profession. For example, not long ago the editor of *English Journal* asked for more contributions from writers directly involved in classroom practice. In the call for submissions, he wrote, "Teachers have much to learn from one another. *EJ* hopes to encourage a new professionalism by publishing the results of disciplined inquiry in your classroom" (Nelms, 1988a, p. 89).

Writing for Publication Helps the Professional Journals

A well-known literary story tells how American novelist James Fenimore Cooper became a writer. Cooper apparently hated writing even a letter. Until the age of thirty, he had never published anything, nor did he have any plans to publish. But one evening he was reading a novel to his wife and thought it so poorly written that he threw it down and said he could do better himself. His wife challenged him to do so, and he began writing (Brooks, Lewis, & Warren, 1973).

Teachers occasionally receive similar challenges: to vent their anger, express an opinion, or share ideas and research. If they, as Cooper did, would accept the challenge to write, they might very well find themselves among the ranks of published writers.

Editors can only publish the articles they receive, and most editors say they would like to receive more. "It is unfortunate," wrote

Donlan (1987), "that so few English teachers write up their classroom experiences in order to share with colleagues and university researchers alike" (p. 1). All editors are anxious to receive well-written, informative articles, and they often tell their readers exactly what kinds of articles they're interested in (see Gebhardt, 1987; Nelms, 1988b; Pradl, 1988; Raymond, 1987). Teachers can help these editors by submitting their best writing to professional journals. Sure, it's risky. Rejection is always a possibility. But as Elbow (1981) said, it's worth the risk, because "we *do* have things we want to tell people even if they haven't invited us to do so" (p. 210).

Writing for Publication Is Rewarding

Outside the university, most teachers don't *have* to write for publication if they don't want to; that, as I see it, is an advantage. Teachers then can write with less pressure, with more care, and choose with more selectivity where they will send their writing. In short, because they don't have to write for publication, they have more freedom. They can write because they choose to, because it matters to them, because they have something they want to say or something that needs saying.

Consider the kind of writing we get from our students. Which is better—the papers we drag out of them, kicking and screaming, or the compositions they generate on their own with just a little prod or guidance? It works both ways, and teachers who write for publication learn that firsthand.

I've talked to various writers about why they write for publication. Some of their reasons for writing really aren't that different from the reasons teachers express. Here are a few of their responses (Crowe, 1986):

> In my own little way, I feel like I'm helping the greater good. (p. 136)

> I like the idea of somebody picking up something that I wrote and being touched by it, or laughing, or thinking, "Wow, she really told that story well." (pp. 143–144)

> I get a real satisfaction when I finish something, and then it's in print. That's really the fun part. There's certainly some ego in it. I guess I really do it mostly for myself . . . Everything I write always has something of me in it. Each time is a growth experience for me. (p. 169)

It's very satisfying. One of the nice things about writing for publication is that when you're finished, you've got a solid thing you can hold in your hand. That's the big difference between that and something like teaching. (p. 197)

You want to be heard, [you] feel like you've got something valuable to say, and you want to share that with an audience. . . . [T]here's also the motivational factor of wanting to help solve problems and improve things. So I think those two things taken together: wanting to have a positive influence and also wanting to be personally part of that and to be recognized . . . are probably the key factors to why I write. (p. 227)

As these writers have said, it is very satisfying to have an article published, but getting published is more than mere ego gratification. For many writers, it's the response to their work that really matters (Fox, 1988). Elbow (1981) explains:

Writing's greatest reward, for most of us anyway, is the sense of reaching an audience. Ideally the audience should love what we write, but in the last analysis, it's enough if we can feel them reading. (p. 212)

And what better audience to reach than one made up of colleagues who share our problems, concerns, and interests? They're out there, our comrades in arms, waiting to read what we have to say.

References

Bartholomy, D. (1983). *Sometimes you just have to stand naked.* Englewood Cliffs, NJ: Prentice-Hall.

Block, L. (1988, June). Messages for your most important reader. *Writer's Digest,* pp. 68–73.

Borstein, J. (1989). A writing teacher risks writing. *English Journal, 78*(5), 60–61.

Brooks, C., Lewis, R.W.B., & Warren, R.P. (Eds.). (1973). *American literature: The makers and the making, Volume 1.* New York: St. Martin's.

Crowe, C.E. (1986). A comparison of elements of writing considered important by professional writers and composition textbooks (Doctoral dissertation, Arizona State University, 1986). *Dissertation Abstracts International, 47,* 517A.

Donelson, K. (1988). Professionalism: English teachers' rights and responsibilities. *English Journal, 77*(4), 47–52.

Donlan, D. (1987). The need for English teachers to contribute to professional literature. *CSSEDC Quarterly, 9*(3), 1–2.

Elbow, P. (1981). *Writing with power.* New York: Oxford University Press.

Fox, M. (1988). Notes from the battlefield: Towards a theory of why people write. *Language Arts, 65,* 112–125.

Gebhardt, R.C. (1987). Editor's note. *College Composition and Communication, 38,* 19–20.

Johnson, R. (1987). Writing from artifacts. *College Composition and Communication, 38,* 342–343.

McCrimmon, J.M. (1984). Writing as a way of knowing. In R.L. Graves (Ed.), *Rhetoric and composition: A sourcebook for teachers and writers* (pp. 3–11). Upper Montclair, NJ: Boynton/Cook.

Nash, T. (1987). By the way, is there any money in this?: Encouraging young teachers to publish. *English Education, 19,* 237–243.

Nelms, B.F. (1988a). Practice and inquiry: *EJ* readers and *EJ* writers. *English Journal, 77*(2), 88–89.

Nelms, B.F. (1988b). What you can do for us. *English Journal, 77*(4), 88–89.

Pickett, N.A. (1988). Editorial: Continuing emphasis in *TETYC. Teaching English in the Two-Year College, 15,* 3–4.

Pradl, G.M. (1988). Editorial. *English Education, 20,* 3–6.

Raymond, J.C. (1987). *College English:* Whence and whither. *College English, 49,* 553–557.

Tchudi, S.J. (1987). Writer to reader to self: Personal uses of writing. *Language Arts, 64,* 489–496.

von Schussler-Schell, S. (1988, March). Passion and professionalism. *The Writer,* pp. 5–6.

10 Professional Writing: Redefining Teaching as Learning

Rod Winters
Orchard Hill Elementary School, Cedar Falls, Iowa

"What we have to learn first is 'how to unlearn.'"
R. Burton, English explorer (Fields, 1984)

Over the past twenty years, many educators have been helping students redefine what it is to write and what it means to be a writer. Rather than accepting a narrow definition that restricts writing to a small, talented minority, teachers have begun celebrating every person as having a story, and they are providing a place to begin telling that story. Passive admiration for the finished copy of published writers has been replaced by firsthand knowledge of the rich and messy endeavor any writer engages in to discover meaning on the page. Embracing a fuller concept of what it means to write and what it means to be a writer has allowed students to identify themselves in these roles. In classrooms scattered all across the nation, this broader perspective has led to a flourishing of writing as student writers discover their own stories.

Is there anything in this experience to help teachers in the classroom find a professional voice? The question is an intriguing one; if students have felt uneasy attempting to write about the classroom, teachers have felt just as uneasy attempting to write about their instruction. Odd though it may seem, the very teachers who helped students broaden narrow riverbeds to allow a full flow of writing seem to suffer drought when asked to write about their own experiences. Having thrown wide the doors to the literacy club for our students (Smith, 1988), perhaps we as teachers must now consider our own membership. The question is, "How do we redefine professional writing to include ourselves?"

Redefinition 1: Writing for Whom?

Professional writing would not seem all that complicated at first glance. Based on our past experience as readers of professional writing, we tend to package it rather neatly—someone telling someone else something which is true for them that the someone serving as audience doesn't already know. Pretty simple. Quite a feat, but pretty simple none-theless. Actually, this commonsense definition is quite a trap; in fact, it's the same trap our students often fall into at the beginning of writing. And our response to such a huge task is often similar to theirs: we freeze.

The only way to unlock those gears for ourselves is to get rid of that tyrant audience sitting on our shoulders, saying "impress me." We don't know what is true for other teachers, let alone how to enlighten them about it. The way out of this trap is not to write for someone else.

Instead, we write for ourselves by becoming our own audience. We listen to ourselves. We listen for our own questions. We listen for our own connections. We listen for our own resolutions. In short, we look for our own observations and our own meanings. We engage in self-talk on paper. My own jottings as a teacher capture this idea:

> Mike wrote another note to me today. It's amazing how his use
> of invented spelling has progressed since we started exchang-
> ing notes in the fall.   (February 1986)

Self-talk in writing can lead to insight. As Nancy Wheeler (1990) comments about a student in her classroom, "because I was writing down what he did, I could reflect on his behavior and theorize about why he did what he did."

We must write first for ourselves and for our own meanings. Indeed, the only way to have anything to say to others is to find something to say to ourselves. Donald Graves once said, "If you have writer's block, lower your standards." A corollary for writing professionally might be: if you can't write, kick out the jury.

Redefinition 2: Writing for What?

Writing primarily for ourselves actually unlocks multiple doors. Keeping ourselves at the center also answers questions about purpose. Once rid of outside expectations, we begin to allow ourselves time. Time to think, time to wonder, time to look for answers to questions, and perhaps even more important, time to become question seekers.

In the process of questioning, a subtle but important shift occurs. Rather than teaching from "a" theory, we begin teaching from our own theory. Once the shift has been made to a personalized system of beliefs and questions, changes occur in the way we approach teaching, the classroom, and our students. Our beliefs and our classrooms are no longer static, but evolve continually through the process of reflecting, rethinking, and readjusting. As Murray explains (1989), we begin "teaching for surprise." When we have done this, we have tapped into the true power of professional writing. Again, a personal jotting is an example:

> I've always had this lurking feeling about outcome-based education. It's hard to put my finger on it, but it just doesn't feel like what I'm all about.   (January 1985)

This entry shows a professional writing about his profession. It's not pretty; it's not very organized yet. But there is a sense of questioning, of reflection, of mulling over experience. There is power.

Redefinition 3: Professional or Personal Writing?

Each time we begin to write professionally, we have to fight our way past a notion that says, "No ideas allowed that aren't objective." If classroom teachers don't get past this idea, we put ourselves in the double-bind of working from personally meaningful questions but valuing only third-person, detached writing.

Fortunately, this narrow conception is slowly giving way to authentic, context-rich case studies along the lines of *Lessons from a Child* (Calkins, 1983). Heralded by many in literacy education, Calkins's book is at least as much a victory for teachers as writers as it is for teachers as readers. The book's language asserts unflinchingly that research needs to be understood in terms of the researcher and the context at least as much as in terms of the content.

This shift to a richer kind of professional writing should not be surprising. There is nothing in the root of *professional* that indicates a dry and unemotional undertaking. Indeed, the root *profess* would seem to indicate almost the opposite. Somehow we have let ourselves believe that professional must always be kept distinct from personal. We have confused scientific with professional. Attempting to write as objectively as possible, we have distanced ourselves right out of the picture.

Professional writing from classroom teachers is anecdotal. It is reflective. It has a sense of classroom action that breathes life into it. We must recognize that classroom teachers are in a unique position to write from their own perspective about the day-in, day-out experience of the classroom. Classroom writing has its own sense of strength and rhythm—strip that ongoing sense of vitality away, and you strip the quality that produces its unique voice. There is no need to try to sound like someone else. There is only one story to tell, and that is our own.

Redefinition 4: Who Am I as a Teacher?

Ultimately, writing becomes a matter of identity. The act of claiming space on the page makes a statement about who we are. If I choose to write, I am reclaiming my right to create meaning. I am making a statement to myself and to others. Without apology, I simply affirm:

> This is who I am.
>
> This is where I am.
>
> This is why I am the way that I am.
>
> Right at this moment.

When I write, my inner voice is given a life of its own. A voice to think, to question, to reflect on that constant stream of information that flows before me. A voice to pose tentative solutions and to make sense of the world.

And that, I realize, is the thought I have been searching for in the midst of this piece of writing. Perhaps the reason many teachers don't write about teaching is that we have forgotten that we can have a voice; forgotten that we have a right to bring to the page the voice of who we are, what we are, and where we are.

We start on our own turf, in our classrooms filled with learning. As Tom Romano has said, "We cut loose in individual voices, growing, changing and maturing by the very act of writing, and each, to quote Whitman, 'singing what belongs to him or her and no one else' " (Romano, 1987, p. 11). Writing for ourselves. Writing for our own meanings. As teachers, as writers, as learners.

References

Calkins, L.M. (1983). *Lessons from a child.* Portsmouth, NH: Heinemann.

Fields, R. (1984). *Chop wood. Carry water.* Los Angeles, CA: Jeremy P. Tarch.

Murray, D.M. (1989). *Expecting the unexpected.* Portsmouth, NH: Heinemann.

Romano, T. (1987). *Clearing the way: Working with teenage writers.* Portsmouth, NH: Heinemann.

Smith, F. (1988). *Essays into literacy.* Portsmouth, NH: Heinemann.

Wheeler, N. (1990). Showing the way: Using journal writing to develop learning and teaching strategies. In N. Atwell (Ed.), *Coming to know* (pp. 129–138). Portsmouth, NH: Heinemann.

11 To Read Like an Author

Alan M. Frager
Miami University, Oxford, Ohio

To have success in writing about education, teachers need to read—in education journals and books—like authors. I owe to Frank Smith (1983) many insights about making this reading-writing connection, as well as the idea for my chapter title. In his characteristic way of looking for an explanation that accounts for the development of a learner's abilities, instead of disabilities, Smith wonders how children ever learn to write, since writing involves "a vast number of conventions of a complexity which could never be organized into formal instructional procedures" (p. 559). By this reasoning, Smith helps us understand how the skills of writing are too multifaceted to be developed through direct instruction alone. Smith also rejects the notion that children learn to write by writing, the trial-and-error or hypothesis-testing approach. This rejection is based on the grounds that children write only infrequently in school and receive very little feedback on their writing. The answer Smith finally suggests to explain how children learn to write: they learn by reading.

This vicarious learning can happen because any writing with which a reader becomes engaged demonstrates how to write, whether the content explicitly discusses writing or any other subject. Any text demonstrates the complex conventions of spelling, usage, style, organization, and tone, among other features of writing, that are used by authors of that type of text. Smith contends that in the moments of ordinary engagement with a book, there is evidence that readers are learning a lot about writing. His example illustrates the meaning of reading like a writer:

> Most literate adults are familiar with the experience of pausing unexpectedly while reading a newspaper, magazine, or book in order to go back and look at the spelling of a word that has caught their attention. We say to ourselves, "Ah, so that's how that word is spelled" . . .
>
> Once more we are casually reading, and once more we find ourselves pausing to reread a passage. Not because of the spell-

ing this time, nor because we did not understand the passage. In fact we understood it very well. We go back because . . . we respond to the craftsman's touch. This is something . . . that we think is not beyond our reach. We have been reading like a writer, like a member of the club. (Smith, 1983, pp. 562–563)

A Stumbling Block for Teachers

As Smith explains, much can be learned about professional writing just through wide and casual reading in one's area of interest within the field of education. Yet before many teachers can make this reading-writing connection, a major stumbling block must be cleared: the conception of professional writing in education which teachers often learn in university coursework. Some university professors use student writing largely for the purpose of evaluation, that is, students write papers or answer essay questions to "prove" mastery of the content.

A shift in audience, from writing for the professor to writing for peers, has the potential to dramatically improve teachers' writing for publication. A teacher's general intent for writing can shift from trying to cover a topic to trying to *uncover* the topic—write something about it in a new or original way. With less reason to prove their worth through writing, teachers can find many other worthwhile purposes for writing about education: to excite, to persuade, to justify, to dramatize, to share. The greater range of purposes for writing creates a need to use forms of discourse other than exposition, such as narration, argument, and description.

More significant, a broad audience of peers is likely to be more receptive to writing based on subjective ways of knowing. In writing to peers, teachers can draw on knowledge that is emotional, physical, and intuitive, and not exclusively intellectual. As Dillon (1987) explains, "This tradition of knowing is perhaps closer to the stereotypical knowledge of the novelist, poet, and artist: experiential, holistic, and subjective" (p. 708). Learning that there are many ways to write about education, and many audiences for different types of writing, can motivate teachers to seek out and apply the writing tools of the novelist, poet, and essayist, instead of mimicking the textbook author's style.

Reading with an Author's Eye

Teachers need to read "like an author" in professional books and journals in education, including those they encountered in their university coursework. What teachers discover in the process of "reading like an author" is that journal articles and books were not necessarily written for the purpose of memory or mastery, but rather to engage the reader, share ideas, and invite interpretation and response. Reading with the eye of an author can help teachers learn much that improves their own professional writing in education. I suggest five specific ways to "read like an author."

Read to Learn What Others Have Written

Read in education journals and books to find the facts, examples, and ideas that will inform your writing and place it in relation to other writing on the same topic. Wide reading in the literature of education shows a writer that whatever the topic may be, others have been interested enough to research and write about it. Teachers should not assume that, because many others have written widely on a topic, there is nothing important left to discuss. On the contrary, knowledge in education, like other social sciences, is the product of the cumulative thinking and writing of practitioners, researchers, journalists, poets, and every kind of thinker in the field. Because people are so complex as individuals, and infinitely more complex in social groups, there will always be room for a new insight or perspective to advance the state of knowledge about teaching and learning.

Through wide reading in the professional literature, teachers learn the context in which to place the ideas they want to discuss in writing. For example, currently much is written about the topic of responding to literature. Consider a teacher who has been successfully using journal writing to help students respond to literature, and this teacher wants to share these insights with other teachers. Through wide reading of the literature, this teacher will find many reports about using journals to elicit responses to literature; by reading these reports, the teacher can judge how "new" her or his ideas really are. If they are new, the teacher will want to summarize in writing the other ideas about using journals, since the other ideas will provide contrast to more clearly illuminate his or her own perspective. If the teacher's insights are very similar to those already reported by others, they can still be shared, but in a different style—perhaps through a narrative, a case study, or a humorous account. In all professional writing, the ideas, facts, and examples written by others may be used, with appropriate credit and references given, to help readers see the network of people who have been interested in the same topic.

Read to Discover the Uses for Writing in Education

For teachers who have the impression that the purpose for reading professional writing is for recall on tests, or perhaps to find research to "prove" the efficacy of an idea or method, a wide world of other uses is there to be discovered. Even a cursory reading of an issue of *English Journal* reveals a wide range of additional purposes: to excite and to explain, to advertise and to dramatize, to review and to reflect, to amuse and to muse, to induce and to dissuade, to brag and to complain. To read like a writer in education journals and books is to look beyond the information each author presents; writers read to discover each author's motives for using the information presented, and by doing so, learn the uses of writing in education.

Read to Learn about Various Professional Journals

Read to develop a greater awareness of different audiences, so you will know where to publish your writing. There may be a wider variety of journals and magazines in education than in any other academic area. In the language arts field alone, there are numerous journals for international, national, and state audiences.

The *Contributors Guide to Periodicals in Reading* (IRA, 1986) provides information about more than 170 periodicals that consistently publish writing about reading and language arts. *Cabell's Directory of Publishing Opportunities in Education* (1984) provides review guidelines for more than 200 education journals that publish writing in all education fields. While teachers can use reference books like these to increase their awareness of opportunities for professional writing in education, they should realize that a good foundation for learning about the expectations of different audiences is best developed through wide reading in different journals.

Read to Discover and Model Different Stylistic Devices

There are numerous lessons about style that teachers can learn by reading like an author. I think the best first lesson to learn is that writers have individual styles. Because there is so much objective, expository writing in professional journals, a teacher might infer that is the only acceptable style. It isn't, and I refer readers to Wayne Otto's columns on reading research, which have appeared in *Journal of Reading* since October 1984. While the content of Otto's columns is the same as that which other writers discuss in their objective, expository articles, Otto's writing about reading research is largely subjective and narrative. It bears some resemblance to that of popular newspaper columnist Mike Royko.

Other lessons about style must be individualized. Writers adopt stylistic devices of other authors to suit their individual standards for taste and their purposes for writing. Reflecting about my own writing, what I have discovered about writing simply and clearly I have learned from reading and modeling my work after the writing of Theodore Sizer and Herbert Kohl; what I know about writing provocatively I have learned from reading Frank Smith and Jonathan Kozol. Whether I have succeeded in learning the styles of these authors is not the point; what matters is that in reading their writing I have responded to their crafting of words and have begun learning to develop greater skill in crafting my own.

Read to Discover the Subjectivity of the Written Word

The cumulative effect of developing a greater awareness of authors' purposes and an understanding of the different networks of influence on authors' ideas is like a slow dawning on a landscape that seems changed in a subtle, but very definite, way. That landscape, which is the state of knowledge in education, will no longer seem dominated by a few familiar landmarks. In the new light that comes from wide reading with an author's eye, the state of knowledge of education will look much more complex, intricate, and variegated than before; there will be more details to observe. It will become clear that the landscape is populated, and its inhabitants have a way of disagreeing and arguing with each other, making what seems to be "one big mess."

To see that knowledge in education is produced by individuals with conflicting purposes and influences is to begin to appreciate the subjectivity of the written word. With so many perspectives, different ways of reasoning, and competing interests in education, the reality described by the words of each author can be seen to be limited by the author's biases, background knowledge, motives for writing, and uses of language.

Understanding the subjectivity of writing can help teachers have a different view of objectivity. Instead of questioning writers' detachment from their experiences, biases, and motives, searching for objectivity means judging the extent to which authors identify and own up to the personal factors that influence their thinking and writing. Teachers may learn to be forthright—"up-front"—with their own biases and motives in their writing, instead of trying to hide these factors.

Conclusion

To teachers who adopt these suggestions about wide and critical reading in the professional literature of education, I promise a feeling of emancipation in writing. Gone will be the stereotypes that have shackled writers in education for decades: the more references, the better; the newer, the better; and (in my view, the most insidious) the more research in the journal where the article appears, the better. Your own reading will free you as you develop your own standards for judging which writing is "better." These standards will not only be guides for improving your own writing, they will free your voice to write what should be written about teaching and learning in the way you feel you can write it best.

References

Cabell, D.W.E. (1984). *Cabell's directory of publishing opportunities in education.* Beaumont, TX: Cabell Publishing.

Dillon, D. (1987). Dear readers. *Language Arts, 64,* 707–709.

International Reading Association. (1986). *Contributors guide to periodicals in reading.* Newark, DE: International Reading Association.

Smith, F. (1983). Reading like a writer. *Language Arts, 60,* 558–567.

III From the Editor's Perspective

12 Writing, Editing, and Miracles

Ken Donelson
Arizona State University

I'm not sure anyone knows how long ago a magazine editor created the rules and regulations for submitting articles, but when Alleen Pace Nilsen and I became editors of *English Journal* in 1980, the rules were already well-established. As other editors over the years have done, we produced a style sheet to help potential authors, we occasionally commented in *EJ* about things that concerned us as editors, and we cheerfully gave frequent talks and workshops that were meant to help past or future contributors.

We did all that, as countless editors have and will, so potential writers would understand what made some manuscripts more attractive than others. We wanted our writers to understand that they didn't need to be part of the "in crowd," and they didn't need to hold to any party line to publish in *EJ*. We wanted writers to know that *EJ* editors wanted fresh ideas and approaches—just what any editors wanted. We hoped for controversy where it was appropriate, but controversy was hardly required. Nothing was required except something worth saying to English teachers, written so busy English teachers would care to read it. That doesn't seem much to ask, but of course, it's everything.

Let me sketch out some assumptions we made as editors, some basic magazine etiquette we mentioned in our style sheet, some reasons why some manuscripts were turned down, some reasons why other manuscripts were accepted and published, and some suggestions for articles that many editors would welcome.

Editors' Assumptions

First, most of the assumptions we made as editors are those Alleen and I make as writers hoping to get our own work published. We assumed that anyone who wanted to publish in *EJ* would examine back issues to learn what *EJ* looked like and what we published and, most important, what audience *EJ* aimed at. Some articles that came our way were doomed for rejection since they had little to do with secondary English teaching and seemed unlikely to interest secondary English teachers.

We also assumed that most writers would know it is considered bad form to submit the same article to two (or more) magazines at the same time. We probably shouldn't have made that assumption, because young writers clearly didn't know it—or if they did, they considered it unfair for editors to demand. But fair or not, editors do, and even slow as some editors are to accept or reject, writers should not send an article to Magazine B until the editor of Magazine A has turned it down. Multiple submissions may not get a writer automatically blackballed, but the author faces the remote but embarrassing possibility of being accepted by two magazines. Unlikely? Of course. But I know it has happened, and the Canadian film magazine that was first to publish an article a few years back missed no opportunity to squirt venom on its editorial pages an issue later after the article in question also appeared in an American journal.

If editors are slow to respond, and some are (editors are human and as busy as the rest of us), a reasonably tactful letter about the status of the article is always in order. An even less polite letter is appropriate if the editor hasn't responded in months. But even if editors are unprofessionally slow, multiple submissions are still no-no's. Indeed, assurance in your cover letter that the article is not being submitted elsewhere gladdens the heart of any editor.

Editors also assume that the article will not be loaded down with lengthy quotations—a problem more common than most contributors would dream. Furthermore, editors assume that the writer has carefully proofread the manuscript. We've all submitted articles with embarrassing, sometimes humiliating, goofs (some editors collect those—with the minimal pay most editors get, these often hysterical goofs are a bonus of sorts). Still, editors do assume that writers have made more than a pass at getting rid of the most obvious typos and misspellings. But with that, editors still prepare to proof and mark up accepted manuscripts as part of their normal work; one more proofing may catch that *public* with an *l* dropped. (That word alone provides sleepless nights for most editors.)

Two other assumptions deserve mention. Cover letters accompanying the articles should be mercifully brief, or briefer. Writers should know who the editor is and address the editor by name, thus demonstrating some familiarity with the magazine (even in August 1990, three years after Alleen and I left the *EJ* offices, I received and forwarded two letters to Ben Nelms, the current editor). The cover letter should identify the article, the author, and probably no more. Sad as it may seem, the editor doesn't care who or what inspired the article, or to whom this is dedicated. Later, if the article is accepted, the editor may care, but not at the time of submission. And a small point—but for nonprofit magazines (and *EJ* is nonprofit) a nice one—stamps attached to self-addressed return envelopes should be clipped, not glued, on. If the article is accepted, the editors will be able to use the stamps. Most busy editors can't take time to soak stamps to recover them for other uses.

Style Sheets Help

Alleen and I developed our style sheet to help potential writers, and we thought the suggestions were helpful even though they were sometimes ignored. We reminded authors to avoid sexist language, partly because we as editors were bothered by it, partly because the National Council of Teachers of English has a formal policy against sexist language in its publications. We also asked writers to avoid clichés, jargon, purple prose, doublespeak, the passive voice, and euphemisms—not a surprise in the carload. We suggested that Anglo-Saxon words almost always had force that Latinate words lacked, and we pleaded with authors to avoid using quotation marks to set off cutesy words, a habit that is almost as bad as any use of exclamation marks.

Finally, we asked writers to avoid long introductions. *In medias res* was good advice when Horace gave it, and it still is. We asked writers to remember the advice they would give to students at all levels: organize the material, stick to the topic, give enough details to make a case but know when enough is enough, and remember that it is the author's job to attract the attention of busy English teachers and then keep their interest.

With the wonderful exception of one English teacher who requested a copy of our style sheet and then returned it quickly with a lengthy and nasty critique, informing us that she did not wish to write for a magazine edited by two people who composed such an inferior style sheet, our suggestions seemed to work.

Reasons for Rejection

We turned down articles for all sorts of reasons. When manuscripts came in, anything from one or two to more than twenty a day, they were logged in. Alleen and I read them within two weeks, and usually faster than that. We weren't trying to impress anyone with our speed, but both of us have had bad experiences with slow-moving editors, and we early on vowed we'd get manuscripts back fast.

Some articles were turned down for the reasons I listed earlier: they weren't aimed at secondary English teachers, or were loaded with footnotes and esoteric enough to tell any editor that this originally must have been intended for *Philological Quarterly* or *PMLA*.

Some were declined even though the authors were obviously sincere and dedicated English teachers. But dedication and sincerity will carry an author only so far, and if the article on Macbeth says what countless other articles have said before, it's not likely to break into print. Whatever the topic, articles must reflect enthusiasm born of new ideas or techniques or methods. Our secondary English teacher readers deserved only the best Alleen and I could put together.

Sometimes we rejected articles we liked. That may sound odd, but we had to reject good articles that were too much like articles we'd used or recently accepted. We also had to reject articles we felt had been done to death in *EJ* or elsewhere. That's obviously a judgment call, but I doubt that most *EJ* readers had any idea how many articles we received on the writing process. It's not a dead topic, but after the first 100 articles, we got a bit particular about accepting one more article on the writing process. The problem an editor faces is simple: How many good articles on the same important topic deserve publication? Worse yet, what if the best article imaginable on the most significant topic imaginable is the 101st one received? The answer, sadly, is that it may be turned down. Is that fair? Of course not, but that's one of the editor's dilemmas.

Occasionally, we rejected articles because they were too timely. Whatever else *EJ* is, it is not *Time* or *Newsweek*. If we were desperate to get something in *EJ*, we might publish it in a month or so, though three months or more was typical. *EJ* is not the place to put red-hot news, nor was it ever intended to be.

One other point about rejected manuscripts deserves mention. When we became *EJ* editors, neither of us had any strong feelings about the kinds of rejection letters we'd write. Early on, we tried writing short, and we hoped helpful, notes to ease the pain. At least they were supposed to be helpful, but that ended almost as fast as it began when an article from an earnest but not particularly adept writer came in. The article was by a college teacher, and while the points it made were fine, the article was pompous and loaded with jargon. In my rejection letter, I tried to be kind and helpful, and

I suggested some tentative solutions to the problems. I said to get rid of the educationese, and further, warmed by my own rhetorical fervor, I said that the first paragraphs weren't clear. I added that I assumed the paragraphs meant _____ , and I then helpfully rewrote them so they did. I closed by wishing the writer luck in finding another publisher.

So much for that, I assumed, until a few weeks later, when another letter came from the college professor. Instead of the thank-you letter I'd anticipated, the manuscript was enclosed, with every change I'd asked for, including my rewrite of the first two paragraphs. Did I realize I'd been snookered? Yes, I did. Did we accept the article? You might pore through *EJ* issues from 1980 on to see if you can be sure about that. Did I feel stupid and amused at the same time? Well, yes I did.

And that's one reason Alleen and I turned to the form rejection letter. After we'd used it for a couple of months, I knew why a form rejection letter is essential for any national magazine, though I knew it hurt some authors' feelings and angered others. Whatever its other faults or merits, the form rejection letter gave us time to do other important things editors do, like edit and cut and read more manuscripts. It ensured that writers would be accepted or get their rejected manuscripts back much faster. I bear personal testimony to the foolishness of giving rejected authors suggestions on how to improve their manuscripts. If we had told all authors the absolute truth, some would have been deeply hurt, and they could hardly afford to believe us. Long and detailed comments may help a few writers, but whether they would or should pay any attention to an editor's subjective judgment is doubtful; in any case, such comments would have taken Alleen and me hours we almost never had to spare. We had time to lose and almost nothing to gain by giving real criticism, which is inevitably subjective. The form rejection letter was the answer. It didn't solve all our editing problems, but it mercifully raised few new ones.

Reasons for Acceptance

We accepted articles for all sorts of reasons, many difficult to explain briefly. Any editor hopes to get fresh ideas about important topics worth bringing to readers, but editors would find words like *fresh* and *important* and *worth reading* impossible to explain or define. When Alleen and I spotted an article that struck us as fresh, clever, witty, significant, new, or different, we knew it. No one had to tell us, and no one had to share our judgment. We could only hope that *EJ* readers would agree with us. It didn't always work that way, but we could be almost dead-certain that if we received a letter from an irked reader that an article "was a tired recital of the obvious . . . something is clearly wrong with the *EJ* editors," we'd soon receive another letter whose writer was pleased that the article "was something I badly needed to hear clearly and cleverly expressed. Keep up the good work." So it goes in the land of editing.

When articles were accepted, they were tossed into a bin, ready for whichever of us had time to edit and mark the manuscripts. Editing meant proofreading and checking factual material and making sure the tone was consistent throughout. Editing also always meant cutting and tightening. If we could cut twelve lines from that manuscript and eighteen lines from this manuscript, we could save a page, and we usually had a one-pager that would neatly fit. All that implied endless arguments within our own minds, but rarely between Alleen and me, about how many examples, good as they might be, were necessary to make a point. We also pondered whether some things weren't already well-known to most English teachers.

Were we looking for any particular topic or point of view? No, we really weren't. We knew what we didn't want to see (e.g., "Grammar for Fun and Profit" or "Another Poetic Must for the Classroom: Rod McKuen"). What we wanted was something fresh and worthwhile, and we picked up each manuscript hoping that *this* was something fresh and worthwhile; amazingly enough, it sometimes was. Was I sick to death with hearing about the writing process? Yes, I was. Hadn't I told Alleen yesterday that I'd gag if I ever saw another one? Yes, I did. Was I pleased when an article on the writing process came along that was fresh and worthwhile? No, I wasn't. Did we accept the article? Of course we did.

Was there one article both of us prayed for, waiting for it to appear? Yes, there was one we eagerly sought: the article that would solve all the problems of English teachers in America and advance education to unheard of heights, in addition to solving the problems of world hunger and cancer and Dutch elm blight and the over-population of rabbits in Australia. It would be witty and profound, convincing and provocative, amusing and solemn, grating and ingratiating, theoretical and practical, controversial and calming. That article never arrived. Or maybe we were out of the office that day.

We accepted at least three manuscripts I remember well because they caused us problems—one anticipated, two surprising. We thought

Ted Hipple's "And Now a Word for the Yearbook: NO" was funny when we first saw it, and it worked beautifully into the January 1986 issue on the English teacher's work outside the classroom. Some journalism people were not happy with the irreverence of the article, proving there are professionals in the world who take themselves and their responsibilities too seriously. The reactions of a few teachers to Mike Jackson's pattern poem, "I'm Pissed," in the March 1984 issue surprised both of us. Looking back, the attacks on our taste were predictable, I guess, but the vehemence of the disgust was a bit puzzling. There were threats to write to NCTE headquarters to lament our professional judgments, more suggestions that English teachers would drop their subscriptions to *EJ*, and considerable worry that the state of the language was in doubt and we had contributed to the decline. One teacher had copied the poem and told us that she was fearful of leaving it on her desk since an innocent student might stop by, see the poem, and be permanently harmed. If all that seemed significant at that time, it paled when we published D.H. Nicholson's poem, "Landgrant Orgy at Illinois" in October 1985. Alleen and I were accused of sexism (that shocked and then amused Alleen) and of showing inexcusable judgment in printing a poem that was so filthy it belonged in *Playboy.* A few people back at NCTE headquarters were disturbed by the poem before it was published and wanted some assurance that we knew what we were doing. Both of us claimed we did, and the poem appeared. An English department in an eastern college signed a collective letter suggesting, none too kindly, that we'd shown poor judgment in inflicting this poem on English teachers, who presumably had the taste and judgment we clearly lacked. Several others again lamented the terrible state of the English language and announced that we were responsible for its decline. (Since then I have noticed that the English language has declined something awful, so herewith I admit my complicity and announce I will no longer contribute to its decline.)

Suggestions for Articles

Occasionally at a workshop, someone would ask us exactly what kind of article we were looking for, and I had the uncomfortable feeling that the writer was seeking clues about that perfect topic we'd not yet seen. But nothing like that ever existed. A perfect topic would be nothing without perfect examples and perfect diction and perfect syntax and on and on.

We resisted suggesting topics, fearful that we'd be deluged with articles on _____ or _____. But as we neared the end of our seven-year term, I decided to suggest some general topics most editors might be glad to see. I wouldn't argue that these are clever or that they will gladden every writer's heart, but some of these could lead to good articles; with a real writer's talent, some could be better than merely satisfactory.

First, any English teacher worth rehiring does something in the classroom that is the envy of colleagues. Whether it is your collection of dime novels used to get a unit on the history of the American novel under way or a knowledge of early ranching in the West that makes Willa Cather or Larry McMurtry or Edward Abbey come alive isn't important. When I was teaching back in Cedar Rapids, Iowa, my closest friend and colleague had become a local expert on Iowa regional art. Another prided himself on his knowledge of the Brontë family. Neither was a world-class authority, but both knew far more about one area than most teachers will ever know. These colleagues could have written a first-rate article on teaching Brontë or using regional art in teaching American literature, though that certainly was not why they picked up their expertise. My wife, Marie, teaches English at Horizon High School in the Paradise Valley School District. She's also danced with the New York City Ballet under George Balanchine. She's also something of an expert on northern New Mexico Indian Pueblo dances, on turquoise jewelry, on teaching mass media (especially old-time radio), and on problems facing high school journalism teachers. Friends in her department, as in almost any other respectable department, have other equally intriguing hobbies or interests. Would one of these interests make a good *EJ* article? Possibly, if the topic were related to English teaching so other teachers might be curious.

Second, in a time when money is tight, when "we don't have money in the budget to do that" is heard throughout the land, teachers have learned to make do or to work around the problem. If some material or activity is basic to a teacher's work and that teacher has figured out a way to get around the money problem, many other teachers would love to hear about it. Most of us have classroom needs that apparently can be solved only by money, so editors would love to hear from creatively optimistic teachers.

Third, most of us desperately searched for a solution to a problem during our first year of teaching. Maybe we needed to find "Five Great Ways to Reduce the Paper Load for English Teachers," or "How

I Faced the World's Greatest Discipline Problem and Won," or "Ten Surefire Ways to Organize Your Teaching Time to Give Yourself Time to Relax," or whatever. Teachers who have survived more than five years have probably found some answers to their first-year worries. Why not help new teachers now?

Fourth, most of us have caught ourselves saying, "Why isn't there a good article I can recommend on _____?" The blank might be filled with unit teaching, or reference sources for ninth graders, or teaching poetry to screaming eighth graders. Maybe we'd like it for ourselves. If no one has written that article, it's possible there's a good reason: it may be unwritable. It's also possible that no one else has worried about the topic or, more likely, that potential writers assume other English teachers already know the answer. One of the more tiresome excuses Alleen and I heard came from English teachers who knew that what they had to say was widely known by every other English teacher in the universe. Nonsense, we said then, and nonsense, I say now. Experienced English teachers can write that article. If they do not, who will? Who else can?

Fifth, beginning teachers tend to be suspicious of theory or anything that isn't clearly and immediately practical. As we teach, we gain a grudging respect for theory or for a technique that's not immediately practical but still important in our teaching. Most experienced English teachers could write a good article on something like "Piaget— From a Frill to a Basic," or "Dewey for Fun but Mostly for Profit," or "Educational Theory Isn't Dull, Just Unused." Maybe that ought to be a requirement for any English teacher who has survived more than ten years in public schools.

Sixth, in addition to being local experts on a particular topic, most of us learn that there is one surefire thing in our teaching, a poem or short story or journal assignment or thesaurus exercise, that always seems to work. While articles on these topics may seem gimmicky, most teachers love them since they're short and specific and helpful. If you know someone who despises gimmicks, call the ideas teaching strategies and watch them become suddenly intellectually and educationally respectable. Experienced English teachers might group these strategies together under an umbrella, for example, "Ten Strategies to Overcome Apathy about Poetry in the Ninth Grade" or "Fifty Surefire Strategies to Wake Kids Up When Spring Fever Hits."

Seventh, most of us have had a class, or a day or so with one class, that we thought was the most exciting group we'd ever taught.

Why not try to recreate that time and that group, and get down on paper what made the time and the people memorable? Most editors admittedly aren't going to wax ecstatic about mere remembrances, but if we can recreate time and place, we might be able to remind ourselves of something we contributed to that time and place, something other English teachers might gain from reading. If we did nothing more than remember when we were once special teachers with incredible capabilities, that too would serve a purpose. It's so easy to become blasé about our work and, unfortunately, about our professional responsibilities. We ought to remind ourselves every once in a while, even in print, how dedicated and caring we are.

Eighth, we often bandy about terms like *great* when we're talking about someone we admire, but we usually never make clear precisely what we mean by *great*. What does the great English teacher do that the merely good English teacher does not? Given the times and the periodic drive by school administrators to install merit pay, maybe this is a good time to figure out what we mean by great English teacher. And it's always time to remember the great teachers we had, the ones who influenced us in some way to become what we are today. What was there about those teachers that so impressed us? Articles about our great teachers could easily, of course, become mushy and sentimental, but it hardly follows that such articles must be faulty. Tributes that attempt to determine specifically what made our English teachers great and what made us know and feel their greatness are uncommon in magazines. I wish they were far more common.

Ninth, most of us have attacked whatever literature text we're stuck with (one we rarely had any say in choosing), because of some inferior content or, more likely for me, some great works it lacks. What story or poem or play or nonfiction is usually ignored by anthology makers but deserves to be more commonly included? Maybe it's that Donne poem you wind up copying every year to include in your remarks about the *carpe diem* tradition. Maybe it's that Updike short story you read aloud each year; you wind up being irritated because you wish your kids could read every word of it on their own. Maybe it's a modern European play, perhaps *R.U.R.* or *Ghosts* or *The Visit*, to get your unit on drama under way. Whatever your choice, why not write an article exploring why that piece may have been ignored and explaining why it is a shame that it's not in more anthologies today. It would be one way to vent your spleen, and it's remotely possible that a publisher might be intrigued by your recommendation. In any case, other English teachers might learn about literature they hitherto have not known. After all, we're all unaware of some writers—maybe you could help rid me of some ignorance.

Finally, as young English teachers, we learned to fear those words, "research tells us that." We fear research because we don't know it and we have no idea how to alleviate our ignorance. We lack statistical tools, and we're sure that's the end of that line of inquiry, since we've known from the beginning of time that English teachers and mathematics are mutually exclusive terms. For these reasons and sundry other spurious causes, we pretend a disdain which is based on and compounded with fear. As we teach we also learn that not all research is drivel, and we learn that some researchers have much to offer us. In literature alone, if we read any research, we learn that Louise Rosenblatt's work is basic to our teaching.

As we teach, we find we are curious about what happens in our class if we try this rather than that. If, for example, we wonder whether teaching literature thematically rather than in our usual chronological format will mean that students will lose out on some significant relationships between authors and literary works, we could be on our way to setting up an experiment, formally or casually. If we do decide to become involved in some sort of research and if we really do want to satisfy our curiosity, we'll need to devise questions to help us look for answers worth discovering. How will we go about measuring differences in the two methods of teaching literature? What differences are worth finding? What differences will establish some sort of proof? Why do we teach literature at all? Indeed, why do we read what we call literature? Who established the canon of great/good literature we think is important? What is good or successful literature teaching?

These and far more questions deserve some sort of answers, no matter how casual the research undertaken. Why do they go ignored? Because they make us uncomfortably aware how little we know about our supposed areas of expertise? Perhaps. Because we are professionally naive or uneducated? Perhaps. Because we lack curiosity or interest? No, that I do not believe. True, if we investigate anything with any likelihood that others will understand what we have done or if we disseminate our findings, we will need to work with people trained in research, but in most school districts those people are not all that difficult to find. Chances are they're more anxious to find imaginative and curious English teachers than the teachers are to find the researchers. Small-scale classroom research need not set out to shake the educational foundations of Western society. Much has been written about simple and complex research in *EJ* and *Language Arts,* and NCTE has published extensively on interpreting and conducting research. Will many classroom teachers do any research, big or small? Probably not nearly enough, but those who do may just possibly make a difference in someone's life, their own if no one else's.

Should all these comments about writing for publication make any difference in a classroom teacher's life? Yes, they should. Why? Because all of us English teachers are lively humans who teach composition and who tell kids every day that writing is important. If it is important, then we—students and teachers—need to practice writing. Piano teachers who teach but cannot play would either be laughed at or scorned. Football coaches who cannot demonstrate skills they think are important won't long be tolerated by players.

English teachers who claim that writing is important but who do not themselves write lack credibility. I don't care what kind of writing they do, only that it is submitted to a newspaper or magazine and aimed at a specific audience to say something the authors think important. If I had my way—and many people are doubtless glad I don't—I'd want those submitted articles on file in the school so parents could examine the kinds of writers these teachers are. If we write clear and intriguing prose, we provide some evidence of our competence. If we write murky and boring prose, we provide evidence of another kind.

So what if you write and that tasteless, abrasive, clod of an editor rejects your work? Don't sulk or curse the fates, tempting as that is. Get the article back into the mail, fast. Somewhere just over the horizon is an editor who needs your article and you. Editors do, you know. Without manuscripts, magazines do not exist. Without you, English teacher and soon-to-be-writer, magazines die.

Believe it or not, editors are human, and they care about getting the best material they can for their readers. They really do care. And please don't think that editors are cynical; that's a face they put on to hide the truth that they believe in miracles. Day after day, editors open the mail and find nothing but run-of-the-mill stuff, but on those rarest of days an article of surpassing fairness appears, and the editors are vindicated. Editors know that miracles don't happen often, but they can testify that they do. Editors believe, and they wait for miracles to happen.

Who wouldn't love and cherish and honor wonderful people like that? Who wouldn't immediately want to write for these unsung noblest of creatures?

13 Inside *Language Arts:* An Editor's Story of One Journal

William H. Teale
University of Texas at San Antonio

This book, *Teacher as Writer,* offers you a great deal of valuable advice about how to write professional articles and how to get them published. In this section three editor colleagues give counsel on everything from what makes a good journal topic, to the steps involved in the submission and processing of an article, to pointers on style and format that you should keep in mind when writing for a journal of the National Council of Teachers of English. From reading my colleagues' chapters, you also can get insight into what kinds of people editors are.

I thought long and hard about what I could add here that would help a teacher writer interested in writing for professional journals. In the end I decided that perhaps the best thing I could do is give you an inside look at one journal, a look not simply at the journal's policies and procedures but also at the feelings and beliefs involved in its creation. So in this chapter, I will try to give you a sense of what *Language Arts (LA)* is about. I think that such an analysis will help you answer questions that are of real interest to you, things like "What kinds of articles is a journal actually interested in?" and "What makes an article a publishable one?"

Language Arts is the official journal of the Elementary Section of NCTE. Its mission is to publish articles about language arts education at the elementary and middle school levels. Although this chapter deals expressly with *LA,* I believe that the ideas it provides relate in a general way to all professional journals in the field of education and in specific ways to several journals published today that focus on language arts and reading education.

In attempting to take you inside *Language Arts,* I will focus on three main topics: people and their ideas make *LA* what it is, *LA* facts and figures for one year, and what all of this means for you.

People and Their Ideas Make *LA* What It Is

When I was in first grade, I never realized that books were written by people. I guess I thought they came from a big printing press, goodness knows where, that spewed them out in some unimaginable way. Today, primary grade teachers place great emphasis on helping children understand what and who authors of children's books are and on helping young children understand that they, too, can be authors. Thus, the children get a much better understanding of what books are and what writing books is all about. The magic of books remains, but the process by which books come into the world is understood.

Of course, you know that real people write all the articles, columns, poems, stories, letters to the editor, position papers, and other quirky kinds of pieces that go into *Language Arts*. But equally important to keep in mind is that people also are at the heart of deciding what does not appear in the pages of the journal.

Sometimes readers of professional journals and persons who are thinking of writing for such journals create a mystique about them, just like my first-grade mystique about books. They imagine that some palpable rules exist somewhere, rules that define what is an acceptable article and what is not, almost like a template in the editorial office of the journal. As each manuscript comes in, it is fed through a machine that checks how well the manuscript fits the template. Those that fit get published; those that don't get sent back. Or maybe they don't have an image of a machine in mind; maybe they see the editor as having certain objective, unbiased standards of writing, rules that are applied to the manuscripts that authors send in: a foolproof, super-duper rubric that is on the cutting edge of writing assessment.

Perhaps the most important thing this chapter can do for you, a writer interested in publishing in professional journals, is to help you understand that the process by which things get published in a journal like *LA* relies completely on people, not on some mechanical process of deciding what gets published and what doesn't. It's sort of like the justice system in the United States; there are principles upon which the justice system is built, but it is people—judges and juries—who make the final decisions.

I'd put it this way. There are "rules" that people use in judging manuscripts, but there are no rules. In other words, what gets into a professional journal gets there not through some kind of scientific process but through a complex social process that involves knowledge, feelings, politics, and even factors like financial and design constraints under which a journal operates. Yes, the quality of writing and the timeliness of the topic remain paramount, but even these elements have a social dimension to them.

To illustrate such factors in action, let's look at how things work for *LA*. I'm the editor, so the buck stops with me. I decide what gets into the pages of the journal and what doesn't, pure and simple. (Actually, this is why editors edit. It's the only perk. An editor gets the pleasure—and it is a pleasure—of being able to include what she or he thinks are the writings that will most advance the thinking of the educators who read the journal.) But I don't operate in a vacuum when making these decisions. There are two things that guide me. One is a group of smart and dedicated people, the individuals who serve on the Editorial Advisory Board of *LA*. The second thing is my own knowledge of the field, of what makes for good writing, and of what would be helpful for the field to hear about.

The *Language Arts* editorial board consists of about forty-five persons whose job is to review manuscripts that are submitted to *LA* for possible publication. Board members represent a wide spectrum of language arts educators. In inviting individuals to become members of the editorial board, I try to assemble a group that has diverse expertise (both in terms of areas of knowledge within language arts education and in terms of grade/age level interest) and diverse backgrounds (they vary in the jobs they hold—classroom teachers, language arts and reading supervisors, curriculum directors, teacher educators, and others; in their cultural and experiential backgrounds; in the areas of the world they come from; and in gender).

Almost all manuscripts that are submitted to *LA* are put through a process of peer review. Two members of the editorial board review each manuscript. They indicate whether they think the manuscript should be published or not, and they write an analysis of its strengths and weaknesses. I value these reviews very much, because I have extremely high regard for the knowledge and good sense of the members of the *LA* editorial board. I find their comments very useful in helping me think about a manuscript.

But, in truth, what the reviewers say is not the final word. I filter their comments through my own reactions to a piece. As I said, I rely on their opinions. About one of every four times, however, they don't agree between themselves. One says accept, the other says reject. So you see, there really is not this set of objective standards about what constitutes a good article for a language arts journal. In such cases I either solicit an opinion from a third member of the editorial board, or I decide that one of the original reviewers is right and the other is wrong and make a final decision about the manuscript accordingly.

On what basis do I make that decision? By relying on the second "thing" I mentioned earlier: my own sense of what a good *LA* article is and what is timely information to publish. Don't ask me to define that here, though. I couldn't. Perhaps this characteristic is what is meant when people talk about the "personality" a journal takes on under a particular editor. It is probably also a large factor in why a professional organization selects a particular person to be the editor of the journal. In any case, I believe it is helpful for you to see how things really work in the decision-making process for a journal. The other refereed journals that focus on language arts education in the elementary and middle school classroom (e.g., *The Reading Teacher*) go through a very similar process in selecting manuscripts to publish.

All of this may lead you to conclude that writing for a professional journal is just an extension of something you learned several years back—perhaps in your middle school years or in high school, certainly by the time you got involved in university-level courses. This something is called "writing for the teacher/professor." The game is to figure out what the teacher or professor wants and then give it to her or him. Make no mistake—there is an element of that in professional journal publication. That's because, as I said before, a journal is produced by real people; whoever makes the decisions for a journal will inevitably have strong beliefs about what is right and what is wrong in the field.

But it is not simply giving editors what they want. It's more the case of giving the field what it needs. An editorial board helps to ensure that breadth of perspective is brought to bear in making a decision on a particular manuscript. Almost invariably, when both reviewers agree that a piece should be published, or both agree that it should be rejected (a phenomenon that occurs with approximately one-half of the manuscripts reviewed for *LA*), I have arrived at the same decision. The only exceptions are the few articles of publishable quality that never make it into the pages of *LA* because of limitations on the number of pages we can include in the eight issues published over the course of a year. Thus, there are shared ideas about what makes a good journal article, not simply maverick editors putting in whatever moves them at the moment.

In another way, too, *LA* is more than a reflection of my beliefs about what is right in language arts education. As an editor, I try to act as a kind of conscience for the field. For instance, I would never publish what I considered to be a bad manuscript, but I have published and will continue to publish manuscripts I disagree with. Why? Because I believe that, above all, the best contribution *LA* can make to language arts education is to extend thinking in the field. And sometimes the best way to do that is to read a well-articulated "opposite" point of view. Otherwise, there is a danger that we get too comfortable and too stale; our old positions become dogma or worse, refuges.

So, what can you take away from this discussion that posits that people and their ideas make a professional journal what it is? I hope you see that writing a journal article is a social event, not a case of filling the slots in a here's-what-makes-a-good-professional-journal-article template. As a social event, factors such as stance, voice, and audience all play an important role in the response it will receive. But equally important is the fact that your article will be responded to from a political perspective and a personal perspective.

A great deal of what goes on in publishing any professional journal can be thought of as invincible. I hope that this discussion brings some of that to light. Please understand that I am not apologizing for this state of affairs. I believe that the procedures *LA* has in place assure that the journal will publish high-quality articles in language arts education, and that it will be equitable in terms of representing topics and constituencies in the readership in a way that promotes growth and dialogue and, ultimately, education of readers. But in the final word, it all comes down to the beliefs of people in the field, not to a set of objective standards or predetermined topics. It is important that, as a potential writer of pieces for a language arts journal, you have a feeling for how such things actually work in publication.

LA Facts and Figures for One Year

Another way of understanding *Language Arts* is to look at it in terms of what has become a cliché from business, its bottom line. In this section, certain basic facts and figures for the 1990–91 publication year for *Language Arts* are presented. I include them because I think they can help teacher writers see the big picture of what is involved in submitting an article to a national journal like *LA*.

During the course of the 1990–91 *LA* publication year, we completed processing of 416 submissions. They included 306 "full-length" articles, 78 short pieces (the equivalent of two journal pages or less), and 32 poems. For purposes of this chapter, I will focus only on the full-length and short articles. Of the 384 total articles processed (full-length articles plus short articles), 81.2 percent were reviewed by the editorial board. The remaining 18.8 percent were either inappropriate for the journal or were deemed by the local editorial review group as not of high enough quality to be sent out for further review. Table 1 summarizes the decisions made on the 384 articles.

What's significant in these facts and figures for you, the teacher writer? The first thing worth noting is that a publication like *LA* processes a great number of submissions each year. Many people write for the audience served by the journal. Coupled with that is the fact that almost nine out of ten submitted manuscripts end up being rejected. I think it's important for you to see these numbers, which give an idea of the extent of competition for the relatively small amount of space in a journal like *Language Arts*. Just because a piece is not accepted by *LA* doesn't mean that it has no audience or that it's not worth publishing. It's important for all authors to keep in perspective the business of publishing in major professional journals.

There are also some things of interest behind the basic figures. I do not know what percentage of articles submitted during the year were authored by classroom teachers. It's certainly not a majority, but it's not insignificant either. We published several pieces by classroom teachers during the 1990–91 academic year. But *LA*, like several other journals in the field, wants to publish even more pieces from authors working with children in the daily world of the classroom.

Table 1 Disposition of Completely Processed *LA* Manuscripts, 1990–91

Action	Full-Length Articles (306)	Short Articles (78)	Total Articles (384)
Publish	16.6%	7.7%	14.5%
Reject, But Invite Author to Resubmit after Revising	13.8%	1.3%	11.2%
Reject	55.2%	55.1%	55.2%
No Review: Unsuitable or Wrong Journal	14.4%	35.9%	18.8%

Another story not told by the figures is what kinds of articles appeared in *LA*. There is no simple answer to this, because such a range of pieces was published. But they had one thing in common: they presented information and insights in a fresh manner. I can't tell you how many manuscripts we received during the year that extolled the virtues of whole language. They were general reviews explaining what whole language is and calling for schools and teachers and administrators and whoever else to make the big switch to whole language teaching. A journal may have been interested in one or two such pieces a decade ago, when people were just beginning to explore what whole language was and what it meant for schools and classrooms. But such articles in the 1990s, even when well-written, are just more of the same. All of these pieces were returned to their authors.

What teacher authors did discuss in articles that were published were specific children they worked with, and programs, activities, and resources that stemmed from their experience in the classroom. Peg Sudol and David Sudol coauthored an article that examined the success and problems Peg encountered in implementing a writer's workshop in an elementary school classroom (April 1991). Twyla Daniel wrote about how the library in her school became a central vehicle in extending the children's literacy, even though the school could not afford a librarian (November 1990). Jean Gunkel provided a description of a Japanese American fourth grader's development of a second language/literacy in a new culture (April 1991). Jennifer Gaskins coauthored an article with Robert Gaskins and Irene Gaskins that described how Jennifer's Resource Room implemented a program designed to help poor readers learn how to decode unknown words as they read text (March 1991). Robin Gutkin told about the great success of Sustained Loud Reading (instead of Sustained Silent Reading) in her kindergarten classroom (September 1990). And Vicki Zack presented a powerful account of using a novel about the Holocaust, Jane Yolen's *The Devil's Arithmetic*, with three of her Grade 5 students (January 1991).

I present this listing not to say that these are topics that should be written about, but rather to illustrate the range of styles and subjects covered in teacher-authored articles. I encourage you to read or reread these pieces to get a better sense of what makes a good classroom-based article. What you'll see is that these authors talked specifics, they talked about learning and teaching, and they talked about children. Furthermore, they did this in straightforward language and in a way that communicated their enthusiasm about what they had to discuss with *LA* readers.

So What Does All This Mean for You?

As I mentioned earlier, there are no rules for writing an article for a language arts education journal. But I hope that by shedding some light on how *Language Arts* works, this discussion has helped you as a teacher writer. When it comes to implications for writers, I resist saying, "Do this, but don't do that" because, inevitably, many authors who follow the do's end up writing poor pieces and some who write wonderful articles do exactly what they're told not to. I feel, however, as if I should end with some words of advice; so here is a brief explanation of things to keep in mind as you plan, draft, rewrite, edit, and proofread.

You're not writing for a journal. You're writing for people who will read what you have to say. In other words, this whole business is not an academic exercise; it's an instance of entering into discussion about real kids and real schools and the important business of teaching with other real people in the world.

Don't pontificate, obfuscate, or otherwise "jargonize." You are writing for real people, not trying to reproduce the language of some poorly written textbook you used in a graduate course last year. Listen to this hypothetical excerpt based on various manuscripts I have reviewed over the past year:

> The purpose of this article is to uncover the assumptions related to literary criticism and children's literature, especially the predominant deconstructionist paradigm as applied to this body of work. Fundamental similarities are assumed to exist between children's literature and other extant forms of literature, so that it is possible to apply to both types of text with equal validity and intentionality the same critical paradigm. Thus, the most basic assumption here is that children's literature has the same nature as adult literature, the productive and receptive literacy levels of the readers of each type of literature notwithstanding.
>
> A more specific assumption based on the more general assumption about equality of forms for critical purposes could be advanced, but an exhaustive survey of the literature revealed that no work on literary criticism of children's literature from poststructuralist or neostructuralist perspectives exists.
>
> Deliberate emphasis in this introduction, therefore, has been placed on assumptions, so as to create a starting point for our discussion. The reason for this choice of emphasis will become apparent when investigating the deconstructionist paradigm, the most dominant of the specific literary theories.

Trust me, not too much becomes apparent in articles like these. You won't fool anyone by hiding behind a veil of important-sounding words that mean little. Above all, *Language Arts* tries to be a journal that talks to classroom teachers. That means saying things in a straightforward manner—not cute, not condescending, just straightforward and respectful.

Find the appropriate journal for your article. Two main things will help you do this. First, read the journal's guidelines for authors. They will give an indication of appropriate topics, formats, and length. Also, read (or reread) an issue or two of the journal. It's important that you do this from your perspective as potential writer. Even though you are a regular subscriber to a journal and you read every issue, you probably approach articles as a reader interested in hearing new ideas or getting new information. When you read from the perspective of potential contributor, you will see new things that indicate a journal's preferences in topics and style. What Journal X thinks is good is not necessarily what Journal Y wants to publish.

For instance, *LA* publishes poetry and short articles of one to three journal pages; other language arts journals don't. *LA* does not publish short pieces that describe specific classroom teaching activities, no matter how great an activity may be. Instead, we want every article to be grounded in theory as it is presented. This doesn't mean that articles cannot be practical; many are. They just can't be mere descriptions of here's-how-to-do-this-great-activity-with-kids-in-your-classroom. *The Reading Teacher* does publish such pieces in its "In the Classroom" section. It's not that one journal is right and the other wrong; they're just different. The more you know about the journal you are submitting to, the better off you will be.

Be tough. Writing is not easy. It takes a great deal of time to write an article for a journal. But even more, it takes a great deal of energy and discipline. Perhaps Donna d'E. Barnes, a second-grade teacher at the North Berwick Primary School in North Berwick, Maine, best summed up the feelings of classroom teachers who want to write (*LA*, April, 1991):

Why Can't I Write?

Why can't I write?
Because . . .   Mrs. Barnes, can I start over? I messed up, and I can't erase the whole thing.

Why can't I write?
Because . . .   Mrs. Barnes, can I read this to you?
                       Mrs. Barnes, do I throw this in the garbage when
                       I'm done?
                       Mrs. Barnes, what is this work? and
                       Mrs. Barnes, I don't want to write about Texas any-
                       more. I want to write about my grampy and my
                       gammy and my aunt and my cousin, and I want
                       to call it "Unexpected Guests." Is that okay? and
                       Mrs. Barnes, here is my book. Should I read it over?
                       and
                       Mrs. Barnes, can I read this to someone else?
Why can't I write?

Why can't I write?
Because . . .   Mom, what's for supper? I'm starving!
Why can't I write?
Because . . .   Mom, is my jeans skirt clean? I need it NOW. and
                       Mom, I've got softball practice at 5:00. Will you drive
                       me? and
                       Mom, Ben doesn't love me anymore, and I'm just
                       going to die.
                       Mom, I made the play, and I'm on my way to Broad-
                       way. and
                       Mom, when are you going to wash this floor? My
                       feet are sticking. and
                       Mom, I need a book for English tomorrow. What
                       should I read?
Why can't I write?

Why can't I write?
Because . . .   Honey, are you going to walk the dog today? I've
                       got a meeting.
Why can't I write?
Because . . .   Put deodorant on the list for the next time you go
                       shopping, Okay?
                       Honey, have you seen my gray slacks? I can't find
                       them anywhere.
                       Do you have any white buttons for my blue shirt?
                       Two of them just disintegrated.
                       Where did you put *Newsweek?*
                       Honey, did you call the plumber yet? The base-
                       ment is still flooding.
                       Honey, we have to go to the Johnson's on Sunday.
                       I know you don't want to; but we, yes WE, have
                       to go.
Why can't I write?

Why can't I write?
Because . . .   I have to answer the phone.
                   "Hello."
Why can't I write?
Because . . .   Mom, I just got a bill from the financial aid office.
                   My loan was reduced, and YOU owe the college $2,000 more!
                   Mom, my stereo broke. What should I do?
                   I'm hungry.
                   I got a B in Economics.
                   Can I come home for the weekend?
                   Will you pick me up? Don't come before 6:00.
                   I have to write a paper.
But, why can't I write?????

You will meet disappointments: an article that ends up going nowhere, a collaboration with a colleague that never gets off the ground, and the inevitable rejection letter (we all get them). However, the rewards are worth it. I wish I had twice as much time to write, because I learn so much from writing and have such a genuinely interesting time doing it. But you do need to prepare yourself mentally for this life of writing.

Finally, please realize that through your writing you have the potential to make invaluable and singular contributions to the education of children. Not only will you touch the children in your classroom, but you will also touch teachers in other parts of the world who work with other children. Classroom teachers have unique perspectives on children's language and literacy learning and on language and literacy teaching. These perspectives need to be shared—through interactions with colleagues in your building, through workshops and conferences, and through writing. Language arts journals want to hear from you.

14 Authentic Voices for an Isolated Profession

Ben F. Nelms
University of Florida

nglish Journal differs from most professional magazines in that it considers all its readers prospective contributors. One thing that the last decade of writing projects has demonstrated with a fair degree of certainty is that classroom teachers—at all levels—are perfectly capable of providing inservice education for one another; one of the lessons of the English Coalition Conference of 1987, if I understand it correctly, is that professionals at all levels may profitably and pleasantly engage in a free exchange of ideas, enlightening and influencing one another no matter at what level they teach. Teachers have much to learn from one another. *EJ* hopes to encourage this new sense of professionalism by publishing the results of disciplined inquiry in English classrooms.

This has been the goal of *EJ* since its inception. W. Wilbur Hatfield, who was its editor for thirty-five years and was associated with the journal even longer than that, wrote in one of his first editorial comments (February 1922):

> We design to make the magazine an open forum for all, conservative and radical alike, who have important ideas and can state them well. Doubtless the progressive bias of the editors will result in a preponderance of the new methods in the magazine, but this on the whole seems desirable, since these are less known.

In describing his editorial ideal, Hatfield borrowed from Edward Bok, who said that "an editor's business is to give his public the kind of thing they want in advance of their demand and of a quality above their expectations." For eighty years that has been the journal's intent.

Portions of this chapter were adapted from editorials first published in *English Journal*.

Practice and Inquiry: What *EJ* Looks for in a Manuscript

What *EJ* seeks—and more and more often finds these days—in manuscripts describing effective classroom practice is evidence of disciplined, professional inquiry. What do my staff and I take as such evidence? On what basis do we judge manuscripts that purport to describe effective classroom practice?

1. *A richness of anecdotal detail that establishes the authenticity of the writer's claims.* To refer to advice often given writers in other genres, the *EJ* staff looks for manuscripts that show rather than tell. Teachers with whom we work, especially junior high school teachers, admire Nancie Atwell's book *In the Middle* (1987). One reason is that it gives such a clear and present sense of the workaday world of the eighth-grade teacher that it establishes a sense of trust, what in classical terms was called ethical persuasion. Teachers sense that where we are Atwell has been, that she knows the territory.

We have discovered that many writers, even classroom teachers, confine themselves to what teachers could do or might do or should do, rather than what someone actually did, an approach that distances themselves and their readers from the actual life of the classroom. We suggest instead that *EJ* writers focus on what happened in the classroom, emphasizing what students accomplished rather than what the teacher proposed. The result will be not only a clearer presentation but also a more palatable one, for it will sound less like a pedagogue's instructions and more like a colleague's invitation to share a finding. Again, early in his editorship, Hatfield set this tone:

> The demand for practical articles on classroom procedure is very strong . . . Lesson *plans* have been offered us and always rejected, because they are hypothetical and unproved. Detailed accounts—including excerpts from stenographic notes—of successful lessons will be something different. (*EJ*, May 1924)

2. *Documentation, in some form, of the effectiveness of the recommended practice.* Our reviewers—and we think our readers, too—are suspicious of the unsupported claim that a practice is "just wonderful." What we like to see, instead, are generous citations of student work: writing samples, quotation of episodes from classroom discussions (actual transcripts or reconstructions), even photographs of student exhibits and productions. Though the length of articles in *EJ* limits the amount of such material we can actually publish, we are happy to consider larger amounts when we review and evaluate manuscripts.

On the other hand, though we welcome documentation in the form of test scores, formal rating scales, or statistical analyses, we do not expect this. Without taking sides in the debate currently raging among educational researchers which pits experimental research against ethnographic research, the quantitative against the qualitative, we think we can safely say that reports of expansive quantitative studies based on massive amounts of statistical data have often been ignored or inappropriately applied because teacher practitioners could not envision the actual, real-life classrooms which had proven most effective. The generalizations may have been clear, but without the actualizing details of context and practice, teachers were skeptical, baffled, or simply indifferent. The translation of generalizations into practice often may have failed to reconstruct the effective classrooms represented in the original research.

3. Explicit awareness of the contextual factors that contributed to the effectiveness of the practice. What works for college-bound seniors in an honors program with classes of twelve to fifteen students will not necessarily, or even probably, be effective in a classroom of thirty-five seventh graders, many of whom are handicapped readers. Yet we receive many manuscripts that either give relatively little information about the context in which the practice worked or show little awareness of the needs of teachers at other levels and with other kinds of students. What kind of adaptations would have to be made if the practice were applied in other settings? At the least, contributors should describe the context in enough detail so readers can determine its "fit" to their own circumstances.

When appropriate, writers should convey a sense of the limitations of the recommended practice and the teacher's successes as well as failures, or perhaps we should say "false starts." Our experience is that no solution works all the time with all students. We need to know something about when and why practices fail, about what alternatives were tried and with what success, and about what was learned in applying the practice and how it was or will be modified.

4. A relatively clear statement of the problem to which the recommended practice may be a possible solution. In this regard, we commend Donald Murray's article (1982), in which he recommends that articles in professional journals begin with leads rather than with introductions.

English teachers are enamored of long, elaborate introductions—fallout, we fear, from the rhetoric textbooks from which we have taught. Yet readers are impatient with an article that takes two or three pages to get to the point, especially if those pages are devoted to tortured analogies, false rhetorical questions, restatements of the obvious, cute scenarios, prolix citation of authorities, or irrelevant autobiographical information. Our readers are busy teachers, with less time for professional reading than they would like. We think they should be able to tell within the first few paragraphs whether an article will address an issue of concern to them. What is the general problem to which this practice may be one possible solution?

5. *The relation between the recommended practice and other published material—whether research, theory, or practice.* To what extent does the recommended practice corroborate, challenge, or qualify work already available in the professional literature? Does it break new ground, or broaden and deepen existing information? We think of *EJ* contributors as a community, almost as a family council. We are pleased when writers display an awareness of what has preceded their contributions in the journal and build on their predecessors' efforts by extending, modifying, supporting, or questioning them.

6. *Sensitivity to the relevance and timeliness of the topic.* Perhaps this criterion should have been listed first. Indeed, the first questions our reviewers are asked to ponder are related to this concern: Is the topic of current interest to the profession? Has it been covered adequately in recent issues of *EJ*? Is it appropriate for our audience, teachers of English in middle, junior high, and senior high schools? Does it make a significant contribution to the literature on the topic? On one level, of course, this is *sine qua non* for any manuscript to be considered publishable.

What we have in mind here, however, is not so much the selection of the topic but the treatment of the topic in the manuscript. Through the years, for instance, we have published hundreds of articles on teaching Shakespeare. That does not mean we won't publish that topic again. Manuscripts on such tried-and-true topics should not belabor the obvious nor repeat what is easily available in other sources. They should emphasize what they add to our understanding of the problem and how material has been adapted to current situations and new or emerging contexts. At one point in our editorship, we had published a number of manuscripts on the use of journals in the English classroom. We continued to receive scores of manuscripts on this topic, and the entire staff agreed, "No more." Then we received Anne McCrary Sullivan's treatment of the subject and realized that she put the whole issue in a new and comprehensive perspective and provided impeccably clear guidelines based on her own experience and previously published accounts. Reviewers recommended unanimously that it be accepted and rushed into print (1989).

Prospective contributors would do well to scan recent issues of *EJ* (from at least the last five years) for previous articles on whatever topic they are addressing. Annual indexes, published in the December issue, make this reasonably easy. If possible, they might even spend an hour or so with ERIC to determine what is readily available in other sources. They certainly need not cite all the materials they find, much less comment on them. But they should get a sense of what is known and what is already recommended or discussed. The most frequent comment we get from reviewers on manuscripts that are not recommended for acceptance is, "nothing new here." In many cases, this comment results not because the authors really have nothing worthwhile to say to our readers, but because they have not written with our readers in mind; they have not considered what readers already know or have available. The unkindest comment of all— one that we get more frequently than we would like—is, "I don't believe this person *reads* the *English Journal.*"

7. *All, any, or none of the above.* It would be rare for a manuscript to address all the concerns listed here; to do so might require a monograph rather than an article. On the other hand, it is extremely rare that we publish articles which address none of these guidelines. Even so, occasionally genuinely unique manuscripts arrive that follow none of these rules; nevertheless, they so impress our reviewers that we accept them. Therefore, we do not mean by this list to discourage submission of any manuscript. Though these are the criteria by which we ordinarily judge descriptions of classroom practice, we remain open to the unusual, the offbeat, the innovative approach. And we do publish material other than descriptions of classroom practice, including position papers and omnibus reviews of exemplary teaching materials.

Telling Stories: Where Classroom Inquiry Fits In

Most of the 1,200 or so manuscripts we receive each year recommend teaching practices for middle school, junior, and senior high school English classrooms. Too often the practices are introduced with a verbal tag such as, "teachers could do so-and-so"; "you might try this in your classroom"; "students can be told"; "the teacher may want to." As a result of these verbal formulas, the text sounds tentative, depicting a hypothetical situation. Perhaps this is understandable when the manuscript is written by a teacher-educator in a college or university, one who is recommending a practice that may not have actually been tried yet. It is less clear why classroom teachers use such language, for they clearly would not recommend a practice unless they had tried it and had evidence from their own students which satisfied them that the practice had achieved some observable success. We suspect that this is a rhetorical element surviving from earlier days, when it was considered impolite for writers to appear too obtrusive in their own manuscripts or boastful about their achievements.

As editors, we encourage writers, "Don't be so polite. Jump right in." *EJ* readers want accounts of practices that have been used in real classrooms. Such accounts are written by teachers who tell stories. Readers may read such a story and "try it on for fit." They may decide it doesn't fit them, or their students. More likely they will say, "I can't do exactly that—I don't need to—but I do see how something similar might work in my classroom." At least readers then have something more concrete than hypothetical suggestions. In such stories you read what students wrote in their journals; you find out what Ramón and Kim and Jimmy said. You will know whether you have Ramóns and Kims and Jimmys in your classroom and whether they would respond similarly.

We make no exaggerated claims for the contribution this writing makes to the growing body of research in our field. We know that it depends heavily on teacher intuition and private judgments. We know that the principles involved need to be tested experimentally by other teachers, subjected to the dialectic of discussion and professional commentary, examined and synthesized by theorists, and verified by more formal research. But we do insist that these stories, reported clearly and carefully by teachers who have lived them, provide valuable insights for practicing teachers and the beginning point for professional inquiry. The stories may even suggest new directions for researchers. Furthermore, stories often report the end point of professional inquiry—the application of principles derived from past experience, theory, and research.

In preparing one issue of *EJ*, we reread George Hillocks's *Research on Written Composition* (1986) as well as all the reviews of it we could locate. Perhaps the most frequent complaint about that work involved not its accuracy or validity or applicability, but the language in which it was reported. For example, Richard L. Larson (1987), certainly one of the more astute readers of composition research anywhere around, concluded:

> In one of the acute ironies in our profession today, a teacher of writing is here addressing other teachers of writing (all of whom value skillful use of language and forceful expression) in a language that, at central points, probably cannot communicate with large numbers of its readers.

In an otherwise favorable review of the book, Russel K. Durst lamented Hillocks's "lack of specific examples that teachers can relate to" (1987). None of this calls into question the importance of Hillocks's research nor even the soundness of his findings, which may or may not be controverted on other grounds. It suggests, however, that for these findings to make an impact on our profession, they must be translated into concrete, dramatic, personal, imaginable scenarios— in other words, stories: stories of teachers and their students struggling to implement what Hillocks called the "inquiry" and "environmental" approaches in real classrooms.

To borrow terms from Sandra Stotsky's perceptive review (1988) of Hillocks, the imbalance in the current, and perhaps unfortunate, debate between proponents of naturalistic or "whole language" approaches and direct or "goal-directed" approaches is troublesome. This imbalance derives from the fact that most naturalistic studies are replete with vivid stories of students and sometimes short on critical examination; on the other hand, the studies of direct instruction abound with generalizations and recommendations, but rarely provide stories of the actual experiences on which the generalizations are grounded. This imbalance in the professional literature makes it difficult for teachers to arrive at rational decisions on an important issue in our profession: the relative merits of naturalistic and direct instruction, of what are loosely called "student-centered" and "teacher-directed" approaches to curriculum and instruction.

Our profession is working toward correcting that imbalance. Arthur Applebee reported in 1988 that roughly one-third of the manuscripts now received by the prestigious research journal *Research in the Teaching of English* are based on qualitative or ethnographic models, and that a similar proportion holds for the articles actually published. Two recent NCTE research monographs (Freedman, 1987; Langer & Applebee, 1987) combined experimental (or at least quasi-experimental) methods with qualitative or descriptive methods. In an editorial in the October 1988 issue of *English Education*, Gordon Pradl issued a ringing call for manuscripts in which teachers tell their stories. It would be wonderful, he said, "to see more teachers detailing their full-bodied stories of celebration, including their classroom lives and their reading and writing, before any real analysis begins to occur." He concluded:

> I have tried to suggest that what moves us as teachers is not sermons disguised as analysis, but the sharing and testing of stories. Finally, I think we need to keep reminding ourselves that we carry the world around in our heads encoded in a series of generalizations. Thus if we hope to gain access to and influence these generalizations, we'll need to return to the experiences that gave birth to these generalizations in the first place. In this way we tap our originating resources and recover the strength that resides in narrative. (p. 133)

Preparing Manuscripts: One Editor's Point of View

What follows are answers to questions most frequently asked this editor (or, in some cases, to questions I wish contributors asked me). Writers for professional journals should keep in mind that editing such journals is often done by professionals on virtually a voluntary basis who make their living doing something else, like teaching full-time. They very rarely have large, highly trained, well-paid staffs. Their staffs, when they are so lucky as to have them, mostly are poorly paid graduate students, who by the nature of their appointments may be around for only a year or two. In other words, these editors need and deserve your patience, and they are not likely to be able to provide the service that, say, a commercial magazine might. What's true of the staff is even more likely true of journal reviewers: they are professionals who volunteer to read manuscripts without compensation. That they do so carefully and promptly is a tribute to the generosity our profession elicits. But there will be delays, and there may be cryptic reviews, particularly of manuscripts not appropriate for the journal or not conforming to the format expected of the journal. Following these suggestions would make editors' lives infinitely easier and assure that your manuscript gets the attention it deserves from the editorial staff.

  1. Read the journal to which you are submitting a manuscript. Unlike freelance magazine writers whose work may appear in hundreds of diverse sources, writers for professional journals are expected to read the journal to which they contribute and know what has already appeared in its pages on the topic addressed. Check the mast page and the calls for manuscripts for information about the kinds of articles solicited and the form in which they should

be submitted. Often journals will have a style sheet or a message to prospective contributors, available upon request.

2. Never submit the same manuscript to two different journals at the same time without informing both that you are doing so. Never submit a manuscript that has already appeared in substantively the same form in another source without informing the editor and, if requested, providing a copy of the previous publication.

3. Avoid clever, gimmicky titles that don't communicate clearly the content of the article. The journal may have restrictions about the length or nature of the title.

4. Edit your manuscript carefully, and have a trusted colleague proofread it for you. Nothing irritates reviewers more than English teachers who submit poorly edited and proofread manuscripts. Remember what you teach your students about the value of peer-response groups. When the competition is keen, often the difference between acceptance and rejection of a manuscript is that the editors are pressed for time and prefer manuscripts that are as nearly ready for press as possible.

5. Always include complete publication information for works cited, in whatever form the journal requires. The need to seek or verify bibliographic information causes unnecessary delays in the publication of your manuscript.

6. You do not need to send an extensive curriculum vita with your manuscript. It will almost certainly not be read. Likewise, your cover letter should be brief. It will most likely not be read by the reviewers of your manuscript. The manuscript must speak for itself. However, always be sure to include complete and current addresses, school affiliation(s), and telephone numbers where you can be reached during working hours. If your manuscript is submitted in response to a special call, this should be indicated in the cover letter.

7. If your manuscript is available on computer disks, let the editor know that in your cover letter. If you know that your disk meets the format requirements of the journal to which you are submitting, go ahead and include the disk. This may save everyone a good bit of time and expense.

8. If you have photographs or other artwork, feel free to submit those with your manuscript, but don't be surprised if the editor accepts the manuscript and not the visuals. If you need to have the visuals

returned, indicate that and send adequate postage and packaging material. If at all possible, avoid using complicated charts and figures that will require special printing procedures and entail additional costs. Or, submit such material as camera-ready copy.

9. Don't be insulted when the editor suggests revisions or edits your manuscript. The better the staff and the more rigorous the publication's standards, the more likely such revising and editing will take place. The acceptance letter should make clear whether and how such changes will be made. It may also ask you to give the editors permission to edit silently in minor ways to conform to the journal's style.

10. And, last but most important, don't be discouraged when a manuscript is not accepted. Remember that journals receive many more good manuscripts than they can use. The quality of the manuscript is seldom the sole consideration in editors' decisions. They must also provide a balance among types, topics, and potential audiences. They may have chosen to emphasize particular themes or topics.

Preparing Manuscripts: Our Readers' Perspective

The list above may or may not be helpful to teachers who want to break into print in professional publications. What may be more helpful is to consider why teachers should write, but to use our major purposes as writers-in-the-trenches as criteria for judging manuscripts. As editors we are very much aware of these criteria, and we suspect that writers whose manuscripts fulfill these criteria are more often successful in getting published and, more important, more effective in communicating with readers.

As simple as this may sound, it needs to be reiterated: teachers need to write for professional publications because there are teachers out there who need help. As editors, we were touched by a handwritten letter handed to us in a professional meeting not too long ago. We used it as the basis for an editorial and for a call for manuscripts (Nelms, 1989). It said, in part:

> I feel we need at least a *part* of an *EJ* issue on the discouragement/despair that so many teachers . . . are feeling. . . . Some of us are faced with such apathy and such an untamed group of young people that we just literally give up. . . . There is little individual teachers can do (often nothing!) in the situation, so they revert to seat work/busy work—no *real* challenge or discussion or lecturing. . . . Please consider this and maybe someone will be able to come up with some workable solutions for those of us in the situation(s) described.

I recently finished reading a book on current research on effective teaching, published by one of the most prestigious educational agencies in the country. It purports to review what has been achieved in such research and to chart new directions for the profession. There is not one single chapter that really speaks to the concerns of our desperate teacher—nor, for that matter, to any teacher struggling with "real, live" classroom problems. The essays dwell on such a level of abstract generalization that not even the most astute reader nor the most dedicated aspirant could translate what is there into a vision of a day-to-day working classroom. Here is not the proper place to debate the bankruptcy of the American educational research establishment, but I simply suggest if anyone is going to help desperate teachers avoid the retreat to worksheets and busy work, it probably will have to be other classroom teachers—those who make the classroom work, those who have been involved in reflection and action research, those who can articulate the "workable solutions" our teacher calls for.

Teachers who need help are all around us. I see them in every school system I have worked with in the past twenty years. Their numbers have not declined through the years. Keeping them in mind will provide one set of criteria for determining whether a manuscript is publishable: Does it address critical issues faced by teachers in real situations? Does it present workable solutions to real problems? Does it articulate these solutions so clearly that other teachers can envision putting them into practice in their classrooms? Does it provide some sort of convincing documentation that the solutions are genuinely effective in achieving important goals? Is it written persuasively?

By such persuasion we do not mean the hard sell of commercial instructional materials nor the authoritarianism of many education mandates, but clear, lucid prose that employs the three classical sources of persuasion: *ethos, logos,* and *pathos.* The *ethos* of the work should persuade the reader that the writer is genuine, knowledgeable, objective, and concerned. The *logos* of the work should present hard evidence that the points made are intellectually sound. The *pathos* of the work should dramatize the classroom situation so clearly that it will appeal to the reader's sense of reality and concern.

Finally, teachers need to write for professional publication to establish their own professionalism. To emphasize this point I will conclude by quoting from a letter we received and published, this one from one of our *EJ* Writing Award winners:

Writing the article about my writing classroom, having it published in *EJ*, and winning the *"English Journal* Writing Award"
for 1989 have been the most rewarding events of my professional life. As I struggled to describe my students and our achievements, I realized anew the power of writing to clarify, to focus,
to enable us to savor our experiences, and to make disparate
incidents and impressions into a meaningful whole. As I worked
to get my points across, the human need to connect and communicate, on which our work as writing teachers is based, was very
real to me. So the actual writing of the article was very satisfying, and I thank you for that particular "call for manuscripts."

Colleagues in my school and district rejoiced with me at the
publication of the article and the *EJ* award, and, thanks in part
to publicity provided by *EJ*, people of my small town also congratulated me and took a new interest in what we're trying to
accomplish in our classrooms. . . .

But long before I received that award and throughout the
months since, *EJ* has been my companion in my efforts to teach
and to learn. Ours is an isolated profession; the opportunities
and demands of our students' presence leaves us with little
time for professional discussions with other teachers. *EJ* helps
overcome that isolation.

That's a bit of what *EJ* means to me: a chance to listen to my
colleagues' authentic, personal, learned, insightful voices; a chance,
perhaps, to add my own voice to the discussion. (Dudley, 1991)

Dudley captures well what it means to write for a publication like
English Journal; she also captures what it means to be an *EJ* reader.
The best way to summarize our criteria for selecting manuscripts
for *EJ* is to say that we look for writers who speak authentically
to such readers.

References

Applebee, A.N. (1988). Musings . . . On publishing in *RTE*. *Research in the Teaching of English, 22*, 239–241.

Atwell, N. (1987). *In the middle.* Portsmouth, NH: Boynton/Cook.

Dudley, M. (1991). Authentic voices. *English Journal, 80*(3), 83.

Durst, R.K. (1987). Review of Hillocks's *Research on written composition. Quarterly of the National Writing Project and the Center for the Study of Writing, 9*(3), 23–25.

Freedman, S.W. (1987). *Response to student writing* (Research Report No. 23). Urbana, IL: National Council of Teachers of English.

Hillocks, G., Jr. (1986). *Research on written composition.* Urbana, IL: ERIC Clearinghouse on Reading and Communication Skills and the National Conference on Research in English.

Langer, J.A., & Applebee, A.N. (1987). *How writing shapes thinking* (Research Report No. 22). Urbana, IL: National Council of Teachers of English.

Larson, R.L. (1987). Review: *Research on written composition. College Composition and Communication, 38,* 207–211.

Murray, D.M. (1982). Write research to be read. *Language Arts, 59,* 760–768.

Nelms, B.F. (1989). Alienated students, alienated teachers. *English Journal, 78*(6), 94.

Pradl, G.M. (1988). Editorial. *English Education, 20,* 127–133.

Stotsky, S. (1988). *Research on written composition:* Response to Hillocks' report. *Research in the Teaching of English, 22,* 89–99.

Sullivan, A.M. (1989). Liberating the urge to write: From classroom journals to lifelong writing. *English Journal, 78*(7), 55–61.

15 An Affiliate Editor's Perspective

Alice K. Swinger
Wright State University, Dayton, Ohio

Alone in my office after the last class and meeting of the day, I tackle the mail. Among the memos, books, and letters are big, brown envelopes. Manuscripts. I pick up one and slit the flap. Hope—the editor's constant companion—reads with me. I hope it says something new. I hope it doesn't put me to sleep. I hope I don't lose my place in a convoluted sentence. I hope I don't need my magnifying glass to read the print from an overused ribbon, or have to decipher a minuscule typeface. I scan the pages; it passes the first screening. I log it in and go on to the next one.

As a former editor of a state English council's affiliate journal, I have often lived that scenario. Accepting a manuscript means taking editorial responsibility for publication; rejecting one means that the journal's subscribers will not read that work and that the writer must seek another publisher. Time and thought are needed to make that decision to publish or not. In this chapter I will describe the decision-making process and some factors related to it.

Editors, Writers, and the Publishing Cycle

Most affiliate editors serve in that role as part of their academic work. They teach full-time and have lots of work but limited staff and little budget. They usually are not paid. Their journals may be published monthly, quarterly, semiannually, or annually according to budgets, readers' demands, or writers' needs. Whatever the schedule, editors' tasks continue throughout their terms of service, changing like seasons of the year with the cycle of publishing.

Your manuscript enters the publishing cycle when it arrives at the office of the editor. The editor or an assistant will log it in with date, title, and your name and address. Depending on the journal's policy, the staff may send a card indicating they have received your article. If readers are used, copies of the manuscript are mailed to members of the review panel; one copy will remain in the editor's file. When reviewers' responses to your manuscript are returned, the editor or editorial staff will decide whether to accept the piece for publication in that journal.

Many affiliate journals do establish panels of readers who review incoming manuscripts, and the process of mailing, reading, critiquing, and returning manuscripts takes time. Readers offer their expertise as a professional contribution. If manuscripts arrive during a particularly busy time, they are probably laid aside for a few days. If they arrive during vacation, other mail lands on top of them. Though reviewers have disciplined reading schedules, they do need time to complete the assigned task. Expect at least three months to elapse from the time an editor receives your manuscript until you receive an acceptance or rejection.

If the journal uses themed issues, your manuscript will be filed with others for that issue. When manuscripts are read, each piece is considered for its contribution to developing and exploring the theme. Even if the journal does not work entirely by themes, an editor may regard several pieces together to form a mini-theme within an issue. Manuscripts are also considered in relationship to others in current and past issues. An editor may reject your manuscript if a similar one has been published recently in that journal or is already accepted for an upcoming issue.

Sometimes, between the time a manuscript is mailed to a prospective publisher and a reply is received, an author decides that journal is not the right choice for the piece. If you do decide that, immediately write to ask for the manuscript to be returned. Don't wait until it is accepted or rejected: the editorial staff will have put unnecessary time into it. Even if you don't want this particular piece published in this journal, you may write other pieces that you will want to have considered. You will, therefore, want to preserve your reputation as a courteous writer.

Even though you may think waiting to hear about the status of your manuscript is tiresome, you should not telephone unless you have a critical need, which does not include impatience or curiosity. If the decision has been made, you will have heard. But if you must know, write a letter of inquiry. This may not bring an affirmative response, but it may bring your manuscript back whether or not the reviewing process is finished.

Improving the Odds for Acceptance

Experience has shown me that writers occasionally need to be reminded of one thing that helps every article submission: polish your manuscript.

Send only your best, finished work. Let the manuscript cool, then reread it. Ask your best friend or severest critic to read your piece to identify grammar problems or trouble spots in your writing. Errors or inaccuracies in your article will be found, if not by the editor, by readers. When in doubt, double-check. If there is a nagging question, do your homework: check the facts.

Successful writers always keep in mind what sells and what doesn't. *What sells:* fresh ideas presented convincingly; say something new, say something old in a new way, or say it to a new audience. *What doesn't:* incomplete development, jargon, verbiage, and excessive length.

The physical condition of your manuscript may be another factor in the editor's decision. Deterrents to acceptance include: errors or illegible printing (e.g., tiny letters in which every *p* looks like a capital and nothing goes below the line). A faint printout is also a problem, one that is easily fixed: buy a new ribbon, change the cartridge, or clean your typewriter.

Although your manuscript must stand on its own, your cover letter is important packaging. A brief cover letter is adequate, and preferable. You may want to mention recently published work and your qualifications for writing the submitted manuscript. Send a self-addressed, stamped envelope, with stamps attached in the manner indicated in the writer's guidelines. Also, keep a record of your manuscript submissions. If your article is returned and you plan to revise and resubmit, you will want to know who has already reviewed the piece.

When a Manuscript Is Accepted

After all the waiting, you will someday receive an acceptance letter telling you the proposed publication date and issue for your piece. With the letter will be a permission form requiring your signature. This represents a contract between you and the publisher. Sign it and send it back immediately. The issue is probably ready to go to press; the layout may be already planned. An editor has little leeway in time or space: the number of pages is established and cannot be changed easily. If a selected piece is withdrawn, the issue may have pages of boring, expensive white space. Each issue must be completely planned, with all pages filled before printing begins. Editors need your signature on that return letter.

Sometimes, but not always, you will have the opportunity to proofread copy before your article is printed. You should mark errors and observe editorial changes, but not revise other parts of your work. If you disagree with editorial changes, you may discuss them. State your reasons; listen to the editor's reasons. You can usually reach agreement. If you cannot, you may choose not to have your piece published in that journal at that time.

You will be sent one or more copies of the issue that has your piece in it. It is considerate to send a letter telling the editor you have received your copy. It is even more considerate if you include a thank you for publishing your piece. (Editors aren't often thanked.)

It is wise to put one of your copies of the issue in a file and circulate the other. If you think you will want more copies, send for them immediately. Periodicals aren't always available months or years after the publication date.

When Your Manuscript Isn't Accepted

Writers know that all manuscripts aren't accepted. When one of yours returns to you unpublished, regard it as a natural event, and don't take it personally. If the rejection letter has a message beyond a form sentence or two (don't expect comments, however), read it to understand what it means for future writing and journal selection. Reread your piece, looking for writing flaws, then correct them. If there are none, adapt the style, introduction, and conclusion to the needs of your second-choice journal. To submit your writing to a new market, compose a new cover letter, print the necessary new copies of the article, and send the package off.

It is important that you regard a manuscript both personally and impersonally. You are responsible for writing well, for producing error-free copy, and for selecting the right publication for your piece. Editors and editorial boards are responsible for creating strong, balanced journals. Not every piece of writing finds its niche the first time it is mailed. Don't lose self-esteem as you search for the best home for your writing.

IV Essential Information
for Teacher Writers

16 Nuts and Bolts of Writing a Manuscript

Gail E. Tompkins
California State University, Fresno

What does Neil Simon do when he sits down to write a script that may become another hit Broadway show? How does Alice Walker capture on paper the characters in her mind? How does Ellen Goodman write her syndicated newspaper columns? Effective writing often appears to have been produced effortlessly, and too often novice writers assume that these experienced and well-known authors write polished compositions in a single draft. Nothing could be further from the truth! Writing is hard work, and it is demanding for all authors. Beginning authors often labor under many myths about how good writers compose. Maybe some of these misconceptions, identified by Brannon, Knight, and Neverow-Turk (1982), are familiar to you: good writers wait for a flash of inspiration before they write; they know exactly what they're going to say before they sit down to write; they always begin with an outline; they never show their writing to anyone until it is finished; they find writing easy and never have to revise; and good writers do not procrastinate. In fact, good writing comes from a process of trial and error; it involves writing and reading, rewriting and rereading.

Through the observation of experienced writers and through research in the field of composition instruction, we can identify some of the tasks involved in writing and suggest strategies for choosing topics, writing the rough draft, revising and editing the manuscript, and submitting it to an editor for review. Writers develop their own writing processes, their rituals and strategies for attacking the writing task. With experience, you will learn a variety of attack plans that you can experiment with as you develop your own unique writing processes.

Undoubtedly, you have already developed some strategies for dealing with writing tasks. Think about the strategies you already use and what you know about yourself as a writer. To help you probe your awareness of your own writing processes, Figure 1 presents a writing profile questionnaire.

1. What sorts of writing do you do most often? Least often? Why?
2. How do you feel about your writing?
3. What experiences have affected your learning how to write?
4. What is the hardest part of writing for you? The easiest part?
5. How do you start a piece of writing? How do you find out what you want to say?
6. What is the ideal writing situation for you?
7. Do you have any special habits or idiosyncracies when you write?
8. How do you decide on the content and form of your writing?
9. Describe the process you go through—step by step—when you write.
10. Do you write more than one draft of a piece of writing? Why or why not?
11. What kinds of revisions do you make? In what order?
12. Are you willing to read your writing to other people? Who do you read it to? Do you ever read a piece of your writing to anyone before it's finished? Do you reread your writing? If so, what do you reread it for?
13. How do you know when a piece of writing is finished?
14. What do you think the characteristics of "good" writing are? Is your writing "good" writing? Why or why not?

Figure 1 Writing profile questionnaire (Adapted from Brannon, Knight, & Neverow-Turk, 1982, p. 8)

Writers use a variety of processes as they write, but elements of these processes can be combined to suggest a plan of attack for teachers as they write for publication in educational magazines and journals. In order to learn to write well, novice writers must shift their attention from the finished product—the manuscript to be sent to an editor—to the process used in creating that product. This shift from product to process is as valuable for adult writers as it is for student writers.

In order to create a well-organized and publishable product, the process that writers use must be considered. Authorities in the field of composition, such as Emig (1971), Elbow (1973), Flower and Hayes (1977), Graves (1983), and Murray (1984), have outlined the cognitive processes that occur during writing. While the names given these actions or behaviors vary, they generally fall into five categories: prewriting, drafting, revising, editing, and publishing. Labeling and ordering these composing actions may be misleading, however, because in practice the writing process is not a series of neatly packaged, linear categories to be completed in a prescribed order. The writing process is cyclical rather than linear, involving recursive shifts back and forth through the various cognitive processes. Some writers begin almost immediately to write a rough draft and then move back to prewriting to gather more details or facts, while others write, re-write, write, rewrite, and write again. Rodrigues (1985) compares the writing process to "a tangled string after a kitten had played with it" (p. 125).

Prewriting: Before You Put Words to Paper

Prewriting has been the most neglected aspect of the writing process, but it is as crucial to writers as a warm-up is to athletes. Researchers recommend that writers spend as much as 75 percent of their total writing time involved in prewriting activities. Writers engage in many types of prewriting, but three of the most important for teachers who are writing for educational magazines and journals are: identifying the topic, choosing the publication(s) they will target their manuscript for, and refining their topics and generating ideas for writing.

Identifying the Topic

Often novice authors have difficulty writing because they attempt to write about something they don't know enough about. But writing grows out of experience, and for the greatest chance of success, writers should choose topics they know well. As you begin to think about possible topics, ask yourself if you already know enough about it or if you can learn enough about your topic to write a paper.

Also think about possible connections among topics or how to twist a topic in an innovative way. For example, one teacher identified wordless picture books as one of the things she knew a lot about and had used successfully in her first-grade classroom, and she decided to use it as the topic for her manuscript. As she reviewed possible publishing sources, she was dismayed to find that articles about using wordless picture books in beginning reading and writing instruction had recently been published in the journals she was considering. She was about to abandon the topic when an ESL teacher joined the discussion and asked about wordless picture books. He wasn't familiar with them, but as the first-grade teacher showed him some wordless picture books and explained how she used them, he thought of ways to use them with his limited English-speaking students. The two teachers decided to collaborate; after the ESL teacher experimented with some wordless picture books that the first-grade teacher loaned him, they wrote an article that was published!

Choosing the Prospective Journal

After deciding the topic for your manuscript, the next consideration will be to which journal or other publication to submit the completed manuscript. It's crucial to choose one or two publications that are appropriate for your topic before you begin to write, because articles on the same topic would be written differently if they were intended for *Language Arts, Research in the Teaching of English,* or *Journal of Reading.* Consider both your purpose and your audience. Why are you writing—to inform? to entertain? to persuade? Who are you writing for—teachers? parents? researchers? In order to choose an appropriate publication, you must answer these basic questions.

Examine several recent issues of the journals, magazines, or other publications you are considering in order to see whether they are appropriate for the kind of article, topic, and audience you have in mind. Choose one or two publication sources as targets for your manuscript. You will model your manuscript on articles in that publication.

Getting Ready to Write

After choosing a topic and identifying possible publication sources, the next step involves collecting resources in order to begin writing. These resources may include articles and books written on the topic, children's language samples, notes you have already written or journal entries, books of children's or adolescent literature, and other materials related to your manuscript.

Donald Graves (1983) called these idea-gathering or prewriting activities "rehearsal," and they may take a variety of forms, including reviewing the literature on the topic, taking notes, talking, brainstorming, teaching a lesson, and collecting student samples. If you are writing for a publication that typically includes quoted or referenced materials, it is especially important to read or review pertinent research, as well as recently published articles and books about the topic.

Many writers like to make notes about how they plan to develop their manuscript. A traditional outline is certainly one possibility, but there are other options. Writers could brainstorm a list of ideas, things to include, or possible directions for the manuscript which can be elaborated while writing. Another option is a cluster or web diagram, in which writers scribble their ideas across a sheet of paper, on lines radiating from a nucleus. Advocates of this approach suggest that these diagrams are more useful than lists because they allow writers to indicate relationships among ideas (Rico, 1983; Pehrsson & Robinson, 1985).

Checklist

As you progress through the prewriting stage, ask yourself these questions:

Am I preparing to write on a topic that I know well?

Have I identified my purpose for writing?

Have I identified the specific audience I plan to write for?
Have I identified the unique characteristics of the publication
I plan to submit the manuscript to?

Have I engaged in rehearsal activities (e.g., reading, taking
notes) before beginning to write?

Have I collected relevant journal articles and books on the
topic (if needed)?

Have I collected student language samples (if needed)?

Drafting: Getting Your Ideas Down on Paper

Authors write and refine their compositions through a series of drafts.
They do not sit down with pencil in hand or with fingers poised
over the computer keyboard and begin to write with their articles
already composed in their minds. Instead, writers begin with tentative ideas that they develop through reading, note-taking, and other
rehearsal activities. They use their rough drafts to pour out ideas,
with little concern for spelling, punctuation, and other mechanical
errors.

During the drafting stage, writers compose quickly without
stopping. Rather than checking the dictionary for the spelling of every
problem word, experienced writers invent a spelling for the word
and continue writing. These rough drafts are often messy, with cross-
outs, arrows, and lines drawn to indicate where a transition is needed.
As a practical matter, authors write only on one side of the sheet
of paper and always double-space, whether writing by hand, on a
typewriter, or on a word processor. You will find that by writing
on every other line you fill up pages more rapidly, thus adding to
your feelings of accomplishment. Also, when the text has been double-
spaced, more room is available for making revisions.

Undoubtedly the most difficult sentence to write is the first
one. It never seems good enough. When writing is viewed as a series
of drafts, however, neither the first sentence nor any of the ones
that follow it need to be good. As you begin to write, focus on pouring
out ideas without laboring over particular words or sentences. The
words and sentences can be refined later in the writing process. In
fact, if you can't think of a particular word, just leave a blank and
continue writing.

As drafting continues, leave space to indicate where you will add a reference later or change an awkward wording. Now you have one or more pages filled with words and you're on your way!

Trouble Spots

The first and last paragraphs may be the two most difficult ones that you write. Again and again editors and reviewers say that they want the first paragraph to reach out and grab them. How do successful authors do it? Look back at the first paragraphs of the articles in the publication you plan to submit your manuscript to. What techniques do these authors use? Some of the more common ones are questions and answers, quotations from published sources, quotations from students, student writing samples, dialogues, and anecdotes. Other articles begin with a traditional thesis sentence. Experiment with a variety of techniques and find one or two that work well for your writing style. Because of the importance attached to the first paragraph, it is often better to leave it until later and move into the manuscript.

The summary or concluding paragraph can also be difficult to write. You may feel that you have already said everything there is to say about your topic. You're out of ideas and out of words. Again, check to see how authors of articles in your chosen publication have handled the problem. One of the easiest ways is to set your manuscript down and leave it for a week. Before you pick it up again, pretend to telephone your Aunt Nellie and tell her in several sentences about your manuscript. What you would say to her would probably make a good summary.

After the First Draft

Writing well takes time. Instead of sitting down and dashing off a finished manuscript in one draft, experienced writers recognize that they must write, read, rewrite, reread, and write and read again and again. Over a period of days or weeks, writers read their drafts, make changes, put the manuscript down, and then repeat the cycle. With each cycle, writers are able to distance themselves from the manuscript and look at it more critically. Throughout these cycles, the focus remains on the content—the ideas and the words used to express the ideas—rather than on spelling and other mechanics. The focus changes to mechanics later in the writing process. It's a waste of time to worry now about how to spell a particular word when you may decide to delete the word in the next draft.

Checklist

During this phase, ask yourself these questions:

> Did I write more than one draft?
>
> Did I write on one side of the paper and double-space my writing in order to leave space for revisions?
>
> In these drafts, did I focus on content rather than mechanics?

Revising: Refining Ideas

Often novice writers break the writing cycle as soon as they complete a satisfactory draft of their composition. Drafting is such an exhausting experience that it seems to be enough. Experienced writers, however, know they must turn to readers for reactions, and then revise on the basis of these comments. Revision is not just polishing writing; it is more than that. Revision is described as working to meet the needs of readers through changing, adding, deleting, and rearranging material. At this stage the emphasis remains on the content of the writing.

Sharing with Readers

In the revising stage, writing is shared with an audience so that the writer can determine how well he or she is communicating. Writing is for readers, according to Frank Smith (1982), and in this stage, writing becomes more public. Experienced writers recognize that through sharing their writing with others, they can learn what they need to revise. It is rarely possible for writers to adequately anticipate what their readers will not understand or will need to know.

Response Groups

Finding an audience is sometimes difficult for teachers who are writing for publication in educational magazines and journals. If you can't locate a group of teacher writers in your community to share your writing with, why not enlist your colleagues, friends, and neighbors to form a response group that meets together to read and respond to each other's writing?

If a response group is not possible, then find a colleague who will read and react to your draft. You want readers to tell you about parts that were unclear, sentences that sounded awkward, words that needed to be defined, or paragraphs that wandered from the topic.

Checklist

Ask yourself these questions during the revising stage:

> Did I have one or more people read my composition?
>
> Did I make changes that reflected the reactions and comments of these readers?
>
> Between my first and final drafts, did I make substantive or only minor changes?

Editing: Putting It into Final Form

In the editing stage, attention switches to the mechanics of writing, such as spelling, capitalization, punctuation, and usage; writers polish their work by rearranging words and correcting specific errors. The goal in this stage is to make the writing "optimally readable" (Smith, 1982).

The approach used to spot and correct such errors is proof-reading, a unique form of reading. Instead of reading for meaning by chunking together words and phrases of text, the proofreader reads space by space and letter by letter. Proofreading is a slow and laborious form of reading (King, 1985). Because writers are familiar with their texts, it is especially difficult for them to proofread their own writing without leaping into meaningful reading and then skipping errorrs. Did you just note the extra *r* in the word *error*, or did you read the previous sentence for meaning?

Writers usually proofread their compositions two or more times, looking for different types of errors on each reading. The purpose of the first reading might be to locate spelling errors, while in the second reading it might be to locate capitalization and punctuation errors. Additional readings can be used to find subject-verb disagreements, nonparallel constructions, overused words, sexist language, and other problems. Books about usage skills, such as Strunk and White's *The Elements of Style* (1979), can be used to help you identify and correct your own errors. It is also helpful to have someone else proofread your manuscript to identify any mechanical errors you may have missed.

Formatting the Manuscript

After proofreading for mechanical errors, writers then put the manuscript into the desired format, according to the style manual used by the selected publication (this is usually specified in the publication's "information for authors"). Style manuals provide information about many aspects of writing for professional publication (and are worthwhile reading), but the most important formatting considerations include:

1. *Title page.* Type the title of the manuscript and the names, addresses, and daytime telephone numbers of all authors. The title of the manuscript is typed again at the top of the first page of text, but the authors' names are not listed there to ensure an unbiased review by the editorial board.

2. *Numbering of pages.* According to some style manuals, page one is the first page of text. In the style of the American Psychological Association, the title page counts as the first page, and page numbers are listed in the upper right corner. Sometimes two or three key words from the title are repeated on each page next to the page number.

3. *Citation of sources in the text.* Style manuals advocate a variety of approaches for listing sources and direct quotations in text. Check the designated style manual, or follow the examples provided in articles from a recent issue of the publication you have selected.

4. *Charts, figures, and tables.* Graphic displays of information are usually placed on separate pages and labeled Figure 1, 2, 3, and so on. They are identified in the text by number, and following the paragraph in which they are identified, a sentence is added stating, "Insert Figure X about here." This sentence is centered between paragraphs, and dashed lines are added above and below the sentence so that it will stand out. This information is added for the editor and type-setter so they will know where to insert the figure in the text; "Insert Figure X about here" does not appear in the published version of your article. Add your figures, each on a separate page, at the end of your manuscript, following the list of references.

5. *List of references.* Each style manual adopts a unique format for listing references at the end of the manuscript. Check the appropriate style manual, or examine how journal articles, books, and other types of references are listed in a recent issue of the publication you have selected. Most style manuals require the same basic information, but the organization of information varies from style to style.

Typing the Final Copy

After the draft has been proofread for mechanical errors and formatted according to the style manual preferred by your publication, the manuscript is retyped or corrected on a word processor and printed out. One last proofreading is necessary to spot any typographical errors in the final copy. Because the sentences are so familiar from numerous rereadings, making it difficult to proofread accurately, some writers proofread their manuscripts backward, from the last word on the last page to the first word on the first page.

Checklist

As you progress through editing, ask yourself these questions:

> Did I proofread my manuscript at least two times?
>
> Did someone else proofread it for me?
>
> Did I locate answers to usage questions in a usage guide?
>
> Did I adhere to the format of the publication I plan to submit the manuscript to?
>
> Did I proofread the final copy for typographical errors?

Publishing: Submitting the Manuscript to an Editor

Now you are ready to submit your manuscript to an editor for review and possible publication. Review one last time the "information for authors" that was printed in a recent issue of the publication to make sure you are following the guidelines exactly. Some editors will reject a manuscript without reading it if the guidelines are not followed! Check the guidelines for the following information:

> Number of copies of the manuscript to be sent to the editor.
>
> Whether a self-addressed, stamped envelope (SASE) is required so the manuscript can be returned if it is not accepted.
>
> Editor's name and address.

If the number of copies is not specified, send two. If the editor does not request a SASE, it is not necessary to send one.

Finally, write a cover letter personally addressed to the editor to accompany your manuscript (see Figure 2 for an example). The typewritten letter should be written in a professional manner and include information about the manuscript being submitted and its appropriateness for this particular publication. The letter can be brief—no longer than four or five sentences—as long as the key information is included.

Writers should follow the editor's guidelines explicitly as they compile the materials to mail. Put all of the specified materials and your cover letter in an envelope addressed to the editor and mail it. Be sure to keep one copy of the manuscript, as well as a copy of the cover letter, for your files.

```
                                         Your Return Address
                                         Date

Dr. William H. Teale, Editor
Language Arts
Division of Education
University of Texas at San Antonio
San Antonio, TX 78285-0654

Dear Dr. Teale:
    I am sending three copies of my manuscript, entitled "Hello History," for your
consideration and possible publication in Language Arts. I believe it is appropriate
for the upcoming themed issue on writing across the curriculum. In this article, I
describe how my third graders read biographies and produced a television show
featuring historical personalities that they called "Hello History." In my manu-
script, I explain how I integrated reading and writing across the curriculum and
how my students worked in cooperative learning groups to prepare their presenta-
tions. This manuscript is my own work and it is not being submitted simulta-
neously to any other journal.
    Thank you for your consideration of my manuscript, and I look forward to
hearing from you.

                                         Sincerely,
                                         Your Name
```

Figure 2 Sample cover letter

It is important to submit the manuscript to only one publication at a time. Some other types of manuscripts can be simultaneously submitted to several publishers, but editors of educational journals assume that the manuscripts being submitted to them are not being submitted to other journals. In fact, some editors require a statement in the cover letter which specifically states that the manuscript is not under consideration by any other journal.

When your manuscript is accepted for publication, the editor often sends a publication agreement form which you are asked to sign and return, stating that the manuscript has not been previously published and that it is your original work. Editors may also accept the manuscript on the condition that certain changes be made. As the author, you will have to decide whether you are willing to make the requested changes. At first, many authors do not want to make the required revisions, but after a bit of reflection, the changes seem more reasonable and most authors are able to satisfy the editors.

Manuscripts are usually published three to twelve months after they are accepted for publication. Authors normally receive one or more complimentary copies of the issue that their article appears in.

Checklist

As you submit your manuscript for publication, ask yourself these questions:

> Did I check the "information for authors" in a recent issue of the publication for submission requirements?
>
> Did I write a cover letter to accompany my manuscript?
>
> Did I submit my manuscript to only one publication at a time?
>
> Do I have some other publishing possibilities in mind in case the manuscript is not accepted by the first publication?

Summary

The guidelines presented in this chapter may lead you to believe that writing for publication in an educational magazine or journal is much like baking a recipe by following the directions in a cookbook. Nothing could be further from the truth! These suggestions provide a skeleton, but content determines whether your manuscript is accepted for publication. If you really know your topic and can tell your story effectively, it is likely to be published. If you're writing for fame or fortune, forget it. Having your article accepted for publication is not easy. Many journals accept only a handful of every 100 manuscripts they receive. These guidelines, however, can lessen your chances of rejection.

References

Brannon, L., Knight, M., & Neverow-Turk, Y. (1982). *Writers writing.* Montclair, NJ: Boynton/Cook.

Elbow, P. (1973). *Writing without teachers.* New York: Oxford University Press.

Emig, J. (1971). *The composing processes of twelfth graders* (Research Report No. 13). Urbana, IL: National Council of Teachers of English.

Flower, L.S., & Hayes, J.R. (1977). Problem-solving strategies and the writing process. *College English, 39,* 449–461.

Graves, D.H. (1983). *Writing: Teachers and children at work.* Exeter, NH: Heinemann.

King, M. (1985). Proofreading is not reading. *Teaching English in the Two-Year College, 12,* 108–112.

Murray, D. (1984). *Write to learn.* New York: Holt.

Pehrsson, R.S., & Robinson, H.A. (1985). *The semantic organizer approach to writing and reading instruction.* Rockville, MD: Aspen.

Rico, G.L. (1983). *Writing the natural way.* Boston: Houghton Mifflin.

Rodrigues, R.J. (1985). Moving away from writing-process worship. *English Journal, 74*(5), 24–27.

Smith, F. (1982). *Writing and the writer.* New York: Holt.

Strunk, W., Jr., & White, E.B. (1979). *The elements of style* (3rd ed.). New York: Macmillan.

17 Searching for Journals: A Brief Guide and 100 Sample Species

Chris M. Anson and Bruce Maylath
University of Minnesota

In every field, three or four species of periodicals are generally considered the most alluring, perched on the highest boughs of academe and holding the admiration of their onlookers, both in and out of the field. They tend to receive the most submissions, are frequently cited in other works, and have the highest rejection rates. In medicine, for example, publishing an article in the *Journal of the American Medical Association* or the *New England Journal of Medicine* brings instant prestige to the authors. The media keep a close watch on these journals for the results of cutting-edge research, and their authors often accept invitations to appear at press conferences or on national talk shows.

For someone just beginning to write and publish in their field, the sight of such unapproachable, brightly plumed journals can carry with it a mixture of awe and frustration. The very best writers with long lists of publications remember moments early in their careers when the initial excitement that accompanied sending an article to a top periodical soon turned to disappointment; they were dabbling among the polished, sophisticated pieces in the journal's issues, measuring their own work against the mature plumage of established authors.

In most cases, however, the two or three most widely cited journals represent only a fraction of the publishing opportunities in a given field. The demoralization so common among aspiring writers often starts because they imagine so few options for getting into print. Setting out to attract only the best and most rarefied journals

Earlier and less complete versions of this list, without the accompanying advice, appeared in C.M. Anson, "A Computerized List of Journals Carrying Articles on Composition," *College Composition and Communication, 37*, pp. 63–76; and C.M. Anson & H. Miller, "Journals in Composition: An Update," *College Composition and Communication, 39*, pp. 198–216.

of your field may be an excellent motivation to write, but it severely limits your range of topics, writing styles, and audiences. Instead of aiming for a golden eagle or an osprey, it helps to look around a bit for other varieties of publication. A range of choices not only boosts your motivation but opens up possibilities for attracting wider interest in your work.

The list of journals in this chapter is intended partly as an illustration of that range in one area of education (writing, literacy, English, and language arts). Indeed, it is broad enough to constitute a full phylum. Just a quick glance at a few of the 100-plus titles will show something of the considerable variety of publishing opportunities in this generalized area of teaching and scholarship. Depending on your own expertise and the focus of your writing, of course, many of the journals may be of marginal interest. We offer the list not only for its obvious usefulness as a source of information on possible publishing opportunities, but also to show how certain types of information can help you tailor a piece for publication or find a market for what you've already written.

The entries are arranged according to a fixed format. Parenthetical letters represent categories of information about the journal—a kind of anatomy. By way of explaining the format for the journal entries, we will offer some seeds of advice for using the list and, more generally, for preparing and submitting articles for publication.

Affiliation (a). While it may seem unimportant, the journal's auspices can tell you a good deal about the sort of material that might find a roost there. Is the journal published by a commercial press, or is it sponsored by a university department? Is it the chief means of professional communication for a large organization or for a small, regional affiliate? Is the organization known for a particular educational, political, or philosophical orientation? (Sending your paper on radical pedagogy to the journal of a highly conservative organization may, if it doesn't doom you to perfunctory rejection, at least limit your chances for publication.)

When published (b). Frequency may be tied to the size of the readership. Journals with small circulations have fewer financial resources to publish issues every month (or even more than once or twice a year). Consequently, when you plan to write and submit a piece for publication, the number of times the journal comes out can affect the timing of the review process. How often the journal comes out can also bear on the backlog of articles waiting to see their way to print. Unless an annual journal receives relatively few submissions worth publishing, its space will fill up quickly months in advance of the issue date, and you can expect a year or more before your accepted piece finally comes out in print. Many editors, however, continue to "build" an issue close to publication by shuffling pieces around and deferring some for later issues, all with the intent of refining the issue's focus. How much of this process takes place often depends on the size of a given issue.

Audience and circulation (c). In many ways, editors are mediators, adjusting an author's ideas (and text) to the expectations and interests of the journal's audience. While a journal's editor may see potential in a manuscript that doesn't quite meet the needs of its audience, it is always wise to keep the journal's audience clearly in mind during all phases of writing, submitting, and revising manuscripts for publication.

We asked editors to describe the interest of their journal's readers in writing, literacy, English, or language arts. Together with the index of interest—see items (i) and (j) below—this category gives a brief but telling profile of the typical subscriber and his or her expectations. Knowing, for example, that a journal's audience consists mainly of "scholars in linguistics, speech, and psychology" (as, for example, *Language and Speech* defines its readers) considerably narrows the focus, style, and content of possible submissions and makes them quite different from submissions to, say, a journal like *WPA: Writing Program Administration*, which caters to "directors of composition programs and writing centers, and English department chairs."

When provided, the journal's circulation appears after the description of its audience. Some periodicals have wide circulation (such as *English Journal*, with a readership of about 45,000), while others reach only a few hundred subscribers. The main difference between high- and low-circulation journals will likely be the complexity of the publication process: editing and producing widely read journals, like *Language Arts* with a circulation of over 20,000, usually involves a team of people working on different aspects of the periodical's design and format as well as in the process through which submissions migrate on their way to acceptance or rejection. In addition, high-volume journals also pass an article through more stages of production (initial copyediting, galleys, page proofs, etc.). Such complexity doesn't mean that you can expect a large-circulation journal to fly faster or slower than a journal with a smaller readership. But the latitude for content, speed of publication, and the like is somewhat wider for a small, local journal than for one whose 40,000 readers all expect to find the spring issue nesting in their mailbox on March 1, plus or minus one day, and, moreover, are used to spying a book review or a research update in every issue.

Focus (d). In this category, editors provide a precis of the journal's usual contents. While this is no substitute for having recent copies of the journal in front of you, such information can help you decide whether your article will fit the journal's needs. Knowing, for example, that *Southern Speech Communication Journal* publishes "quantitative studies of oral and written language" might be useful as you think about how best to cast your case study of a new method of speech instruction. At the very least, it gives you a place to start when you write a letter of inquiry or call the editor for advice.

Subscription information (e) and (g). This information is included for two important reasons. Writers who aspire to publish in their field should first and foremost be readers of their field's work. The whole business of knowledge production in a field thrives on communally based understandings. If you don't know what is going on in your discipline, you risk writing something already widely understood by a journal's audience. Several editors told us this in passing; some even wrote it into their tips for potential submitters of manuscripts. (Note, for example, *College Teaching*'s interest in "*new ideas or approaches; we reject many mundane manuscripts,*" or the advice of *Freshman English News:* "Be aware of the current research and articles in the field that have already been published on your topic. Too many submissions reflect a lack of scholarly awareness.")

Second, reading widely in your field's journals, especially at its fringes, can broaden your perspectives on what you do and suggest alternative flyways for publication. When we first compiled the list in this chapter, we became excited about several new possibilities for publication. The *Journal of Natural Inquiry*, to take one example, suggested a likely place to send some ethnographic work we have been doing. Likewise, once we had examined some back issues, *English for Specific Purposes* gave us impetus to write up some research on how writers adapt to new professional communities. We were impressed and encouraged by these attractive periodicals; yet had we not compiled the list, we might never have known enough about them to consider either writing or submitting material. In workshops that we run on the publication process, participants often react with awe when we dump copies of seventy or eighty journals on a table in the middle of the room. Consequently, we're now compelled to provide a half-hour "browsing break"—often the most significant note-taking episode of the workshop.

On the surface, the list may look hopelessly diverse. What interest could a teacher of fifth-grade English in a rural middle school possibly have in a journal like *Memory and Cognition?* In truth, that teacher may never conduct the research or gain sufficient expertise in this area of language studies to write and submit an article to the journal for publication. Nevertheless, the journal makes for some interesting reading and could broaden the teacher's thoughts about daily work. We know several graduate students who, largely because they started reading beyond the narrower boundaries of their degree programs, ended up writing quite interdisciplinary dissertations and going on to publish further research on the same scholarly intersections.

Address for submissions (f). Throughout our many discussions and correspondence with the editors of journals represented in the list, we learned much about the nature of the infamous Editor. For many writers poking through their shells into publication, it is not uncommon to think of journal editors as powerful judges who hold the beaks and feathers of people's professional lives in the palms of their hands: with one slash of a pen, the Editor can banish them forever to the bush. For this reason, many writers feel reluctant to call or write to an editor, who surely must be too busy to respond to petty inquiries or who will take offense at being bothered by someone who has not established a national reputation as a scholar.

Nothing could be further from the truth! The sooner you can reject the myth of the godly editor, the more comfortable you'll feel working with an editor, even before you write a piece or send it in. Editors of most scholarly and educational periodicals, especially those sponsored by nonprofit organizations, are appointed to their position and usually continue their usual work as teachers, administrators, and scholars (albeit on a lesser scale). In short, they're like anyone you're likely to meet at your own school or place of work—as receptive to your ideas, as willing to talk with you, as happy to share advice. And, like you, they're looking for publishing opportunities (in this case, from the perspective of solicitation instead of submission).

Far from being bothered by your phone calls or letters, editors actually welcome such queries. They can encourage you to send in a manuscript or, before you waste your own time and the time of reviewers, can let you know that your piece would not meet the journal's needs. Your chances of timely publication elsewhere are greatly increased, because you don't need to wait for weeks or months to hear from an editor who could have discouraged your submission from the start.

If you choose to query an editor, it helps to plan what you want to say in light of what most editors want to know:

> What is your contribution about, exactly? How does it fit the publishing mission and audience of the journal? Again, it helps greatly to become familiar with the journal's focus and readership before contacting the editor.
>
> What sort of article is it? Is it based on research? Is it informal and anecdotal? Is it purely instructional? Heavily theoretical? Is it a review essay on several new books or a short book review of a single work?
>
> How long is the manuscript, in pages or number of words? (Keep in mind that along with audience and focus, an editor's chief concern is often space.) In working out the length of your manuscript, try to be more specific than "around twenty pages." Calculate the number of words on a page by adding the number of words per line for a few lines and taking the average number of words per line, then multiplying by an average number of lines per page. An editor will know exactly whether an article of 25,000 words will be too long, but "twenty pages" may say little.
>
> Finally, how usable is your article in its current state? Occasionally, an editor may want to know how long it will take you to finish the piece. One of us queried an editor and learned that the next issue's focus coincided with this author's topic. As close as the editor was to the publication date, he still wanted material. With the article already finished, the editor was able to include it easily. That couldn't have happened if it hadn't been ready to go. (Nevertheless, we still recommend contacting editors before you're far along in the process.)

These questions may seem routine, but several editors told us that they often receive very vague letters of query. A letter asking whether an editor has any interest in reviewing an article on peer-group conferences is far less useful than one explaining that the article involves a quantitative descriptive study of high school students' revisions when they do and do not engage in peer revision sessions. At the same time, it's important not to become so prolix in the letter that you might as well have sent the article itself. The chief benefit of the letter (or call) of query is that you can gauge an editor's interest and possibly save weeks or months of waiting for the entire submission and review process to unfold.

Index of interest (h) and (i). We asked editors to provide us with two bits of information from which we could create an "index of interest" in the general topics of composition, writing, and literacy: "extremely interested," "very interested," "somewhat interested," or "occasionally/marginally interested." We then asked them to estimate the total number of articles published in the journal over the past five years and the total number that focused on writing or literacy. The result is a simple ratio (10/100, 75/80). Together, these two items fairly accurately reflect the journal's interest in publishing articles on the subject at hand. In a few cases, the ratio does not reflect the indicated interest. These journals may be trying to increase their coverage of the subject and may therefore be good places to try your ideas first.

The index of interest is, of course, an artifact of our list. In normal circumstances, your thorough familiarity with the journal will be the best index of its interest. Anytime you're not sure whether your article will be met enthusiastically—at least in terms of its focus—it helps to call or write to the editor.

Tips (j). Finally, we asked editors if they had any advice for potential submitters of manuscripts. About half responded to this question, and we found their comments interesting and useful enough to include in the list.

Generally, the comments fell into three groups: those preoccupied with the style or format of a submission; those that encouraged submissions on the subject of writing; and those that elaborated further on the focus and audience of the journal. In essence, the editors collectively gave us two fundamental tips for anyone thinking about submitting a manuscript for publication.

Be meticulous. Editors must be exacting in their own work, and often expect nothing less than perfection when it comes to following their guidelines (many strongly encourage writers to obtain a copy of their style sheets or requirements for preparing manuscripts). If the journal uses the American Psychological Association's reference format, get the manual and follow it. If you need to provide margins of 1½" on both sides, do it. If the editor asks you to clip the stamps on your SASE instead of pasting them on it, don't paste them. In short, do exactly what is required, and no less.

Know the journal. The suggestion of *Exercise Exchange* is telling: "Become familiar with journal format and topics of interest. We are happy to supply a copy of [the] journal to prospective authors." In the subscription information, many journals include a price per copy. If you can't locate the journal in a library or colleague's office, it is probably a good idea to send for two or three recent back issues. Sometimes if you subscribe in the middle of a publication year, you can get previous issues for perusal.

Some Further Reflections and Advice

Whenever the urge arises to write a piece for publication, it is wise to consider the type of journal best suited to your purposes. In the early stages of a new interest, for example, before you've delved fully into the subject in a scholarly way, consider starting modestly. Perhaps a local affiliate journal or newsletter might welcome a short article on your topic. A good, class-tested teaching strategy might find a more receptive audience in a small regional periodical with a circulation of 500 or less than it would in a major, research-oriented journal whose readers are more interested in complex empirical designs than in classroom applications.

This is not to say that you can make light of publishing in a smaller or less nationally visible journal, simply tossing off an article in a few hours and dropping it expectantly in the mail. Some journals with fairly limited circulations still subject submissions to blind review. In addition, most have high editorial standards. But your chances of publication may be greater if the journal has little or no backlog and receives only a few good submissions per issue. In contrast, consider the periodical that has already accepted the next four full issues of material and receives a hundred manuscripts a month. In short, learn to "read" a journal's disposition. Sometimes you may be surprised: a small, regional journal may well want a report of your extensive research project, perhaps to give some balance to more practical pieces.

On the matter of National Council of Teachers of English state and regional affiliate journals, we did not find any editors unwilling to consider out-of-state or out-of-region submissions. Editors of affiliate journals are usually happy to review and publish works from people who live in other parts of the country, even though their primary audience will be in their own region. If you harbor any doubts, please follow our perpetual advice: call the editor!

A Journal List

What our long list gains in breadth it loses in depth. For purposes of your own writing and publishing, a smaller but more descriptive list can be a valuable asset. The best way to keep such a list is in your own personal "publishing journal." You might use our format (explained below) as a guideline for beginning, but by all means adapt it and add to it as you accumulate your own information. Keep in mind, too, that information presented in this list will change over time; therefore, you would be well-advised to obtain a current issue of the journal before submitting your article.

Title of the Journal [occasional acronyms are spelled out in brackets].

(a) The journal's auspices or the organization responsible for its publication.

(b) Number of times published per year; when published (month abbreviated Jan, Feb, Mar, etc.; seasons Sp, S, F, W; BiM = bi-monthly; Occ = occasional).

(c) In addition to those generally interested in writing and literacy, any particularly appropriate readership (standard abbreviations for school level: JH, SH, C, K-12): approximate circulation.

(d) The journal's emphasis in writing or literacy.

(e) Subscription costs. R = regular cost per year; S = student cost per year; I = cost to institutions per year; RT = cost to retirees per year; +F = add for subscriptions to foreign countries; M = cost of membership in sponsoring organizations, which includes free subscription to the journal; +___B = cost per year when more than X subscriptions are mailed in bulk to the same address; C = cost per copy; D = recommended donation.

(f) Complete address for submissions (J = the journal's title).

(g) Complete address for subscriptions. If same as (f), this line is omitted.

(h) Interest in publishing articles on writing and literacy. Ex = extremely interested, V = very interested, S = somewhat interested, Occ = occasionally/marginally interested.

(i) Publishing ratio for articles on writing and literacy—first number is total of articles published on writing and literacy in last five years, second number is total number of articles published on all topics in last five years.

(j) Editor's advice to potential submitters of manuscripts (ms. = manuscripts).

ADE Bulletin

(a) Association of Departments of English. (b) 3: F, W, Sp. (c) Administrators of English departments, directors of communications and rhetoric programs, heads of humanities divisions: 2000. (d) Administration, organization, staffing of composition programs; theoretical matters concerning pedagogy; relationships between the study and teaching of literature and composition. (e) R$15; I$30; M$100. (f) J, 10 Astor Place, New York, NY 10003. (h) Ex. (i) 55/165.

Adult Basic Education Journal

(a) Commission on Adult Basic Education. (b) 3. (c) Adult basic educators, adult learners: 2000. (d) Emphasis on written literacy. (e) (1, 2 or 3 yrs.): R$20/$39/$58; +F$10/$20/$30. (f) J, Dr. Thomas Valentine, College of Education, 416 Tucker Hall, Univ. of Georgia, Athens, GA 30602. (f) J, Commission on Adult Basic Education, PO Box 592053, Orlando, FL 32859. (h) Ex. (i) 100%. (j) Format for submissions will be sent on request.

Adult Education Quarterly

(a) American Association for Adult and Continuing Education. (b) 4: Sp, S, F, W. (c) Adult and continuing educators interested in conducting research. (d) Research, philosophical analyses, theories, interpretive literature reviews relating to writing in adult education: 5000. (e) R$36; +F$7. (f) J, AAACE, 1112 16th St. NW, Suite 420, Washington, DC 20036. (h) Occ. (j) Occasionally interested in articles on theory and research of written literacy. Please write for author guidelines.

Adult Learning

(a) American Association for Adult and Continuing Education. (b) 8: Jan, Feb, Apr, May, June, Sep, Oct, Nov. (c) Adult and continuing education administrators, practitioners, and students: 4500. (d) Practice-oriented articles for adult educators. (e) R$37; +F$8; C$5. (f) J, AAACE, 1112 16th St. NW, Suite 420, Washington, DC 20036. (h) S. (i) Read several issues of magazine; obtain author's guidelines, then call or write with query; unsolicited ms. also accepted.

Alberta English

(a) English Language Arts Council of the Alberta English Teachers Association. (b) 2: Dec, Mar. (c) Individuals interested in English language arts: 1200. (d) Provides a forum for teachers of English language arts to express their views on issues relevant to the teaching of language arts. Essays, poetry, curricular ideas, student poetry and writing, etc. (e) R$6; M$15. (f) J, Alberta English Teachers Association, 11010-142 St., Edmonton, Alberta T5N 2R1, Canada. (h) V. (i) 20/60.

American Educational Research Journal

(a) American Educational Research Association. (b) 4: Sp, S, F, W. (c) Educational researchers. (d) Empirical and theoretical studies and analyses significant to the understanding and/or improvement of educational processes and outcomes. (e) R$28; S$20; I$35; +F$6; M$45; C$10. (f) J, Hilda Borko, Dept. of Curriculum and Instruction, College of Education, Univ. of Maryland, College Park, MD 20742. (g) J, 1230 17th St. NW, Washington, DC 20036-3078. (h) V. (i) 20/130. (j) Articles must be written in a style and format that will provide access to their content for researchers, practitioners, and policymakers in a broad range of education-related fields.

The American Scholar

(a) Phi Beta Kappa Society. (b) 4: Dec, Mar, June, Sep. (c) General audience of teachers and scholars across disciplines: 26,000. (d) Material covers a wide range of subject matter in the arts, sciences, current affairs, history, and literature, as well as poetry. (e) R$21 ($38/2 years); I$25 ($48/2 years). (f) J, 1811 Q St. NW, Washington, DC 20009. (h) Occ. (i) Small percent. (j) Write for guidelines.

Arizona English Bulletin

(a) Arizona English Teachers' Association. (b) 3: Sp, F, W. (c) Teachers K-C: 300. (d) All subjects pertinent to K-C, with emphasis on writing, literature, and methodology. (e) R$20; S$10; I$25; +F$5; 3yr.M$50. (f) J, c/o Carol Williams, English Dept., Arizona State Univ., Tempe, AZ 85287. Coeditors: Carol Williams and Ken Donelson. (g) AETA, PO Box 9353, Phoenix, AZ 85068-9353. (h) Ex. (i) 30/70. (j) We are interested in reading quality ms. for K-12 and college audiences.

California English

(a) California Association of Teachers of English (CATE). (b) 5: Jan/Feb, Mar/Apr, May/June, Sep/Oct, Nov/Dec. (c) K-C Eng. lang. arts teachers. (d) Integrating the English language arts with each other and other subject areas; practical applications: 3300. (e) M$35; S$8; I$15; RT$20; C$3. (f) Wanda Burzycki, ed., *California English*, 14401

McDonough Hts. Rd., Healdsburg, CA 95448. (g) CATE Membership Office, PO Box 4427, Whittier, CA 90607. (h) V. (i) 350/720. (j) We prefer articles that relate to actual classroom experience and can be applied to more than one level of teaching.

Carleton Papers in Applied Language Studies

(a) Carleton University, Ottawa. (b) 1: Sp. (c) C, K-12. (d) Provides a forum for research-in-progress pertaining to the underlying theoretical principles of language teaching, learning, and research. Of particular interest are such themes as pedagogical implications of research on writing, discourse analysis, and syllabus design, as well as approaches to communicative language teaching. (e) R$8 (US). (f) J, Centre for Applied Language Studies, Rm. 215, Paterson Hall, Carleton Univ., Ottawa, Ontario K1S 5B6, Canada. (h) V. (i) 13/32.

Carolina English Teacher

(a) South Carolina Council of Teachers of English. (b) 1. (c) English/ language arts teachers, E-C: 350. (d) Articles, reviews, and descriptions of techniques and methods with direct bearing on the teaching of composition and literature. (e) M$10. (f) J, Dept. of English, Francis Marion College, Florence, SC 29501. (h) Ex. (i) 35/50.

CEA Critic

(a) College English Association. (b) 3: Nov, Apr, July. (d) Literary and composition pedagogy: what we teach and how (shorter pieces on classroom practice should be submitted to *CEA Forum* [see below]). (e) (1 or 2 yrs.): R$25/45; I$30/54; S$8/12. (f) J, English Dept., Youngstown State Univ., Youngstown, OH 44555. (h) V. (i) Occ.; 1 in each of last several issues. (j) See Jan. 28, 1991, letter from Bowers & Brothers.

CEA Forum

(a) College English Association. (b) 2: Jan, Aug. (c) Anyone interested in the teaching of writing, the teaching of fiction and nonfiction prose, and professional concerns: 1400. (d) Teaching texts of various sorts in the composition and literature classroom. Emphasis on pedagogy and current professional issues. (e) (Includes subscription to *CEA Critic):* R$25; I$30; C$3. (f) J, English Dept., Youngstown State Univ., Youngstown, OH 44555. (g) J, Marion Hoctor, College English Association, Nazareth College of Rochester, Rochester, NY 14618. (h) Ex. (i) Past 2 yrs.: 13/27.

Childhood Education

(a) Association for Childhood Education International. (b) 5: F, W, Sp, S, and Annual Theme. (c) Teachers K-8, ECE (early childhood educators). (d) Whole language instruction, literacy, writing in classrooms. (e) R$38; +F$2; S$20; I$65. (f) J, ACEI, 11141 Georgia Ave., #200, Wheaton, MD 20902. (h) Ex. (i) 25/150. (j) Timely articles dealing with the education, care, and well-being of children (birth through early adolescence) are welcome.

Cognition and Instruction

(a) Erlbaum, Inc. (b) 4: Sp, S, F, W. (c) Scholars, teachers, and researchers interested in the relationships among cognition, learning, and instructional methodology. (d) Interdisciplinary; publishes articles on a range of topics concerning learning and cognition, including language processes (example: "Knowledge Organization and Text Organization"). (e) R$37.50; I$105; +F$20. (f) J, Lauren Resnick, Learning Research & Development Center, Univ. of Pittsburgh, 3939 O'Hara St., Pittsburgh, PA 15260. (g) J, Lawrence Erlbaum Associates Inc., 365 Broadway, Hillsdale, NY 07642. (h) Ex. (i) 5/55.

Cognitive Psychology

(a) Academic Press. (b) 4: Sp, S, F, W. (c) Scholars, teachers, and researchers interested in cognitive psychology. (d) The analysis and understanding of cognitive processes and skills, including those in the production of written discourse. Topics range from perception, attention, and memory to language and judgment decisions. (e) R$64.50; I$129; S$32.25. (f) J, Dr. Douglas L. Medin, Dept. of Psychology, Univ. of Michigan, 330 Packard Rd., Ann Arbor, MI 48104-2994. (g) J, Academic Press, Harcourt Brace Jovanovich, 1250 6th Ave., San Diego, CA 92101. (h) S. (i) 5/75. (j) The critical question is always what the bearing is of some particular set of findings on theories of cognition.

College Composition and Communication

(a) National Council of Teachers of English (Conference on College Composition and Communication). (b) 4: Feb, May, Oct, Dec. (c) Emphasis at the college level: 12,000. (d) Publishes articles pertaining to the theory and practice of composition and the teaching of composition, and to research on composition at all college levels; articles that explore the relationship of literature, language studies, rhetoric, or logic to the teaching of composition. (e) M$52; I$59; +F$9; S$21. (f) J, Richard C. Gebhardt, Bowling Green State Univ., Bowling Green, OH 43403.

(g) J, National Council of Teachers of English, 1111 Kenyon Rd., Urbana, IL 61801. (h) Ex. (i) 150/150. (j) See author's guide printed in February 1991 issue.

College English

(a) National Council of Teachers of English. (b) 8: Sep–Apr. (c) Emphasis at the college level: 16,000. (d) Publishes articles on: the working concepts of criticism—structure, genre, rhetoric, the role of readers, etc.; the nature of critical and scholarly reasoning; the relevance of ideas in other fields to ideas about how English is studied, taught, and learned; the structure of the field and profession; the social agencies and consequences of the study and teaching of English in the U.S.; curricular, pedagogical, and educational theory. (e) M$40; I$47; +F$6; S$16. (f) J, Dept. of English, Univ. of Massachusetts–Boston, Boston, MA 02125. (g) J, National Council of Teachers of English, 1111 Kenyon Rd., Urbana, IL 61801.

College Teaching

(a) Heldref Publications. (b) 4: F, W, Sp, S. (c) Dedicated college teachers and administrators; those interested in faculty development: 2500. (d) Covers ideas, methods, and philosophies for all academic disciplines—classroom activities and techniques; book reviews; special section on teaching writing, writing as process, appears once a year. (e) R$42; +F$6; C$8.75. (f) J, Heldref Publications, 4000 Albermarle St. NW, Washington, DC 20016. (h) V. (i) 35/180. (j) Interested in *new* ideas or approaches; we reject many mundane manuscripts.

Communication Monographs

(a) Speech Communication Association. (b) 4: Mar, June, Sep, Dec. (c) Members of SCA; libraries; scholars interested in communication in its various forms; 3500. (d) Publishes the best original scholarship dealing with human communication processes, including, occasionally, those of writing. (e) M$50; I$90; S$25. (f) J, Judee K. Burgoon, Dept. of Communication, Univ. of Arizona, Tucson, AZ 85721. (g) J, Speech Communication Association, 5105 Backlick Rd., Annandale, VA 22003. (h) S.

Communication Research

(a) Sage Publications. (b) 6: BiM. (c) College professors and students: 2000. (d) Primary focus is on communication theory and research. (e) R$45; I$160. (f) J, Anenberg School for Communications, 3502

S. Hoover St., Los Angeles, CA 90089-0281. (g) J, Sage Publications Inc., 2455 Teller Rd., Newbury Park, CA 91320. (h) S. (j) Our primary criteria for manuscripts is that they test communication theory.

Communitas

(a) Minnesota Community College Faculty Association. (b) 2: F, Sp. (c) Teachers SH and C: 2000. (d) Focus is on research and teaching stratagems in all disciplines, comparative studies (multicultural, global studies, etc.), and issues in undergraduate education; emphasis is on composition research, rhetoric, and pedagogy. (e) R$8; S$5; I$8; RT$5; +F$14; C$4. (f) J, Chief Editor, MCCFA, 165 Western Ave. N., St. Paul, MN 55102. (h) V. (i) 8/35. (j) We welcome manuscripts for an audience of college faculty and administrators.

Community College Review

(a) Department of Adult and Community College Education, North Carolina State University. (b) 4: Apr, July, Oct, Jan. (c) Community and junior college students and faculty; departments of higher and graduate education. (d) Research-based articles relative to community college education. (e) R$35; I$35; S$20; RT$35; +F$4 (Canada +$2). (f) J, Dept. of Adult and Community College Education, North Carolina State Univ., Box 7801, Raleigh, NC 27695-7801. (h) Ex. (j) Write for copy of guidelines.

Composition Chronicle: A Newsletter for Writing Teachers

(a) Viceroy Publications. (b) 9: Sep–May. (c) Composition teachers, researchers, administrators, scholars, graduate students: 700. (d) Primary focus on news and how-to articles about writing and literacy issues related to writing. (e) R$25; S$20; +F$5; photocopy rights $90. (f) J, Viceroy Publications, 3217 Bronson Hill Rd., Livonia, NY 14487. (h) V. (j) Do not send articles; query first. Articles should be brief (up to 2000 words) and readable by a wide range of writing teachers.

Computers and Composition

(a) Computers and Composition, Michigan Technological University, and the University of Illinois, Urbana-Champaign. (b) 3: Nov, Apr, Aug. (c) All teachers of writing; generally at college level but occasionally K-12 interests: 700. (d) Explores effects of computers on writing and on teachers and their classrooms, on writing processes, and on the exchange of written materials. (e) R$10; I$20; +F$15; C$5. (f) J, Gail Hawisher, English Dept., University of Illinois, 608 S. Wright

St., Urbana, IL 61801. (g) J, Cynthia L. Selfe, Humanities Dept., Michigan Technological Univ., Houghton, MI 49931. (h) Ex. (i) 75/75.

Critical Inquiry

(a) University of Chicago Press. (b) 4. (c) Scholars and broadly educated general readers in criticism, literature, history, philosophy, film, music, and the fine arts. (d) An interdisciplinary journal devoted to critical thought in the arts and humanities. (e) R$29; I$62; S$20; C$6.50; +F$4.50. (f) J, University of Chicago Press, 5720 South Woodlawn Ave., Chicago, IL 60637.

English Education

(a) National Council of Teachers of English (Conference on English Education). (b) 4: Feb, May, Oct, Dec. (c) Educators of teachers of English at all levels, K-16; inservice leaders, consultants, and supervisors: 3300. (d) Research and practice relating to preservice and inservice education of composition teachers. (e) M$55; I$59; +F$9; S$21. (f) J, Gordon Pradl, New York Univ., 635 East Building, New York, NY 10003. (g) J, National Council of Teachers of English, 1111 Kenyon Rd., Urbana, IL 61801. (h) V. (i) 20/75. (j) Special focus on the education of writing teachers.

English for Specific Purposes: An International Journal

(a) Pergamon Press. (b) 3: F, W, Sp. (c) Those interested in varieties of English found in different disciplines or discourse communities. (d) Publishes articles focusing on English in particular professional and academic communities, with special attention to the variety of texts produced and received in such communities. (e) R$30. (f) Ann M. Johns, Academic Skills Center, San Diego State Univ., San Diego, CA 92812; **or,** John M. Swales, English Language Institute, Univ. of Michigan, Ann Arbor, MI 48109; **or,** Tony Dudley-Evans, English for Overseas Students Unit, Univ. of Birmingham, Edgbaston, Birmingham, UK B160SH. (g) Pergamon Journals Inc., Maxwell House, Fairview Park, Elmsford, NY 10523. (h) Ex. (i) 25/60. (j) Many of the journal's readers live outside the U.S., in other English-speaking countries, or the Third World. Most readers are teaching the special Englishes of academic and professional communities to adult speakers of other languages. Research, particularly qualitative, is of great interest to them; however, they are often uncomfortable with heavily statistical studies.

English in Texas

(a) Texas Joint Council of Teachers of English. (b) 4: F, W, Sp, S. (c) English language arts teachers K-C: 2500. (d) Address topics of interest to teachers of English/language arts through C. More emphasis on theory and the translation of that theory into practice in writing in other language arts. (e) R$15. (f) Edward Wilson, PO Box 999, Spring, TX 73898-0999. (g) Texas Council of Teachers of English, C.E. Ellison HS, 90 Elms Rd., Killeen, TX 76541. (h) Ex. (i) 250/300. (j) Articles must have a strong voice and little academic posturing.

English Journal

(a) National Council of Teachers of English. (b) 8: Sep–Apr. (c) JH, SH English teachers and English education scholars: 45,000. (d) One-third of what is published relates to composition; constantly looking for new material and research presented from the point of view of classroom teachers. (e) M$40; S$16; I$47; +F$6. (f) J, Ben Nelms, Univ. of Florida, 200 Norman Hall, Gainesville, FL 32611. (g) J, National Council of Teachers of English, 1111 Kenyon Rd., Urbana, IL 61801. (h) Ex. (i) 200/600. (j) See "Editorial Comments" in February 1988, February 1989, and September 1990 issues.

English Quarterly

(a) Canadian Council of Teachers of English (CCTE). (b) 4: Sp, S, F, W. (c) K-C, general—teachers, administrators, consultants, specialists: 1100. (d) Any topic of concern to English teachers K-12. (e) M$50 Canadian; S$25 Canadian. (f) J, Dr. David Dillon, Faculty of Education, McGill Univ., 3700 McTavish St., Montreal, Quebec H3A 1Y2, Canada. (g) J, CCTE Membership, 1243 Wood Place, Oakville, Ontario L6L 2R4, Canada. (h) Ex. (i) 31/59.

The English Record

(a) New York State English Council (NYSEC). (b) 4: W, Sp, S, F. (c) English teachers K-12 and C: 1200. (d) Includes much material on the teaching of writing; recent issues have published articles on reading and writing, the research paper, controlled composition as a teaching technique, etc. (e) R$25; I$25; S$15; RT$15. (f) J, NYSEC, PO Box 948, Schenectady, NY 12301. (h) V. (i) 50/120.

Exercise Exchange: A Journal of English in High Schools and Colleges

(a) College of Education and Human Services, Clarion University. (b) 2: F, Sp. (c) Classroom teachers: 400. (d) Practical, classroom teaching applications, especially writing instruction, suitable for use by HS and C instructors; new perspectives on prewriting, revision, paragraphing, responding to student writing, grading and evaluation, etc. (e) R$5; I$6. (f) J, 101 Stevens Hall, Clarion University, Clarion, PA 16214. (h) V. (i) 90/140. (j) Become familiar with journal format and topics of interest. We are happy to supply a copy of journal to prospective authors.

Feminist Studies

(a) Feminist Studies. (b) 3: Sp, S, F. (c) C (professors, graduate/doctoral students, undergraduates): 7400. (d) Composition: scholarly interdisciplinary; fiction, book reviews. (e) R$24; I$48; F(for R)$28; F(for I)$52; C(for R)$10; C(for I)$20. (f) J, c/o Women's Studies Program, Univ. of Maryland, College Park, MD 20742. (h) S. (i) 0/90. (j) 3 copies of ms.; 30-35 pp. in length including notes; 0-200 word abstract for routing purposes.

Focus: Teaching English Language Arts

(a) Southeastern Ohio Council of Teachers of English. (b) 2: W, S. (c) Teachers K-C: 400. (d) Issues are thematic, with occasional issues devoted to various aspects of writing. (e) M$12. (f) J, Ron Luce, editor, PO Box 212, Murray City, OH 43144. (h) S. (i) 3/10. (j) Check with editor for upcoming themes. Normally, only pieces reflecting the theme are considered.

Focuses

(a) Appalachian State University; Southeastern Writing Center Association (founder and financial supporter). (b) 2: W, S. (c) College directors of writing, writing center directors and staff, computer-using writing instructors, classroom teachers of writing in general. (d) Issues of writing as discipline, rhetorical theory, composition theory and practice, writing centers. (e) M$8 (of SEWCA), R$10, I$15, CR$5, CI$7.50. (f) William C. Wolff, editor, J, Dept. of English, Appalachian State Univ., Boone, NC 28608. (h) Ex. (i) All articles focus on writing. (j) Typewritten, double-spaced ms. in rev. MLA style. Send 3 copies, 2 without reference to author's or institution's ID. 2500-5000 words (10-20 pp.) including works cited. Follow NCTE guidelines for nonsexist use of language.

Foreign Language Annals

(a) American Council on the Teaching of Foreign Languages (ACTFL). (b) 6: Feb, Apr, May, Sep, Oct, Dec. (c) Teachers and administrators, all levels: 6500. (d) Dedicated to advancing all phases of foreign language education; includes articles on innovative and successful teaching methods, educational research or experimentation, and concerns and problems of the profession. (e) R$65; S$55; RT$25; F$75. (f) J, ACTFL, 6 Executive Plaza, Yonkers, NY 10701. (h) Ex. (i) 20/150. (j) 20 pages maximum; broad range of topics.

Freshman English News

(b) 2: F, S. (c) Rhetoric and composition theorists; composition instructors; writing program and writing center directors and staff: 900. (d) Publishes a wide range of articles in rhetoric and composition, including rhetorical traditions and theories, theories of cognition and the composing process, composition and cultural criticism, pedagogical methods, and personal reflections on the teaching of writing. (e) R$8; I$20; +$10B4; C$4.50. (f) J, Christina Murphy, Box 32875, Texas Christian Univ., Fort Worth, TX 76129. (h) Ex. (i) 85/85. (j) Be aware of the current research and articles in the field that have already been published on your topic. Too many submissions reflect a lack of scholarly awareness.

Houston English Journal

(a) Houston Area Council of Teachers of English. (b) 1: Annual. (c) K-12: 400. (d) Primarily a forum for teachers to share their writing: research, creative, expository. (e) M$7. (f) J, P. Wayne Stauffer, 11814 Flushing Meadows, Houston, TX 77089. (h) V. (i) 8/15. (j) We want to provide a springboard for future publication to teachers who are doing what they ask of their students—writing.

Human Communication Research

(a) International Communication Association. (b) 4: S, F, W, Sp. (c) Communication researchers, social psychologists, discourse analysts, applied linguists. (d) Primary focus is on communication behavior studied social scientifically. (e) R$36; I$96. (f) J, Dept. of Communication, Univ. of California, Santa Barbara, CA 93106. (g) J, International Communication Association, 8240 Burnet Rd., Austin, TX 78756. (h) O. (i) 5/120.

Illinois English Bulletin

(a) Illinois Association of Teachers of English. (b) 4: F, W, Sp, late Sp. (c) K-12, C, established and new teachers. (d) Practical emphasis, implications of research in classroom for busy classroom teachers; some issues include miscellaneous topics in language study and literature, and one issue is composition-oriented. Includes articles in which teachers publish student writing, ideas for encouraging student poets, writing assignments based on literary works, topics for composition in elementary schools. (e) R$15; S$3; I$15; RT$3; D$20. (f) J, English Dept., Univ. of Illinois, 608 S. Wright St., Urbana, IL 61801.

Indiana English

(a) Indiana Council of Teachers of English. (b) 3: W, Sp, F. (c) Teachers at all levels: 800. (d) Emphasizes all elements of the teaching of writing E-C. (e) M$10; S$3. (f) J, Dept. of English, Indiana State Univ., Terre Haute, IN 47809. (h) Ex. (i) 54/126.

InLand: A Journal for Teachers of English Language Arts

(a) Inland Northwest Council of Teachers of English (INCTE) and Idaho Council of Teachers of English (ICTE). (b) 2: F, Sp. (c) English language arts teachers and students K-C: 800. (d) Articles on the focus of each issue as well as other topics accepted; creative writing, shorts, book reviews, letters. (e) R$8; M$15 ICTE; M$15 INCTE; C$4. (f) J, Driek Zirinsky, Dept. of English, Boise State Univ., Boise, ID 83725. (h) Ex. (i) 100/150. (j) Calls for ms. available on request.

Iowa English Bulletin

(a) Iowa Council of Teachers of English. (b) 1: Sp. (c) English teachers, all levels: 800. (d) Interests in all areas of the composing process, especially pedagogical implications K-C. (e) R$5. (f) J, English Dept., Drake Univ., Des Moines, IA 50311. (h) Ex. (i) 38/50.

IRAL: International Review of Applied Linguistics in Language Teaching

(b) 4: Feb, May, Aug, Nov. (c) University institutions, linguists, linguistic researchers, translators: 1900. (d) Second language teaching, institutional linguistic research. (e) R104DM; I166DM. (f) J, Julius Groos Verlag, PO Box 10-24-23, 6900 Heidelberg, Germany. (h) S. (i) 15/85.

Issues in Writing

(a) Department of English, University of Wisconsin–Stevens Point. (b) 2: F/W, Sp/S. (c) Academic and nonacademic writing professionals; teachers C: 500. (d) Focus on all aspects of the teaching and production of public writing; prefer articles that encourage stimulating dialogue across traditional rhetorical boundaries, forms, and roles. (e) R$10; I$10; +F$3. (f) J, Dept. of English, Univ. of Wisconsin, Stevens Point, WI 54481. (h) Ex. (i) 20/20. (j) Please send for "Guidelines for Authors" or read "Notes to Contributors" included in each issue. The editors are glad to work with prospective authors to produce publishable manuscripts.

Journal of Advanced Composition

(a) Association of Teachers of Advanced Composition. (b) Semiannual. (c) Teachers of advanced composition: 1000. (d) Composition theory, as well as the entire field of advanced composition: advanced expository writing; business, technical, and professional writing; writing across the curriculum. (e) R$15 ($40 for three years); IS$20. (f) J, Dept. of English, Univ. of South Florida, Tampa, FL 33620. (g) J, Dept. of English, Univ. of Idaho, Moscow, ID 83843. (h) Ex. (i) 85/120. (j) *JAC* is a journal of *theory*, not pedagogy or empirical research.

Journal of Basic Writing

(a) City University of New York. (b) 2: F, Sp. (c) Teachers of basic writers HS and C: 2000. (d) Theory and practice of teaching basic writing in today's colleges (and some HS). Explores connections between basic writing and other areas (linguistics, rhetoric, cognitive theory, ESL, literature, other language skills, technology, etc.). (e) R$8; I$12; +F$5; C$4.50. (f) J, Instructional Resource Center, City Univ. of New York, 535 East 80th St., New York, NY 10021. (h) Ex. (i) 65/65.

Journal of Business Communication

(a) J. (b) 4: W, Sp, S, F. (c) Univ. and college faculty. (d) Business, management, and organizational communication, both written and oral. (e) M$40; S$20; R$20. (f) N.L. Reinsch, editor, J, Box 8347, Abilene Christian Univ., Abilene, TX 79699. (g) John D. Pettit Jr., College of Business, Univ. of North Texas, Denton, TX 76203. (h) V. (i) 53/108. (j) Please send 5 copies.

JBTC [Journal of Business and Technical Communication]

(a) Sage Periodicals Press. (b) 4: Jan, Apr, July, Oct. (c) Academic and industrial audience: 400. (d) Articles on the impact of new technologies on professional writing; innovative instruction in industry and academe; empirical research in government, industrial, and academic settings; theoretical approaches to business and technical writing; also book and software reviews and commentaries on state of profession. (e) R$30; +F$6; I$75. (f) J, Dept. of English, 203 Ross Hall, Iowa State Univ., Ames, IA 50011. (g) Sage Publications Inc., PO Box 5084, Newbury Park, CA 91359. (h) Ex. (i) 40/45.

Journal of Communication

(a) University of Pennsylvania and Oxford University Press. (b) 4: W, Sp, S, F. (c) Scholars, researchers, scientists in communication and related fields, government and academic institutions: 6000. (d) Writing, language, and discourse in the media, journalism, and communications policy. (e) R$30; I$65; +F$14; C$8.95 (individuals), C$18 (institutions). (f) J, Univ. of Pennsylvania, 3620 Walnut St., Philadelphia, PA 19104-6220. (g) J, Journals Dept., Oxford Univ. Press, 2001 Evans Rd., Cary, NC 27513. (h) Occ. (i) 4/150; 30 on press, journalism, etc. (j) Most likely to find research and book reviews related to literacy, from media literacy to computer literacy and impact of print and journalistic practice on what is written.

Journal of Developmental Education

(a) Appalachian State University. (b) 3: F, W, Sp. (c) Instructors and administrators of basic writers: 5000. (d) Teaching methods of basic composition; evaluation of basic writing programs. (e) R$17; I$24; S$6. (f) J, Center for Developmental Education, Appalachian State Univ., Boone, NC 28608. (h) V. (i) 15/65. (j) Our focus is on developmental writing or basic composition skills at the postsecondary level. Write for Author's Guidelines if interested.

Journal of Learning Disabilities

(a) Donald D. Hammill Foundation. (b) 10: Monthly, except June/July, Aug/Sep. (c) Teachers C and K-12: 10,700. (d) Primary focus is on assessment, intervention, and research for students with learning disabilities. (e) R$45; I$90; F$105. (f) J, Dept. of Special Education, EDB 306, Univ. of Texas, Austin, TX 78712-1290. (g) J, 8700 Shoal Creek Blvd., Austin, TX 78758-6897. (h) V. (i) 110/450. (j) We follow APA (3rd ed.) format. Author guidelines are available.

Journal of Memory and Language

(a) Academic Press, Inc. (b) 6: BiM. (c) Interdisciplinary. (d) Articles contribute to the formulation of scientific issues, theories, and debate in the areas of language comprehension, human memory, psycholinguistics, and other language processes, including the production and comprehension of language, and issues in the field of cognitive science. (e) R$64.50 (domestic), $83.50 (foreign); I$129 (domestic), $152 (foreign); S$32.50 (domestic), $34.25 (foreign). (f) J, Dept. of Psychology, Univ. of Illinois, 603 E. Daniel St., Champaign, IL 61820. (g) J, Academic Press Inc., Journal Promotion Dept., 1250 Sixth Ave., San Diego, CA 92101. (h) Occ. (i) 5/240.

Journal of Reading

(a) International Reading Association. (b) 8: Sep–May, with combined Dec/Jan issue. (c) Educators in the field of reading/writing for adolescents and adults: specialists, coordinators, school supervisors, classroom teachers, ABE and adult program personnel, and college professors of education: 20,000. (d) Interconnections between reading and writing; emphasis on communication processes, including producing and comprehending texts. (e) M$30. (f) J, IRA, 800 Barksdale Rd., PO Box 8139, Newark, DE 19714-8139. (h) V. (i) 50/350. (j) Must show interconnections of writing and reading.

Journal of Reading Behavior

(a) National Reading Conference. (b) 4: Mar, Jun, Sep, Dec. (c) Teacher-trainers, researchers, and theorists, all levels. (d) Publishes studies that investigate the impact of all language processes upon literacy. (e) M$70; I$50; S$35. (f) J, Univ. of North Carolina at Greensboro, School of Education, 336 Curry Bldg., Greensboro, NC 27412. (g) J, NRC, 11 E. Hubbard, Suite 200, Chicago, IL 60611. (h) Ex. (i) 20/120.

Journal of Teaching Writing

(a) Indiana Teachers of Writing. (b) 2: F/W; Sp/S. (c) K-C: 1500. (d) Focus on relationship of writing theory and practice; teacher/researcher emphasis; authors from all academic levels. (e) R$15; I$20; +F$5; M$20. (f) J, Barbara Cambridge, editor, 425 University Blvd., Indianapolis, IN 46202. (h) Ex. (i) 100%. (j) We welcome ms. from classroom teachers and faculty that demonstrate the relationship of theory and practice. Reading an issue of *JTW* is advisable to learn the type of article and audience.

Journal of Technical Writing and Communication

(a) Baywood Publishing. (b) 4: W, Sp, S, F. (c) Academic and industrial technical writers; others interested in technical writing: 1000.

(d) Expresses views of communicators in the field of technical writing, rhetoric, theory, and visual communication; records their achievements; promotes their research; and acts as a forum for their professional activities. Papers cut across professional lines and deal with speculative as well as functional subjects. (e) R$25; I$75. (f) J, David L. Carson, 9 Shepherd Dr., Troy, NY 12180. (g) J, Baywood Publishing Co., 120 Marine St., Farmingdale, NY 11735. (h) Ex. (i) 200/200. (j) Submit according to instructions contained in front and back inside covers of journal.

Kansas English

(a) Kansas Association of Teachers of English. (b) 2: Nov, Mar. (c) E-C English: 500. (d) Rhetoric and composition theory, teaching composition (K-C). (e) M$12.50. (f) J, English Dept., Fort Hays State Univ., Hays, KS 67601. (h) Ex. (i) 15/40.

Kentucky English Bulletin

(a) Kentucky Council of Teachers of English/Language Arts. (b) 3: F, W, Sp. (c) E-C English teachers: 800. (d) Emphasizes composition, writing, and literacy. (e) R$10; M$10; +F$10; C$5. (f) J, Dept. of English, Western Kentucky Univ., Bowling Green, KY 42101. (g) J, Elizabethtown Community College, College St. Road, Elizabethtown, KY 42701. (h) Ex. (i) 80/100+.

Language and Speech

(a) Kingston Press Services, Ltd. (b) 4: Mar, June, Sep, Dec. (c) Scholars in linguistics, speech, psychology: 1100. (d) Research papers in psycholinguistics, the production and perception of speech, the nature of writing and reading, etc. (e) R$90. (f) J, Haskins Laboratories, 270 Crown St., New Haven, CT 06501-6695. (g) J, Kingston Press Services Ltd., 28 High St., Teddington, Middlesex TW118EW, England. (h) Occ. (i) 3/100. (j) Must be high-quality research, relevant to psychological or linguistics theories.

Language and Style

(a) Queens College of the City University of New York. (b) 4. (c) 750. (d) Style in all its manifestations, including in all the arts and all social and cultural contexts. (e) R$16; +F$2; I$22; I+F$25; C$5. (f) E.L. Epstein, editor, J, Dept. of English, Queens College, CUNY, Flushing, NY 11367. (g) J, Editorial Services, Kiely Hall 1310, Queens College, CUNY, Flushing, NY 11367. (h) Occ. (j) Publishes articles in English, French, and German, 4,000-25,000 words, double-spaced in duplicate. References and appendices follow text.

Language Arts

(a) National Council of Teachers of English. (b) 8: Monthly, Sep–Apr. (c) Elementary and middle school classroom teachers, school district lang. arts educators, teacher educators in elem./middle school lang. arts education: 20,000. (d) Focuses on processes of composing and learning to compose, as well as methods of instruction in composition appropriate to children from preschool through middle school age. Articles on composing considered for all issues; occasionally an issue will be themed specifically to focus on composition. (e) I$47; +F$6; M$40; S$16. (f) J, William Teale, Division of Education, Univ. of Texas at San Antonio, San Antonio, TX 78285-0654. (g) J, NCTE, 1111 Kenyon Rd., Urbana, IL 61801. (h) Ex. (i) 200/400.

Language Arts Journal of Michigan

(a) Michigan Council of Teachers of English. (b) 2: F, Sp. (c) Teachers K-C. (d) Composition research and pedagogy, particularly classroom applications. (e) R$15; S$10; I$15; M$15. (f) J, Dept. of English, Central Michigan Univ., Mt. Pleasant, MI 48859. (g) Michigan Council of Teachers of English, PO Box 1152, Rochester, MI 48063. (h) V. (i) 29/91. (j) Our focus is on classroom practices grounded in research. We accept articles, interviews, annotated bibliographies, review-essays, and occasionally announce special focus issues. Ms. should be 6-15 pp., double-spaced, MLA internal style, with SASE. Please send 3 copies.

Language Learning: A Journal of Applied Linguistics

(a) Research Club in Language Learning. (b) 4: Mar, Jun, Sep, Dec. (c) Interdisciplinary: those interested in the learning of language. (d) Publishes research articles in applied linguistics, understood to be the application of linguistic method and philosophical perspective to problem areas usually viewed as lying outside the narrower, more traditional concerns of linguistics proper. Welcomes studies in psycholinguistics, anthropological linguistics, sociolinguistics, language pedagogy, and second-language acquisition. (e) R$36; I$60; +F$20-$25. (f) J, John A. Upshur, TESL Center ER-601, Concordia Univ., 1455 de Maisonneuve Blvd. West, Montreal, Quebec H3G 1M8, Canada. (g) J, 178 Henry S. Frieze Bldg., 105 S. State St., Ann Arbor, MI 48109-1285. (j) APA publication format.

Language Sciences

(a) Pergamon Press p/c. (b) 4. (c) Research-level readership. (d) Emphasis on sociolinguistics, psycholinguistics, pragmatics, child language, sign language, and general linguistics studies. (e) I$180. (f) Dr. Fred C.C. Peng, Dept. of Linguistics, Int'l Christian Univ., 10-2, 3 Chome, Osawa, Mitaka, Tokyo 181, Japan. (g) Pergamon Press p/c, Headington Hill Hall, Oxford OX3 OBW, UK (h) S. (i) 3/48 (3 yrs. only). (j) Research level only, please.

The Leaflet

(a) New England Association of Teachers of English. (b) 3: Oct, Jan, May. (c) E-C teachers: 850. (d) Applications of research and methodology of teaching writing in K-12 and some college. All aspects of English teaching. (e) M$25; S$5. (f) J, Barbara A. Vonvillas, 4 Ruth St., Middletown, RI 02840. (g) J, New England Association of Teachers of English, PO Box 234, Lexington, MA 02173. (h) V. (i) 20/80. (j) Articles with strategies are the most useful.

Liberal Education

(a) Association of American Colleges. (b) 5: Sep–June. (c) College and university administrators and faculty. (e) R$30, I$30 (members of AAC); R$36, I$36 (others). (f) J, AAC, 1818 R St. NW, Washington, DC 20009. (h) Occ. (j) Interested in receiving 1500-2000 word essays reflecting informed opinion on undergraduate curriculum issues.

Management Communication Quarterly

(a) Sage Publications. (b) 4: Aug, Nov, Feb, May. (c) Teachers, scholars, practitioners: 1000+. (d) Articles advance both theory and practice in field of management communication for impact on organizational/managerial effectiveness; field research in writing on the job using a broad range of methodologies; nonresearch pieces including refereed book reviews, guest commentaries, notes from professionals in the field. Many articles focus on such areas of composition research as managerial speaking and writing, managerial writing processes, linguistic and psycholinguistic analysis, and discourse analysis. (e) R$30; I$85; C$10; +F$6. (f) J, Larry R. Smeltzer, College of Business, Arizona State Univ., Tempe, AZ 85287-3706. (g) J, Sage Publications, 2111 W. Hillcrest Dr., Newbury Park, CA 91320. (h) S. (i) 20/90.

Maryland English Journal

(a) Maryland Council of Teachers of English. (b) 2: Sp, F. (c) English and language arts teachers K-C: 400. (d) Pedagogically oriented articles; applied theoretical language issues; reviews of literature; creative writing and nonfiction essays. (e) R$8; I$10; M$10 (3 years $25); C$4. (f) J, Judy Fowler and Stephan Martin, Dept. of English, Univ. of Maryland-Baltimore County, Baltimore, MD 21228. (h) Ex. (i) 52/60.

Memory and Cognition

(a) Psychonometric Society. (b) 6: BiM. (c) Experimental psychologists and those interested in memory, cognitive processes, language comprehension, and production: 2380. (d) Publishes articles concerned with a broad range of topics in human experimental psychology; encompasses reading, writing, and other language processes. (e) R$38; S$18; I$84; +F$8. (f) J, Dr. Margaret Jean Intons-Peterson, Dept. of Psychology, Indiana Univ., Bloomington, IN 47405. (g) Psychonometric Society Publications, 1710 Fortview Rd., Austin, TX 78704. (h) S. (i) 5/308. (j) Write to editor for six pages of useful advice on manuscript submission.

Minnesota English Journal

(a) Minnesota Council of Teachers of English. (b) 2: F, W/Sp. (c) Teachers C and K-12: 450. (d) Primary focus is on college and secondary school rhetoric, composition research, and pedagogy. (e) R$25; S$10; I$25; M$25. (f) J, Languages and Literature, College of St. Scholastica, Duluth, MN 55811. (g) J, Education Dept., College of St. Catherine, 2004 Randolph Ave., St. Paul, MN 55105. (h) Ex. (i) 20/75. (j) We are delighted to read ms. for K-12, college audiences.

Mississippi Council of Teachers of English

(a) Mississippi Council of Teachers of English. (b) 2: F/W, Sp/S. (c) Teachers K-C: 250. (d) Practical articles on teaching writing in JH, SH, and C. (e) M$10. (f) J, Dept. of Languages & Lit., Delta State Univ., Cleveland, MS 38733. (h) V.

Modern Language Journal

(a) National Federation of Modern Language Teachers Association. (b) 4: Sp, S, F, W. (c) Language teachers, all levels: 6500. (d) Methods, pedagogical research, and topics of interest to all language teachers. (e) R$17.50; I$30; +F$5.50 or +$15 (air). (f) J, Dept. of German, Ohio

State Univ., Columbus, OH 43210. (g) J, Univ. of Wisconsin Press, 114 N. Murray St., Madison, WI 53715. (h) Ex. (i) 10/110.

Nebraska English and Language Arts Journal (NELAJ)

(a) Nebraska English and Language Arts Council. (b) 4: Sp, S, F, W (occasional double issues). (c) K-C: 450. (d) Emphasis on reading and writing of literature, teaching established authors, strong creative writing accepted. (e) R$20; S$5; I$20; M$20. (f) J, Dept. of English, Univ. of Nebraska, Kearny, NE 68849. (g) Jan Strange, J, 8109 Imperial Circle, Lincoln, NE 68506. (h) V. (i) 35/50. (j) Contributors urged to submit ms. for K-12 and college audiences; creative writing, especially poetry, is welcome.

The New Advocate

(b) 2: F, W/Sp. (c) Teachers C, JH. (d) Primary focus is on literature for children and writing as it ties in to the study of literature. (e) R$27; I$45; C$10. (f) J, Dr. Joel Taxel, 125 Alderhold Hall, Univ. of Georgia, Athens, GA 30602. (g) J, 480 Washington St., Norwood, MA 02062. (h) Ex. (i) 90/100. (j) Read back issues of our journal for style and appropriateness of ms.

New Mexico English Journal

(a) New Mexico Council of Teachers of English. (b) 2: Sp, F. (c) K-C. (d) Focuses on teaching of English: composition, literature, and related articles. (e) M$15; R$10. (f) J, 121 Sunland Dr., Clovis, NM 88101. (h) E. (i) 34/66. (j) Will read all ms. for K-12 and college audiences.

North Carolina English Teacher

(a) North Carolina English Teacher. (b) 4: F, W, Sp, S. (c) Teachers 6-C. (d) Emphasis on English pedagogy. (e) R$25, 2 yrs. $35. (f) J, Box 7266, Wake Forest Univ., Winston-Salem, NC 27109. (g) Collett Dilworth, Exec. Dir. NCETA, East Carolina Univ., Dept. of English, Greenville, NC 27834. (h) V. (i) 20/50. (j) We are pleased to have submissions on English pedagogy from all interested parties.

Ohio Journal of the English Language Arts

(a) Ohio Council of Teachers of English Language Arts. (b) 2: F, Sp. (c) Teachers K-C: 3400. (d) All issues themed. Composition/rhetoric themes used commonly. (e) R$18; S$9; I$18; RT$9; M$18. (f) J, Gary

M. Salvner, editor, Dept. of English, Youngstown State Univ., Youngstown, OH 44555-0001. (g) Hazeldean Myers, 7843 Stanburn Rd., Worthington, OH 43235-1882. (h) Ex. (i) Est. 60/100. (j) Ms. should be on topics of interest to teachers of English and language arts, K-C.

Oklahoma English Journal

(a) Oklahoma Council of Teachers of English. (b) 2: F, Sp. (c) Classroom teachers, K-grad. school: 500. (d) Composition K-C, basic research through classroom teaching techniques. Many articles on composition each year. (e) R$20; S$6. (f) J, Kevin Davis, East Central Univ., Ada, OK 74820. (h) Ex. (i) 40/60. (j) Reaches a broad audience of educators, elementary through college.

Oregon English Journal

(a) Oregon Council of Teachers of English. (b) 2: F, Sp. (c) Teachers, administrators, curriculum specialists K-C: 1200. (d) Composition at all levels; also creative writing. (e) R$15; I$15. (f) Ulrich H. Hardt, editor, Portland State Univ., PO Box 751, Portland, OR 97207. (g) David Freitag, 13044 SE King, Portland, OR 97236. (h) V. (i) 40/60. (j) We are very interested in receiving ms. focusing on composition, especially if they are appropriate for the elementary level.

Poetics

(a) Elsevier Science Publishers. (b) 6. (c) Scholars and researchers in literary studies: 1000. (d) Theoretical foundation and methodological aspects of empirical research in the field of literary communication, theory of literary text structures, general theory of discourse, and relation of literary theory to adjacent disciplines. (e) Dfl.349.00 per volume of six issues (includes shipping). (f) J, Cees J. Van Rees, Dept. of Language and Literature, Tilburg Univ., PO Box 90153, 5000 LE Tilburg, The Netherlands. (g) J, Elsevier Science Publishers B.V., Journals Dept., PO Box 211, 1000 AE Amsterdam, The Netherlands.

Pre/Text: A Journal of Rhetorical Theory

(a) Victor Vitanza, University of Texas at Arlington. (b) 4: Sp, S, F, W. (c) Multidisciplinary: 500. (d) All aspects of rhetorical theory. (e) R$15; I$45; +F$15. (f) J, Dept. of English, PO Box 19035, Univ. of Texas at Arlington, Arlington, TX 76019-0035. (h) Ex. (i) 20/40. (j) Please contact the editor.

Quarterly

(a) National Writing Project and Center for the Study of Writing. (b) 4: Jan, Apr, July, Oct. (c) K-C. (d) Articles reflecting current thought on composition theory and practice; also research and reviews. Reports news about Center activities, but also accepts articles from outside. (e) R$6. (f) J, Center for the Study of Writing, School of Education, Univ. of California, Berkeley, CA 94720.

Quarterly Journal of Speech

(a) Speech Communication Association. (b) 4: Feb, May, Aug, Nov. (c) Interdisciplinary. (d) Articles, research reports, and book reviews of interest to persons across a broad spectrum of the communication arts. (e) M$40. (f) J, Dept. of Speech Communication, Tawes Hall, Univ. of Maryland, College Park, MD 20742. (g) J, SCA, 5105 Backlick Rd., Bldg. E, Annandale, VA 22003. (h) Occ. (i) 10/100.

Radical Teacher

(b) 3. (c) Teachers working from K-C. (d) Three critical areas: classroom practices that stress the teacher's political experience and development to students and subject matter; the political economy of education and related institutional struggles; socialist theory from feminist, Marxist, and Third World perspectives from the teaching of reading to the application of computer science. (e) R$8; I$11; $35 sustaining; $4 part-time/unemployed/RT; +F$3 (surface); +F$10 (air). (f) J, PO Box 102, Cambridge, MA 02142. (h) V. (j) Send proposals first.

Reader

(a) Department of Humanities, Michigan Technological University. (b) 2: F, Sp. (d) Essays in reader-oriented theory, criticism, and pedagogy; relationships between reading and writing. (e) R$8; I$10; +F$2. (f) J, Dept. of Humanities, Michigan Tech. Univ., Houghton, MI 49931. (h) V. (i) 15/52.

Reading and Writing: An Interdisciplinary Journal

(a) Kluwer Academic Publishers. (b) 4: Mar, June, Sep, Dec. (c) Teachers C and K-12; psychologists: 300. (d) Focuses on research on pedagogy of writing/spelling at all levels; information processing and writing; linguistic aspects of writing/spelling, composition; relationships between reading and writing. (e) R$50; I$117; C$10. (f) J, Dr. R. Malatesha, The Reading Center, 104 Gundersen Hall, Oklahoma State Univ., Stillwater, OK 74078. (g) Kluwer Academic Publishers, PO Box 358 Accord Station, Hingham, MA 02018-9900. (h) Ex. (i) 10/50 since 1989. (j) We will be delighted to receive manuscripts related to current research on writing/spelling; models of writing/spelling; information processing and writing; and orthography.

Reading Research Quarterly

(a) International Reading Association. (b) 4: Sp, S, F, W. (c) Primarily researchers at the university level. (d) Reports of experimental or descriptive research on reading and theoretical discussions of the reading process, including relationships between reading and writing. (e) M$38. (f) J, 257 Arps Hall, Ohio State Univ., 1945 N. High St., Columbus, OH 43210. (g) J, IRA, PO Box 8139, Newark, DE 19714-8139. (i) 10/100.

Reflections on Canadian Literacy

(a) University of Calgary. (b) 4: F, W, Sp, S. (c) K-12, C teachers, consultants, and researchers: 500. (d) Reading and writing processes, instruction, and connections. (e) R$28; I$35; +F$3; C$5 (Canadian). (f) J, Dept. of Curriculum and Instruction, Univ. of Calgary, Calgary, Alberta T2N 1N4, Canada. (h) V. (i) 30/130. (j) Topics relevant to teachers. Manuscripts need to be written in a teacher-friendly style.

Research in the Teaching of English

(a) National Council of Teachers of English. (b) 4: Feb, May, Oct, Dec. (c) Interdisciplinary, preschool to adult. (d) Original research on the relationships between language teaching and language learning at all levels. Reflects a variety of methodologies and modes of inquiry current in the field: studies of instruction, historical influences, linguistic and cognitive development, interrelationships among reading, writing, and oral language skills. (e) R$15; I$20; +F$3. (f) J, Harvard Graduate School of Education, Larsen Hall, Appian Way, Cambridge, MA 02138. (g) J, National Council of Teachers of English, 1111 Kenyon Rd., Urbana, IL 61801. (h) Ex. (i) 75/100. (j) Write for guidelines.

Rhetorica

(a) International Society for the History of Rhetoric. (b) 4. (c) International, scholars of rhetoric: 700. (d) Articles, book reviews, and bibliographies that promote the study of both the theory and practice of rhetoric in all periods and languages, and its relationships with poetics, philosophy, politics, religion, law, and other aspects of cultural context. (e) R$30; I$40; M$25; C$6.50 (individuals), $10 (institutions). (f) J, Dept. of Communication Studies, Northwestern Univ., 1815 Chicago Ave., Evanston, IL 60208. (h) Ex. (i) 30/90. (j) The journal is devoted to the history of rhetoric; essays on theory or contemporary applications normally are not suitable.

Rhetoric Review

(a) Rhetoric Review Association of America. (b) 2: F, Sp. (d) Explorations in histories and theories of rhetoric: theory and method; professional, provocative, practical essays structured for classroom exchange; and personal essays about writing, language, or the teaching of writing. (e) R$12. (f) J, Dept. of English, Univ. of Arizona, Tucson, AZ 85721. (h) V. (i) 76/80.

Rhetoric Society Quarterly

(a) Rhetoric Society of America. (b) 4: W, Sp, S, F. (c) CCCC members; speech communications teachers and scholars: 700. (d) Interdisciplinary: rhetorical theory, criticism, pedagogy, and research; history of rhetoric. (e) R$20; S$5; I$30; +F$5; M$20. (f) J, Dept. of English, St. Cloud State Univ., St. Cloud, MN 65301. (g) J, Rhetoric Society of America, [same as (f)]. (h) Ex. (i) 25/125. (j) We look for papers that reflect with some explicitness a theoretical and historical interest in and awareness of the field of rhetoric.

Rocky Mountain Review of Language and Literature

(a) Rocky Mountain Modern Language Association (b) 3: Apr, Aug, Nov. (c) C, HS: 700. (d) Journal's emphasis is on research in English, foreign, and classical languages and literatures (articles can be published in foreign languages), linguistics, literary theory; also includes book reviews. Conference includes these topics as well as composition teaching, writing programs, children's literature, etc. (e) M$15; MS$10; MRT$10; I$20; C$5. (f) J, English Dept., Boise State Univ., Boise, ID 83725. (g) J, Secretariat, RMMLA, English Dept., Boise State Univ., Boise, ID 83725. (h) S/Occ. (i) 5/95. (j) We prefer manuscripts for college audiences.

Southern Speech Communication Journal

(a) Southern Speech Communication Association. (b) 4: F, W, Sp, S. (c) Educators and professionals, C and some secondary and professional communication. (d) Quantitative studies of oral and written language; communication instruction. (e) M (patron) $70, (sustaining) $25, (regular) $15, (student) $10; +F$8; C$5. (f) J, Keith V. Erickson, Dept. of Speech Communication, Univ. of Southern Mississippi, Hattiesburg, MS 39406. (h) Occ. (i) 1/100. (j) Relate the topic to human communication, interaction, or rhetorical concerns, not literary.

Sunspots

(a) Southland Council of Teachers of English. (b) 5. (c) All levels of English. (d) Informational to members. (e) Comes with membership to SCTE/CATE. (f) J, Kay Burkhart, 2530 S. Cardillo, Haciendo Hts., CA 91745. (h) V. (j) Short paragraphs/essays only. Long articles should be submitted to *California English*.

Teachers and Writers Magazine

(a) Teachers and Writers Collaborative. (b) 5: Sep/Oct, Nov/Dec, Jan/Feb, Mar/Apr, May/Jun. (c) Teachers K-C: 2000. (d) Primary focus is on the teaching of imaginative writing. (e) R$15; S$15; I$15; +F$2.50; M$35; C$4. (f) J, 5 Union Square West, New York, NY 10003. (h) Ex. (i) 70/75. (j) We are looking for clear and informal articles and essays about innovative ways to teach writing, especially imaginative writing.

Teaching and Learning: The Journal of Natural Inquiry

(a) Center for Teaching and Learning, University of North Dakota. (b) 3: F, W, Sp. (c) K-C: 1400. (d) General education emphasis with primary focus on qualitative, descriptive, naturalistic, experience-based, or phenomenological research. (e) R$12; I$12; RT$12; +F$7; C$4. (f) J, Center for Teaching and Learning, Box 8158, Univ. Station, Grand Forks, ND 58202. (h) V. (i) 15/48. (j) Keep "qualitative thought" in mind. We tend not to publish single-classroom activities, statistical or quantitative work (e.g., surveys), or explanations or theories already accepted and in practice. We are *keenly interested* in reflective essays, deep and thick descriptions of practice, case studies, and the like. Our readers are generally progressive in their educational attitudes and preferences. We are more interested in literacy and writing than suggested in the ratio of articles published.

Teaching English in the Two-Year College

(a) National Council of Teachers of English. (b) 4: Feb, May, Oct, Dec. (c) Instructors in two- and four-year colleges: 3500. (d) Articles and reviews on trends in teaching composition, especially in freshman and sophomore courses, and pieces containing tips for two-year college instructors. (e) R$15; I$15; +F$3. (f) J, Box 1266, Hinds Community College, Raymond, MS 39154-9799. (g) National Council of Teachers of English, 1111 Kenyon Rd., Urbana, IL 61801. (h) Ex. (i) 125/175. (j) Every teacher of writing should write!

Technical Writing Teacher

(a) Association of Teachers of Technical Writing. (b) 3: W, Sp, F. (c) Academic and business: 800. (d) Articles on research, theory, and pedagogical methods; reviews, annual bibliography, special research issue in fall. (e) R$20; I$50; +F (Canada) $5, (other countries) $10; C$8. (f) J, Dept. of Rhetoric, 202 Haecker Hall, Univ. of Minnesota, St. Paul, MN 55108. (g) V. (h) 35/125.

Tennessee English Journal

(a) Tennessee English Journal. (b) 1: F. (c) Teachers K-C. (d) Primary focus for articles is on teaching. (e) R$10; I$15. (f) J, Dr. Anne Sherrill, editor, Dept. of English, 22990A, E. Tennessee State Univ., Johnson City, TN 37614-0002. (g) Ms. Carolyn Phipps, 7091 Crestridge, Memphis, TN 38119. (h) Ex. (i) 30%. (j) Please submit 3 copies, limited to 8 pp., double-spaced, MLA style.

Text: An Interdisciplinary Journal for the Study of Discourse

(a) Mouton, Inc. (b) 4: Sp, S, F, W. (c) Interdisciplinary: 1500. (d) An international journal for the publication of papers on discourse (text, conversation, messages, communicative events, etc.). (e) R$75; S$34.90; I$75. (f) J, Teun A. van Dijk, Dept. of General Literary Studies, Section of Discourse Studies, Univ. of Amsterdam, Spuistraat 210, Amsterdam, The Netherlands. (g) J, Walter de Gruyter Inc., Subscription Dept., 200 Saw Mill River Rd., Hawthorne, NY 10530.

Theory Into Practice

(a) Ohio State University, College of Education. (b) 4: W, Sp, S, F. (c) K-12, C educators: 4000. (d) Theme issues on educational topics, some relating to writing and literacy. (e) R$22; I$45; +F$5; C$6. (f) J, College of Education, 101 Ramseyer Hall, 29 W. Woodruff Ave., Columbus, OH 43210. (g) J, College of Education, 174 Arps Hall, 1945 N. High St., Columbus, OH 43210. (h) V. (j) Check to see if a theme issue is planned related to topic.

Virginia English Bulletin

(a) Virginia Association of Teachers of English Language Arts. (b) 2: May, Oct. (c) Teachers K-12: 2700. (d) Periodic focus on composition: pragmatic application for teachers K-12, often with short student samples. (e) R$10; S$2. (f) J, Division of Curriculum and Instruction, Virginia Tech, Blacksburg, VA 24061-0313. (g) Leon F. Williams, 5556 McVitty Rd., Roanoke, VA 24018. (h) V. (i) 40/200.

Washington English Journal

(a) Washington State Council of Teachers of English. (b) 2: F, Sp. (c) Teachers, K-C: 400. (d) *WEJ* seeks to publish ms. that address the concerns of language arts teachers, K-C. (e) M$15; C$3. (f) Jan Slater Chappuis, editor, J, Curriculum Specialist, Central Kitsap School Dist., PO Box 8, Silverdale, WA 98383-0008. (g) Elaine Cockrell, WSCTE Membership, 1 Jeffrey Place, Longview, WA 98632. (h) Ex. (i) 50/70. (j) We welcome ms. for K-12 and college audiences.

Western Ohio Journal

(a) Western Ohio Council of Teachers of English/Language Arts (WOCTELA). (b) 1: Sp. (c) Teacher K-C: 200. (d) Primary focus: writing concerns at all levels—rhetoric, pedagogy, politics, critical literacy, creative writing. (e) M$12. (f) J, Jim Brooks, DEV, Sinclair Community College, 444 W. 3rd St., Dayton, OH 45402. (g) WOCTELA, 5840 Hunter Rd., Enon, OH 45323. (h) Ex. (j) We will consider all types of ms.: classroom narratives, research, commentaries, creative writing, criticism.

Wisconsin English Journal

(a) Wisconsin Council of Teachers of English. (b) 3: Sp, F, W. (c) ELED, JH, SH, C: 700. (d) Always have articles on writing; occasionally thematic issue on composition. (e) R$2.25; I$7.50; journal free with membership. (f) J, Dr. Rhoda Maxwell, English Dept., Univ. of Wisconsin, Eau Claire, WI 54701. (h) Ex. (i) 80/118 (last 3 yrs.) (j) Ms. 5-10 pp., double-spaced, MLA style.

WPA: Writing Program Administration

(a) Council of Writing Program Administrators. (b) 2: F/W, Sp. (c) Directors of composition programs and writing centers; English department chairs; other 2- and 4-year college and university administrators: 650. (d) Administration of writing programs; teaching writing or research in composition when these deal with the relationship of those activities to writing program administration. (e) R$15; I$20; +F$1.50. (f) J, Christine Hult, Dept. of English, Utah State Univ., Logan, UT 84322-3200. (g) J, WPA, Dept. of English, Miami Univ., Oxford, OH 45056. (h) Ex. (i) 50/50. (j) See author's guide in the front of each issue.

The Writer

(a) The Writer, Inc. (b) Monthly. (c) HS and C. (d) Writing: how-to's and how and where to sell and market literary work. (e) R$25.50; +F$8. (f) J, 120 Boylston St., Boston, MA 02116. (h) V. (i) 90-95%. (j) Read several issues first to determine style, focus, tone. Articles by published writers preferred. Always willing to read submissions, but we make no assignments. All material submitted on speculation. Responsive audience of writers eager to master basics of writing and selling for publication. Not literary discussions.

Writer's Digest

(a) F & W Publications. (b) 12: monthly. (c) 250,000. (d) How to write for publication. (e) R$21. (f) J, 1507 Dana Ave., Cincinnati, OH 45207. (h) Focus is on writing technique, for improved style and sales to publishers. (j) Write to editor for guidelines.

Writing!

(a) Field Publications. (b) 9: Sep–May. (c) SH, JH: 110,000. (d) Primary focus is on junior/senior high writing skills and notable writers. (e) B$6.50 (over 15). (f) J, 60 Revere Dr., Northbrook, IL 60062-1563. (g) Field Publications, 4343 Equity Dr., PO Box 16730, Columbus, OH 43285-6730. (h) S. (i) All. (j) Interested in articles addressed to JH, SH students, including interviews with writers.

The Writing Center Journal

(a) Affiliated with the National Writing Centers Association. (b) 2: F/W, Sp/S. (c) K-12, C. (d) Writing lab/center instruction. (e) R$10. (f) J, Humanities Dept., Michigan Technological Univ., Houghton, MI 49931. (h) Ex. (i) 70/70. (j) The editors are soliciting manuscripts that address the following: critical theory and writing center instruction; politics of writing center instruction; students' perspectives of the writing center; cultural diversity in writing center instruction; collaborative learning and the writing center; theories of learning and writing center instruction; writing centers and community involvement; literacy programs in the writing center.

The Writing Instructor

(a) English Department, University of Southern California. (b) 3: W, Sp, F. (c) Secondary and C writing teachers: 800. (d) The interaction of theory and practice in the composition classroom; essays on student as communicator or audience; teacher as communicator, facilitator, audience, or student; educational institution as rhetorical scene; larger community's view of writing. (e) R$18; I$35; +F$4; C$2. (f) J, Univ. of Southern California, 817 W. 34th St., UUC 4th Floor, Los Angeles, CA 90089. (h) V. (i) 90/90. (j) We are interested in articles which are theoretically current, and which bridge the informed critique of that current theory with the real world of classroom praxis.

Writing Lab Newsletter

(a) Department of English, Purdue University; official publication of the National Writing Centers Association of NCTE. (b) 10: Monthly, Sep–June. (c) Directors, tutors, and other writing center staff, JH, SH, C: 1100. (d) Promotes communication and interaction among people who teach in writing labs and other tutorial centers. Includes articles, reviews, announcements, and queries on individualized instruction, administration, and the structures and services of specific writing labs and centers. (e) R$10 (US); R$15 (Canada). (f) J, Dept. of English, Purdue Univ., West Lafayette, IN 47907. (h) Ex. (i) 250/250. (j) Articles must be relevant to the tutorial setting of writing labs and centers, not classroom instruction.

Writing on the Edge

(a) Regents of the University of California. (b) 2: Sp, F. (c) College teachers and professional writers: 350. (d) Personal essays, academic articles, fiction, poetry, and interviews on writing and the teaching of writing; new approaches to composition, such as cross-disciplinary writing, computers in the classroom, and collaborative writing; interviews with professional writers and writing teachers. (e) R$15; S$12; C$8; +$5B5; lifetime $200. (f) J, Campus Writing Center, Univ. of California, Davis, CA 95616. (h) V. (i) 1/10 (1 yr.). (j) We have no rules; we especially appreciate interesting manuscripts with a strong sense of the author's voice.

Written Communication

(a) Sage Publications, Inc. (b) 4: Jan, Apr, Jul, Oct. (c) Interdisciplinary: 1200. (d) Devoted to the advancement of knowledge of writing through theoretical, historical, and empirical research. It is a cross-disciplinary journal that addresses substantive issues in writing from perspectives such as rhetoric, discourse analysis, pragmatics, sociolinguistics, psychology, linguistics, journalism, and anthropology. Among topics of interest are the nature of writing ability, the assessment of writing, the impact of technology on writing, social and political consequences of writing and writing instruction, nonacademic writing, literacy, social construction of knowledge, cognition and composing, structure of written text, gender and writing, and connections among writing, reading, speaking, and listening. (e) R$39; I$108; +F$6. (f) J, Dept. of English, 164 W. 17th Ave., Ohio State Univ., Columbus, OH 43210-1370. (g) J, Sage Publications Inc., 2433 Teller Rd., Newbury Park, CA 91320. (h) Ex. (i) 90/90. (j) See "Guidelines for Submission" at the front of each issue as well as "Editors' Comments" in the January 1991 issue.

The Written Word

(a) CEGA Services. (b) Monthly. (c) Providers of literacy services, libraries, community colleges. (d) Adult functional illiteracy, family literacy, workplace literacy, innovative program ideas. (e) R$15; +F$5. (f) CEGA Services, PO Box 81826, Lincoln, NE 68508. (h) Ex. (j) We do not publish scholarly works but are very interested in receiving news releases, announcements about new materials/publications and conferences, and brief descriptions of successful literacy programs.

18 Beating the Odds: Getting a Manuscript Published

Margaret A. Deitrich
Austin Peay State University, Clarksville, Tennessee

Many writers seem to have the knack of beating the odds and getting their manuscripts accepted. This chapter presents five simple hints that capture their successful strategies.

Schedule Blocks of Time for Writing

The first strategy for writing successfully is to simply spend time writing. No editor can publish the idea that you talk about or mean to write about, but never actually get written. The writers who get published allow themselves time to write and protect that writing time from other intruding events.

Choose Your Journal Carefully

Knowing your audience and the available publications that are read by that intended audience is an important step in the publishing process, one that needs to occur early in the framing of an article. In Chapter 17 of this volume, Chris Anson and Bruce Maylath provide a comprehensive listing of journals that may be appropriate publication sources. In addition, several other publications, usually available at the public library, contain publishing information about educational journals and periodicals. These references provide excellent summaries of various journals in education:

Cabell, D.W.E. (1989). *Cabell's directory of publishing opportunities in education* (2nd ed.). Beaumont, TX: Cabell Publishing Company.

> This reference summarizes 400 journals in the areas of education and describes for each journal the kinds of manuscripts sought, manuscript guidelines, descriptions of the review process, acceptance rates, and types of readership.

Collins, M.E. (1988). *Education journals and serials analytical guide.* New York: Greenwood Press.

> Listings for each journal in this reference include a description of target audience, publication data, circulation information, and procedures for manuscript selection.

Loke, W.H. (1990). *A guide to journals in psychology and education.* Meluchen, NJ: Scarecrow Press.

> Serving as a guide for journal selection in the areas of education and psychology, this reference lists data about journal readership, manuscript length, topics, and acceptance criteria.

Wang, A.Y. (1989). *Author's guide to journals in the behavioral sciences.* Hillsdale, NJ: Erlbaum.

> This reference addresses all journals indexed in *Psychology Abstracts.* It provides a description of each journal, types of papers accepted, style requirements, acceptance rates, and review periods.

From these sources, make a list of journals that look promising for your type of article. Spend as much time thinking about the choice of a journal—and the selection of two or three alternates—as you do with the concept of the manuscript itself. A good strategy is to locate these journals and review several issues from the latest publication year. Investigate the format, style, content, types of articles, length of articles, and deadline dates. Investigate whether the journal has themed issues that may relate to your interests. Many writers gather information about a range of possible publication sources for their particular kind of article. Constructing a personal chart with essential information will enable you to retrieve quickly the necessary points needed for matching a journal and prospective article.

Be sure to peruse the journals you already know. You probably have read many issues of certain journals, but always focused on the content of the articles rather than on the specific features of the writing itself. Notice how leads are handled and whether student writing or pictures are included. Consider the tone of the articles and their comprehensiveness. Look specifically for articles about your intended topic; if a piece has just been published that relates to your article, the editor may be reluctant to print another.

Include Classroom Examples

Writers are often given the advice that examples and quotations make writing more vivid. Writing that shows the work of students and uses their language allows readers to envision the classrooms that are being described. Readers can remember the first grader who, after reading *Goldilocks and the Three Bears*, remarked critically, "I don't very much like the way she messed up the bears' house." And we are moved by the fifth-grade student from China who wrote in her journal how happy she was to be able to hear and see the beauty of the world after reading about Helen Keller. Readers tend to forget some of the content of articles, but the examples about students remain and allow readers to think about the learners in their own classes.

Allow Time to Revise and Polish

Writers who publish successfully spend extensive amounts of time solving the problems that arise in their manuscripts. They may use various kinds of references, including these handbooks and guides:

Axelrod, R.B., & Cooper, C.R. (1985). *The St. Martin's guide to writing.* New York: St. Martin's Press.

> This book guides the writer through the entire writing process, as well as providing help with grammar, usage, style, punctuation, and mechanics.

Hodges, J.C., Whitten, M.E., Horner, W.B., Webb, S.S., & Miller, R.K. (1990). *Harbrace College Handbook* (11th ed.). New York: Harcourt Brace Jovanovich.

> This revised edition has practical, concise examples that demonstrate the principles of writing. Major topics include grammar, mechanics, punctuation, spelling, and effective sentences.

Lester, J.D. (1991). *A writer's handbook: Style and grammar.* New York: Harcourt Brace Jovanovich.

> Lester's publication addresses the science and art of writing. It discusses style, how to construct a composition, the importance of revising, ways to eliminate biased language, and how to edit nonstandard English.

Norton Textra Writer 2.0. (1989). New York: W.W. Norton.

> Using the computer more effectively while composing is the purpose of the Textra Writer software. This version adds new printing and formatting capabilities and provides information about split screen, works cited, and endnotes. This program can be used with various computers and is designed to help the writer become an efficient computer user.

Zinsser, W. (1985). *On writing well* (3rd ed.). New York: Harper & Row.

Zinsser's book contains three parts with Part 2, nonfiction writing, receiving the major emphasis. Zinsser contends that much of today's best writing is occurring in nonfiction, and he provides extensive examples of effective writing. Part 3 describes the advantages of using the computer while composing. (Revised editions of this book have been published fairly regularly, so consult your library or bookstore for the latest version.)

Writers may use other references as sources of additional information. It may be useful to read journal articles about writing for publication and descriptions by journal editors about the kinds of articles they seek. Among these, the following articles are representative:

Gebhardt, R.C. (1987). Editor's note. *College Composition and Communication, 38,* 19–20.

Gentile, L.M. (1984). Writing and publishing in reading: Some suggestions for practicing educators. *Reading World, 40,* 26–33.

Henson, K.T. (1986). Writing for publication: Playing to win. *Phi Delta Kappan, 67,* 602–604.

Jalongo, M.R., & McCraken, J.B. (1986). Writing for professional publication in early childhood education. *Young Children, 41,* 19–24.

Nelms, B.F. (1988). What you can do for us. *English Journal, 77*(4), 88–89.

Another valuable resource that provides critical details about manuscript preparation is the style sheet furnished by the journal itself. Style sheets describe the particular journal's specifications for manuscripts, including the style, format, length, and other requirements.

Recycle the Manuscript

Writers who get published are tenacious. They view rejection letters as an inevitable part of the writing experience and recycle their manuscripts.

Rejection can be difficult to handle, especially the first time an article has been submitted for publication. Ask yourself how committed you are to getting the manuscript published. If you are focused on that outcome and believe the article's content is good, you have two options. The first is to review your notes on suitable publications, check the journal's publication guidelines, and resubmit the article immediately. Mail it! The second option is to let the article incubate a bit, make the suggested revisions, and then submit the article to a different journal. Look again at the articles journals are publishing and make adjustments to the manuscript as needed.

The writers who beat the odds and get published are those who have made the commitment of time and effort, those who read the journals they select for their own work. Their advice is straight-forward: The time to start is now! Get that burning idea on paper. It may seem like an insurmountable task, but manuscripts do get published.

19 Confessions of a Computer Convert

Thelma Kibler
New Mexico State University

I dug in my heels. I resisted with every spurious argument I could muster: I don't think that way. I failed typing in high school. I have an established routine that works for me. I only write with pencil on yellow legal tablets at the kitchen table. I'm writing something important, and I don't want to rock the boat. Later, later, I'll learn to compose at the computer, but I don't think it will work for me.

Two years later, when I was still saying "later, later," I moved to a new university, and they placed a computer and printer in my office. It sat there, and since I kept bumping into it, I finally found myself using it—just to do simple things, mind you, just handouts, tests, and syllabi.

Gradually, I became a computer convert, and a fanatical one at that. As a convert, I can't write a memo or letter in longhand. My excuses: It takes too long. I'm out of rubber cement for cut-and-paste. Later, later, I'll write it when I've got my computer. In just two years, I have discovered several ways in which the computer can increase the number of articles I submit to journals for publication.

For most of us, time is the big oppressor: we just cannot find sufficient time to write and revise the article for which we have ideas. Fragmentary ideas pass through the mind while we are riding in the car, facing a classroom of students, or washing the dishes; these are good ideas, ideas that would find a readership and be helpful to others. If only we had the time to think them through, polish them up, and send them off. The computer can help by allowing the writer to reallocate time to those tasks that will improve the product.

Text editing is certainly the most obvious and useful capability of the word processor. It saves time and effort at all stages of the process, from prewriting to composing the cover letter. The computer enables the writer to make additions easily and also handle deletions and rearrangements that were tedious and debilitating in longhand. Often the mere thought of the effort needed to manually rewrite a piece, or even cut-and-paste it, lures us to be too easily satisfied with first-draft attempts. Ah, the joy of that computer magic to delete or move text:

> Each maimed and misconceived passage can be made to vanish instantly, by the word or by the paragraph, leaving a pristine green field on which to make the next attempt. (Fallows, 1982, p. 84)

The ease of moving whole chunks of text within the piece, to new files, or to other disks is an equally powerful and efficient maneuver. By going through the steps of the writing process, I will share some computer practices that can be adapted to your personal writing procedures.

Prewriting

The investment in a few extra disks is a worthwhile expenditure. The most helpful disk is one used for recording ideas for possible future articles. On this *in-progress disk,* I make a file for each potential piece or topic of interest and do my jotlisting there—tentative titles, flashes of insight, possible quotes. The following example is part of the initial jotlist for this article:

> Jotlisting, idea collecting, note collection
>> possible articles, interests
>> titles
>
> Works in progress
>> begin file for article
>> possible articles on same disk, some stage of progress
>>> as writing one, an idea for other occurs
>
> Cook article—"Step 1 Keep your inner editor in its place":
>> reminder that the critic if comes into play too soon overpowers the artist within, blocking creative flow then emit "technically competent but uninspired work." p. 30

As Cook (1987) reminds us, we should not rush a piece; it needs time to cool. Having several articles in progress allows time for re-flection and for ideas to gel. This working file is speculative and probably includes more content and a wider range of subtopics than will eventually appear in the finished piece. With additional research and thought, an accumulation of ideas, quotes, relationships, and references results in a more comprehensive preview of possibilities.

The computer also allows the writer to move the jotlisted items around freely and discover idea clusters or tentative plans for organization. The ease of rearranging enables me to try different sequences until I feel comfortable with one. I find it helpful to make printouts of my different jotlists, then compare them and add notes right on the printout. Yes, this computer convert still finds it convenient to make arrows, scratch marks, and visible traces of my thoughts. And the printout can be taken to the sink, armchair, or bed for further contemplation. The ease of tinkering around with ideas on the computer enhances the probability of more thorough prewriting, which may produce a better product and save time in drafting.

Another disk that writers might find helpful is solely for *references*. In the olden days, pre-computer, I would jot down bibliographic information on whatever paper was handy, or sometimes make a copy of an article for future reference. When it was time to list references, I would waste time relocating the information, often finding that it was incomplete—no volume number, no month. Now when I find a useful article, I record the reference as soon as possible on my reference disk, using a consistent format. I have chosen APA style, but if another style is needed for a particular journal my citations can be altered easily; at least the complete information is readily at hand. Writers might choose to list the references by broad fields, (e.g., whole language, assessment, composition), or by potential article, or in an alphabetized listing regardless of topic. With the cut-and-paste capabilities of the computer, it is necessary to type the reference only once, though it can be used again and again.

The references for this chapter were drawn from my reference disk. I inserted that disk, called to the desktop a list of references, and immediately removed the disk so that during the cut-and-paste procedure I would not accidentally erase the items I used from the disk. Then I chose and compiled the reference list used here, saving it at the end of the file for the drafted article.

Writers also might have a separate file in which to keep *notable quotes*. Too often in the past I vaguely recalled a quote or phrase that I would like to use, but could not locate it. Now, as a computer buff, I mark pertinent quotes as I read. After reading an article, I place it next to the computer so I can easily add the quotes to my notable quote file and the bibliographic information to the reference file. Both of these files may be kept on one disk for ease in recording. Should the disk get full, one file can be moved to a new disk.

Drafting

Successful writers often advise the novice writer to plunge ahead. The best strategy is to just begin writing and get rid of the blank page staring at you. Writing to discover content, forms, and language is a powerful tool for effective writing (Murray, 1982), but when writing in longhand or at a conventional typewriter, it seems discouraging to write a lot only to throw it away or recopy it in different form. It is hard to cross out or discard those wonderful words that took hours to get down in the first place. Thus, the writer may be reluctant to put time or effort into freewriting, attempting to get a good, usable draft on the first try. When using a word processor, however, the remarkable ease of manipulating and saving text gives freedom to engage in freewriting without worrying about wasted time.

I find that the ability to save text in another file frees me to be more tentative and risk-taking in my initial drafting. I am more willing to try something that I may or may not use. If it is questionable that I'll use it, I can save it for further consideration and not succumb to the sensation that I've destroyed or discarded precious text.

Sometimes I am writing along and a fleeting idea comes to mind, an idea that I could not remember if I waited until I finished writing the current section. I have discovered that I can insert possible ideas as they occur, and later shift that temporary text to other locations and perhaps elaborate if the idea is worthwhile. For example, as I was writing an article about persuasion, I thought of some possible implications that should be included. I quickly noted the ideas as follows:

> Learners volunteered no instances of seeing print models of persuasion and showed little experience generating written persuasion, and that largely in self-sponsored notes and letters. Their self-reports support the contention that little experience with persuasion is school-sponsored. The students' perceptions indicate that a child's concept of persuasion is rooted in oral regulatory interactions.
> IMPLICATION: Need for print models???
>   Need for experiences with written persuasion

I then continued writing the text, but the idea was saved and had not really interrupted my flow of thought. I could decide later if the noted implications would contribute to the piece. (Note: The above example was transferred from the original persuasion draft to this piece without retyping. I did have to be careful in the cut-and-paste maneuver not to erase the section from the persuasion file.)

Sometimes I wish to try an alternative approach to a portion of a draft, but do not want to erase the first attempt. I am careful to *save* the first: then rename it, make alterations, and *save* the renamed file. I now have two files and can quickly print them out for comparison. When making different versions of the same piece, the file titles should start with the same word so they appear on the menu in succession. Similarly, when writing a longer piece, I make a file for each section so that I can print only the section I'm working on at that point. A sample menu would list the separate files contributing to the article:

ESL conclusion

ESL findings

ESL intro

ESL method

Even as I continue to draft or revise, I may do further jotlisting at the end of these different files. With the files on the same disk, it is easy to flip back and forth during the drafting process. I can jot an idea in one file, save it, and return to the desktop file on which I'm concentrating. Listing on the menu is alphabetical, so if I have a file I wish to access frequently, I rename it by putting an *a* in front of the file name. Then it is always at the top of the list.

Revision

The novice writer, particularly when writing in longhand, frequently doesn't revise sufficiently. Composing the first draft is often so laborious that the thought of rewriting is overwhelming, tempting the writer too soon to consider a piece completed. The relative ease of text editing with a computer makes revision less formidable. Further, while editing even at superficial levels, the writer has time to ponder more substantial questions and possibilities (Bridwell, Sirc, & Brooke, 1985).

On the other hand, writers should be cautioned against over-revision. Text editing now is so easy that it is possible to revise the life, the fire, the personal voice right out of the piece, resulting in bland, technically correct prose that no one wants to read. One measure to prevent this sterilization of text is to always save your original. This version can be compared to further drafts to check that the revisions improved the piece without eviscerating it.

The computer allows me to play with the format, attempting to get the article into a shape that makes it look its best. In an instant, I can flip from single-space to double-space, change headings, and arrange white space. Although these superficial matters are less important than content, they may produce an appearance that is more effective.

Revision also takes place through the production of hard copies. Since the computer monitor offers a limited view of a piece, it may be helpful to make a hard copy on which to identify chunks of text and note possible rearrangements. One approach is to periodically print a copy to see how the piece is shaping up—format, length, quotes, sequence, paragraphing, redundancies. The printout gives a sense of what the article will look like. The author, with printout in hand, can more easily shift to the role of reader, looking at the draft dispassionately and employing the perspective of self-as-critic.

Easily accessible copies also allow you to receive feedback from outside readers. One of my friends, who gets published frequently, never submits anything until at least three people have read it. Family members as well as colleagues can be asked to review close-to-ready copies.

When the piece is ready for a selected audience, it can be transferred to a disk reserved for finished, submitted articles. If the piece is subsequently rejected, the writer can easily make the needed alterations prior to sending it to another publisher.

Collaborative Writing

The computer can also contribute to efficient collaborative writing. If members come to the planning session with hard copies of jotlisted ideas for the others to peruse, the printed words guide discussion in a way that fast-fleeting oral language cannot. All ideas are considered with fewer oversights and more focused discussion. In my experience, the print form of brainstorming more clearly communicates intended meaning than do less explicitly stated oral explanations. The result often is more of the ideas being adopted by the collaborators.

When the writing tasks have been assigned, drafting proceeds as it would for an individual piece. However, by having brief sharing meetings with the computer printouts in hand, the writers can continuously monitor for redundancies and inconsistencies. This also gives an opportunity to check on format and style options, which can be readily modified for greater effect. Thus, the finished piece more easily will take a coherent form and look less like the stereotypic "committee work." This works even when the individuals do not use the same software program; there are, of course, considerable benefits when the same software program is used. Writers can transfer sections others have written to their own disk, so that each person has the whole piece for reference as they proceed with revision.

Final and Crucial Note

When adapting various timesaving techniques to computer composing, the writer must not forget the most obvious and basic tenets of word processing: (1) During writing, save the text frequently, and (2) always, always, have a backup copy of anything valued. In the category of "would you believe," I was almost finished with this piece about advice for computer writers when my machine ate the disk on which the article was written—and I did not have a backup copy. I always make a backup, but this time I did not. What a hard way to learn a lesson! It cost dearly to have a computer programmer retrieve the article. And temporarily, I had doubts that I truly was a computer convert.

References

Bridwell, L., Sirc, G., & Brooke, R. (1985). Revising and computing: Case studies of student writers. In S. Freedman (Ed.), *The acquisition of written language* (pp. 172–194). Norwood, NJ: Ablex.

Cook, M. (1987, September). Seven steps to better manuscripts. *Writer's Digest*, pp. 30–34.

Fallows, J. (1982, July). Living with a computer. *Atlantic*, pp. 84–91.

Murray, D.M. (1982). *Learning by teaching*. Montclair, NJ: Boynton/ Cook.

V The Craft of Writing for Publication

20 Finding Voices in the Silence

Renée Casbergue and Patricia J. Austin
Tulane University, New Orleans

Emptiness. Writing begins when I feel the familiar but always terrifying "I have nothing to say." There is no subject, no form, no language. Sometimes as I come to the writing desk I feel trapped in an arctic landscape without landmarks, an aluminum sky with no East or West, South or North. More often I feel the emptiness as a black pit without a bottom and with no light above. No down, no up. Soft furry walls with no handholds. Despair.

(Murray, 1989, p. 20)

As teacher writers, we have been there with all other writers, feeling the emptiness. Yet like other writers, we were able to overcome the fear of having nothing to say and discovered, perhaps through the writing process itself, that the words were there. Once we viewed writing for publication as a means of conversing with our colleagues in a community of learners, we were able to relax and begin the conversation. The initial emptiness, though, highlights a dilemma faced by novice and professional writers alike. The dilemma? Simply stated, "Where do the ideas for writing come from?"

Authors' Perspectives

In trying to answer that question and in considering how our ideas for published pieces evolve, we began to realize that where we get ideas cannot be divorced from the issue of why we write. Often, we write to share ideas and enthusiasm with other teachers. We do something in our teaching that we want the world to know about. Some ideas focus on small arenas, offering suggestions for specific lessons. Other ideas focus on larger arenas, positing designs of programmatic scope. The idea is the "something that works." Our intent as writers is to share that "something" as a recipe or formula to recommend to others.

Other times, we write to reflect on and more fully understand our experience. Something happens in our classroom or we read something in the literature that stirs reflection. We write, perhaps to clarify our own understanding, and certainly to share our reflection with others. Idea and intent are intertwined as teachers write to make sense of experience.

Ideas for writing, then, come from both our teaching experiences and our reflections about them. In a sense, the ideas are always there; a writer's task is to recognize them. In both teaching well and writing well, as Calkins (1990) said, we need to linger longer to see and feel things that we might otherwise pass by. Donald Murray (1968) proposed that writers spend part of their time in a state of open susceptibility, aware of and uniquely receptive to impressions and ideas.

But are ideas really just out there waiting to be harnessed by teachers? Does this notion truly reflect the way teachers get ideas when they write for publication? To find out, we decided to talk to teachers who had recently published articles in professional journals in the field of literacy. We asked each teacher to describe how the ideas for specific articles emerged and to discuss more generally their impressions of where ideas come from.

From conversations with these authors, we found that like us, they had difficulty separating their source of ideas for writing from their purposes for writing. Nancy Gorrell, discussing her formulation of an article published in *English Journal* (Gorrell, 1989), captured the nature of this difficulty. She described the process of coming up with ideas as interactive. Regarding herself as a writer, she views her teaching through a writer's lens. As she envisions a potential article, she adjusts her teaching. The adjustments represent innovations that are tested and then shared with other teachers. For her, and many of the other teachers we interviewed, writing shapes practice and practice shapes writing.

Nonetheless, as the fifteen teachers we interviewed discussed their publications with us, we discovered that they share common thoughts on sources for ideas. Most often, teachers' ideas for writing derived from a degree of frustration, followed by successful innovation. Other times their ideas arose from reactions to professional literature. Occasionally, ideas took shape from personal reflection on experience. In each case, the teachers wrote to share their ideas with their colleagues.

Beyond Frustration: Sharing Success

Frustration with traditional methodology and students' lack of response and investment in their learning spurred many teachers we spoke with to develop and test alternative methods. Richard Paul told us that the idea for his article emerged in response to dissatisfaction with the recommended methods for teaching critical reading. His article in the *Journal of Reading* (Paul, 1990) reported his alternative strategies for helping students respond critically to content text.

Frustrated by her high school students' inability to respond adequately to their reading, Norma Greco sought an explanation by tracing the historical evolution of critical theory in the literature. She became aware of the dissonance between theory and practice in her own teaching. In response, she developed activities that reflected the most current theoretical views, then reported those activities in an article published in *English Journal* (Greco, 1990).

Sandra Bidwell described her frustration with her students' level of investment in their own learning. Upon initiating the use of drama to heighten students' interest and increase their involvement in reading, she explored professional literature on instructional uses of drama. Her reading led to refinements in teaching, from which she developed her article in the *Journal of Reading* (Bidwell, 1990) as a means of providing guidelines for other teachers facing the same frustration.

As a result of being frustrated and dissatisfied with the status quo of practice, these teachers developed alternatives, often seeking insight from professional literature. Patricia Cordeiro described this process as circular. She told us that theory underlies the work she does in the classroom. She writes about her work and in the process discovers new theoretical perspectives. These new perspectives bring her full circle to redefinition of instructional practice and innovation. Because the teachers we spoke to moved beyond frustration, and because they recognized that their approaches were different from those of many of their colleagues, they decided to write accounts of their experiences.

In general, accounts of classroom experience can serve to confirm the results of a particular methodology, affirm the effectiveness of modifications or adaptations that teachers develop for certain techniques, or recommend a specific unit or assignment with which they have had success. The ideas for our writing are drawn from our frustration and our success.

Beyond the Literature: Sharing Applications

Another common source of ideas for writing is the desire to respond to professional literature. While Bidwell and Greco described the professional literature as an information source that they turned to out of frustration, they also used it to provide theoretical support for practices they had developed intuitively. Other teachers told us that the literature itself served as the primary catalyst for their published work.

Some recognized the potential of approaches and techniques as appropriate for populations different than those described in their professional reading. Carol Fuhler, for example, realized that despite the growing enthusiasm for literature-based instruction for regular students, its use was rarely considered for special needs populations. Similarly, Susan Davis and Janice Winek recognized the potential of a technique typically used for research writing in colleges as helpful for their advanced junior high school students. Both Fuhler and Davis told us that they thought other teachers could benefit from their application of literature to practice and therefore submitted manuscripts for publication (Davis & Winek, 1989; Fuhler, 1990).

Other teachers recognize the potential for research literature to suggest classroom practice. In response to their extensive reading of literature related to children's difficulties with expository text, Evelyn Cudd and Leslie Roberts developed a method of using paragraph frames to enhance children's abilities to deal with exposition (Cudd & Roberts, 1989). Cudd told us that her writing is often prompted by a desire to translate current research into practical applications so that it is useful to other classroom teachers. Linda Rief also told us that much of what she writes is in response to the professional literature. Her article in *Language Arts* (Rief, 1990) arose from activities she designed in response to literature suggesting that teachers should do what they ask students to do.

Ideas for writing can also arise out of a more direct response to professional reading. Patricia Johnston told us that the idea for a study she conducted arose from dissatisfaction with the official picture of literacy represented in the literature. Her article in *Language Arts* (Johnston, 1989) took shape after she presented her research. Based on feedback from her audience, she was able to focus more clearly on a better image of literacy development.

Each of these teachers found the professional literature a valuable source of ideas for their own writing. Clearly, they viewed professional publication as an opportunity for dialogue. They approached their reading of the literature as a means to engage in that dialogue by finding new applications, by translating theory to practice, or by adding new insight. In making current theory and practice accessible to a wider audience, they were in essence inviting others to participate in the conversation.

Beyond Practice: Sharing Reflections

Ideas for writing also emerge as teachers reflect on their experience. Sometimes that reflection leads to innovative practice. An author of numerous published poems, Jane Ellen Glasser described reflecting on her own early attempts at writing poetry, in which she modeled her work on writers she admired. Acknowledging the need for her students to read like writers, she developed an approach to teaching poetry that strengthened the connection between reading and writing in that genre. That approach, as well as the insightful poetry created by her students in response, provided the fodder for her article in *English Journal* (Glasser, 1990).

Not all reflection on experience results in direct suggestions for practice. Sometimes reflection leads instead to research. In reflecting on his own process of discovering meaning as he writes, Bill Talbot considered the extent to which this was true for children as well. He told us that he was prompted to study children's learning through writing when he heard a child say, "I didn't know what I had to say until I wrote it." An account of his classroom research resulted in his first publication in a national journal (Talbot, 1990).

The notion of discovering meaning through writing was mentioned by many of the teachers we talked to, and in fact seemed to provoke truly reflective pieces in which the author's purpose is simply to present "something that happened" for other teachers to consider. Cordeiro stated that she writes not merely to report experience to others, but also to understand experience herself. She told us that as she writes, she makes discoveries. The process of writing and reflecting allows tacit knowledge to emerge at a conscious level. Cordeiro's articles in *Language Arts* (1988, 1990) offer pictures of classes she has taught, approaches she has used, and interactions with children. They are there for our consideration, not necessarily for our replication. Her ideas for writing come as she contemplates her experience with children and seeks better understanding through writing.

The desire to share insight through reflection also prompted Vicki Zack's article in *Language Arts* (Zack, 1991). She described her concern with "what's happening in the emotional realm as well as the literary realm" as the source for her reflection on children's responses to literature about the Holocaust. She did not intend the article as a recipe for teaching the Holocaust and hoped that it would not be used in that way. The how-to, she said, is too dependent on what children bring to the situation. It is unlikely that the exact set of circumstances surrounding the use of that particular book would ever arise again. Instead, her intent was to share an experience, to present what had happened once in such a way that others could consider broader implications for teaching. She spoke of wanting to hear more of what other teachers bring to literature and what they take away from interacting with children about literature. In a sense, she spoke of wanting to begin a conversation.

For these and other teachers, reflective pieces stem from the rich context of teachers and children interacting as learners. Ideas for such articles emerge from those aspects of classroom life that teachers feel the need to talk about. They want to share their experience, but they also want to hear about the experience of others. Through their writing, they attempt to open a dialogue. For them, what is worth talking about is worth writing for publication.

Harnessing the Ideas

Our discussions with these teacher writers confirmed for us that ideas for writing really do lurk everywhere, waiting for our attention. These writers added further insight and practical advice, however, as they discussed what prompted them to recognize those ideas and eventually write for publication.

Many of the teachers told us that they did not initially realize that they had ideas worthy of publication. They only began to consider offering their ideas to a broader audience when their colleagues praised their efforts as unique or intriguing. Their advice to teachers seeking ideas for writing: write about those classroom practices that you find yourselves talking about with your colleagues.

A number of teachers also mentioned that ideas for articles originally took shape as they wrote for different purposes. Jackie Swensson told us that her article, published in *English Journal* (1990), evolved as a result of presenting at professional conferences and being asked by participants for more information. Bidwell and Cudd also told us that their articles originally took shape as they presented their ideas at local and national educational conferences. They advised teachers with an interest in publication to consider crafting any type of professional presentation into an article to be shared with an even larger audience.

Some authors credited professors with nudging them to rework their ideas into articles for publication. Cordeiro said that her content pieces were originally papers submitted to fulfill course requirements during her graduate studies. Bidwell also told us that her article was first written in response to a course assignment. Obviously, teachers who are interested in publishing in professional journals could look back to papers they have already written and gather ideas for publication. They can also approach required papers as an opportunity to write for publication. As Gorrell views her teaching through a writer's lens, always open to new ideas, so teachers might also approach their coursework from a writer's perspective.

A few teachers mentioned that their ideas were sometimes stimulated by calls for manuscripts in professional journals. When topics listed in requests for submissions seemed to fit what they were doing in their classrooms, these teachers recognized the value of their practices or reflections and thus were prompted to write for publication. These writers viewed issues raised in calls for manuscripts as frames for stories they wanted to tell.

A final observation made by many of these teacher writers is perhaps most revealing about the process of identifying ideas. Almost all of them spoke with animation about manuscripts they are now working on. Some reported having multiple articles in progress at once. Having published, they now view themselves as writers, participants in professional dialogue. They have engaged in the conversation and now find that they have much to contribute.

Coming Full Circle

We began with a dilemma, a question: Where do ideas come from? With the thoughts of those teachers who have harnessed ideas, we have attempted to illustrate that, as Graves (1989) says, "Life presents us with edges, questions, moments, and experiences to listen to and to observe." The ideas are there in our frustration and our success, in our response and reflection. Indeed, we have something to say. "Emptiness cannot be maintained. The silence will fill. . ." (Murray, 1989, p. 20).

References

Bidwell, S.M. (1990). Using drama to increase motivation, comprehension, and fluency. *Journal of Reading, 34,* 38–41.

Calkins, L., with Harwayne, S. (1990). *Living between the lines.* Portsmouth, NH: Heinemann.

Cordeiro, P. (1988). Playing with infinity in the sixth grade. *Language Arts, 65,* 557–566.

Cordeiro, P. (1990). Problem-based thematic instruction. *Language Arts, 67,* 26–34.

Cudd, E.T., & Roberts, L. (1989). Using writing to enhance content area learning in the primary grades. *The Reading Teacher, 42,* 392–404.

Davis, S., & Winek, J. (1989). Improving expository writing by increasing background knowledge. *Journal of Reading, 33,* 178–181.

Fuhler, C.J. (1990). Let's move toward literature-based reading instruction. *The Reading Teacher, 43,* 312–315.

Glasser, J.E. (1990). The reading-writing-reading connection: An approach to poetry. *English Journal, 79*(7), 22–26.

Gorrell, N. (1989). Let found poetry help your students find poetry. *English Journal, 78*(2), 30–34.

Graves, D.H. (1989). *Discover your own literacy.* Portsmouth, NH: Heinemann.

Greco, N.A. (1990). Re-creating the literary text: Practice and theory. *English Journal, 79*(7), 34–40.

Johnston, P. (1989). A scenic view of reading. *Language Arts, 66,* 160–170.

Murray, D.M. (1968). *A writer teaches writing.* Boston: Houghton Mifflin.

Murray, D.M. (1989). *Expecting the unexpected.* Portsmouth, NH: Heinemann.

Paul, R.H. (1990). Reading between the lines in content areas using classifying reasoning. *Journal of Reading, 34,* 92–97.

Rief, L. (1990). Cutting loose: Getting it write. *Language Arts, 67,* 473.

Swensson, J.E. (1990). *WriteNow:* An alternative in-house publication. *English Journal, 79*(7), 60–62.

Talbot, B. (1990). Writing for learning in school: Is it possible? *Language Arts, 67,* 47–56.

Zack, V. (1991). "It was the worst of times": Learning about the Holocaust through literature. *Language Arts, 68,* 42–48.

21 Beginnings: Effective Starting Points for Professional Writing

Eileen Tway
Miami University, Oxford, Ohio

Bang! You're dead," the child shouted in the back of the room. A ripple of surprise and interest went through the third-grade classroom, but then everyone went back to work. Bobby was simply talking to himself and acting out as he wrote his adventure story. He is typical of writers who "live" a story and get involved in it from the inside out, which is what any writer of fiction or fact must do to create authentic writing. And the authenticity and involvement must start right at the beginning to capture a reader's attention. If a writer does not start with a bang, the piece will be dead.

Good beginnings touch the heart, emotions, and interests of the reader; in short, a writer who wants to reach readers must start in a way that will hook the reader's attention. Authors use anecdotes, provocative questions, quotations, and challenges to capture the reader's interest. This chapter started with an anecdote about a child's active involvement in writing, an anecdote that has implications for all authentic writing. Many writers of educational material use the anecdote effectively to get started. Others depend on various other kinds of hooks for readers.

Anecdotes

Donald Graves, author, researcher, and proponent of the writing process approach to writing instruction, is a master at using the anecdote to get into writing. The anecdotes he writes have human interest and help make an important point right up front. A good anecdote lets the reader know what to expect in the rest of the piece. Consider the following Gravesian opening paragraph:

> I don't like welfare. Peter wouldn't like it either . . . if he knew we were on welfare, writer's welfare. Each day Peter waits in line in his second grade classroom, to receive whatever praise

may come his way on writing assignments about subjects that have been carefully chosen to stimulate him into "creativity." He writes for others, not for himself. He writes to communicate with one person, the teacher. He is dependent on the teacher for criticism, topic, writing time (always between 1:00 and 1:40 after lunch, when few professional writers can write). Opportunities for writing are carefully controlled and only come when the teacher makes writing assignments. (Graves, 1976, p. 645)

What reader could resist following up on this anecdote and finding out how Graves proposed to get rid of the "welfare mess," where children are totally dependent on the teacher?

Barbara Kamler, in writing a guest article for Donald Graves's research column in *Language Arts,* also used a typical Gravesian beginning:

Jill was in a slump. She was stuck for a good topic to write about. Her teacher Judy Egan knew it. The last two topics Jill chose had not worked. She was not interested in "The Day I Changed My Room Around" and she knew nothing about "Cats." The result: two stories lacking in detail and interest for both reader and writer. In the writing conference Jill did not respond to her teacher's questions about content. She had little information to add to either piece. At the conclusion of the conference, the soft-spoken woman broached the issue of topic by first empathizing with Jill's problem. (Kamler, 1980, p. 681)

Readers are drawn in by the possibilities presented in this situation and will want to continue—to see how the teacher handled the problem, and how Jill found what she really had to say and share.

Provocative Questions

Judith A. Schickedanz and Maureen Sullivan (1984) started their article with a question in the title, "Mom, What Does U-F-F Spell?" and then used an anecdote about the question to begin their piece about early literacy development.

My first instinct [explained the child's mother] was to say that u-f-f did not spell anything. But I've learned that Cindy usually has a reason when she says or does something, so I decided to take a look. Sure enough, the top of one of the dials on the stove had been worn down so that the o in the word "off" now resembled a u. (Schickedanz & Sullivan, 1984, p. 7)

Schickedanz and Sullivan proceeded to discuss the question they had explored in a three-month study of literacy development in both the home and nursery school. They were particularly interested in how literacy events "actually kick into action, or what course they take once started" (p. 7). Their article's lead invited the reader to wonder about the significance of questions such as Cindy's in early literacy development.

Walter E. Sawyer (1978) began an article on writing with a title question: "How Do the Children Write? Ask Heidi Seibert." His opening paragraph set the stage:

> Educators seeking answers to the questions which continually plague them are often directed to several sources: university courses, professional books and journals, and fellow professionals. In seeking to learn more about the manner in which children go about the task of writing[,] another logical source of information is the young writer. Such a writer is Heidi Seibert, a fifth grade student at the Waterford-Halfmoon Elementary School in Waterford, New York. She has been a successful writer in the classroom and has contemplated a career in writing. (Sawyer, 1978, p. 816)

Sawyer was then ready to take the reader directly to the fifth-grade writer, to get some answers and learn what Heidi had to say. Sawyer has made a good case for going to the student to find out how young writers write.

Quotations

Dorothy Grant Hennings (1982) started each chapter of her language arts textbook with a quotation from either *Alice's Adventures in Wonderland* or *Through the Looking Glass.* The quotations set the tone for each chapter and for the entire book: exploring the wonderland of language.

Jennie Ingham (1982) began Chapter 1 in her book, *Books and Reading Development*, with a quotation about research:

> [R]esearch is always a venture into the unknown, there is no ultimate "should be."

Ingham proceeded to ask what the ingredients of reading success are, and concluded that there is no simple, straightforward answer. Again, the quotation she used set the tone for the book: there is no set outcome for research; it is an exploration to see what is there—in this case, what makes for reading success. The reader must be willing to explore with the writer and to receive with open mind whatever turns up.

Challenges

Joannis Kelly Flatley and Adele Ducharme Rutland (1986) presented a challenge at the beginning of their article on "Using Wordless Picture Books to Teach Linguistically/Culturally Different Students":

> Mobility of a population presents a challenge for the classroom teacher. Students speak many languages and dialects and represent many cultures and subcultures. The classroom teacher is expected to teach this diverse population to read and learn in standard English. How do classroom teachers provide reading instruction for limited and non-English speaking students . . . and those who speak nonstandard English dialects?

As the title implies, the authors took up this challenge in their article and offered at least a partial solution through the use of wordless picture books to stimulate language development.

To start his article, David M. Considine (1987) made this challenging statement:

> The American classroom has traditionally been a chalk-and-talk environment in which students passively listen to the verbal presentations of teachers.

Considine supported his statement by citing other writers on the subject. He then proceeded to address the challenge of an outdated system by discussing the importance of the new literacies—visual, computer, and media—and their place in the modern classroom. He concluded the article with a paragraph, starting:

> If today's classroom is to meet the challenge presented by the new literacies, our vision and self-image will have to change remarkably. A new, more holistic version of learning is needed, and central to that will be the recognition and realization that . . . there is more to read in our society than just print. (Considine, 1987, pp. 639–640)

Considine tied his opening paragraph and closing paragraph together, with a good "sandwich" of discussion in between. Using the challenge is an effective way to work out the unifying theme of an article.

Which Technique to Choose?

The question for writers looking for good beginnings now becomes one of choosing which kind to use: anecdote, question, quotation, challenge, or another idea. A helpful technique to use is freewriting, exploring to see what works. According to a report by Deborah Fox and Charles Suhor (1986), some writers may profit from the unblocking effects of freewriting. Actually, all writers can use freewriting to get "warmed up" to their subjects.

A look at Peter Elbow's definition can be a guide to understanding just how freewriting works. Elbow (1973) defines freewriting as "automatic writings," "babbling," or "jabbering" exercises.

> The idea is simply to write for ten minutes (later on, perhaps fifteen or twenty). Don't stop for anything. Go quickly without rushing. Never stop to look back, to cross something out, to wonder how to spell something, to wonder what word or thought to use, or to think about what you are doing. . . . The easiest thing is just to put down whatever is in your mind. (Elbow, 1973, p. 1)

Stimulating the flow of ideas by "letting go" and writing whatever comes to mind can, as Fox and Suhor say, unblock a writer's mind and give a beginning point. As the writer sifts through the freewriting, insight may come as to what kind of beginning to use.

If the beginning is still not readily apparent, even after freewriting, but the flow of writing is started, the writer may go on to do the entire first draft, and then discover an effective way to begin or to introduce the piece. In fact, for many writers the entire first draft may well be a freewriting activity.

An offshoot of freewriting that can be used when the writer has a preconceived notion of what is to be written is to try multiple beginnings or different kinds of openings, until one seems right. Also, after the first draft is completed, a writer may discover that some story or thought in the middle or toward the end would be better at the beginning.

Donald Graves (1983) suggests that in drafting, a writer may need to try a different perspective or point of view to get a broader understanding of what he or she is trying to say. Looking at one's ideas from different angles or perspectives will often trigger an idea for getting started.

Some helpful steps in drafting, according to Graves, include the following:

1. Jot down three or four topics that you know about and would like to explore further.
2. Choose one of these topics and brainstorm about it by rapidly writing down words and phrases that come to mind.
3. Begin to write "junk." Just write as fast as you can, without stopping or changing anything—almost in the manner of freewriting.

4. Put what you have written in perspective, writing what came before and just after.

5. Try writing from a different point of view, imagining how someone else perceives the topic.

6. Look over what you have and then begin to polish. Put the piece in the form you want.

At the sixth stage, when the writer begins again—after the first draft—to polish and get the piece ready for publication, he or she should ask, "Does the beginning live up to its promise when the piece is done? Does it all fit: the beginning, middle, and end?"

In answering these questions, the writer may need to begin again and again, but it is all worthwhile because if the beginning is not effective, the piece will probably die, that is, never see the light of publication. Good beginnings promise a lively, engrossing piece of writing.

In summary, to make a lively beginning, writers need to reach into their own experience, whether for an anecdote, question, or quotation they like, or a challenge they have found. Just as Jill had problems writing about topics she knew and cared little about, all authors have the same problem if they write without commitment or personal investment. The teacher told Jill: "It really is easier to write if you have a lot of information about a topic" (Kamler, 1980, p. 681). Together, the teacher and Jill explored some topics that Jill really knows. Choosing a good beginning for writing depends on the same kind of knowledge; it has to ring with authenticity.

"Bang! You are really alive," readers can say about authors who allow the authenticity of personal experience or strong belief to lead them into their writing.

References

Considine, D.M. (1987). Visual literacy and the curriculum: More to it than meets the eye. *Language Arts, 64,* 634–640.

Elbow, P. (1973). *Writing without teachers.* New York: Oxford University Press.

Flatley, J.K., & Rutland, A.D. (1986). Using wordless picture books to teach linguistically/culturally different students. *The Reading Teacher, 40,* 276–281.

Fox, D., & Suhor, C. (1986). Limitations of free writing. *English Journal, 75*(8), 34–36.

Graves, D.H. (1976). Let's get rid of the welfare mess in the teaching of writing. *Language Arts, 53,* 645–651.

Graves, D.H. (1983, May). Unpublished interview. Durham, NH.

Hennings, D.G. (1982). *Communication in action.* Boston: Houghton Mifflin.

Ingham, J. (1982). Why a book flood? In J. Ingham, *Books and reading development* (2nd ed.). Exeter, NH: Heinemann.

Kamler, B. (1980). One child, one teacher, one classroom: The story of one piece of writing. *Language Arts, 57,* 680–693.

Sawyer, W.E. (1978). How do the children write? Ask Heidi Seibert. *Language Arts, 55,* 816–820.

Schickedanz, J.A., & Sullivan, M. (1984). Mom, what does U-F-F spell? *Language Arts, 61,* 7–17.

22 Decisions Authors Make While Writing

Doris L. Prater
University of Houston at Clear Lake

Writing well is a complex and time-consuming task. Elbow (1981) reminds us that this task is made more complex because it calls on the two opposite skills of creativity and critical thinking. That is, both intuition and conscious control are used in producing the final product. In preparing a manuscript for publication, a writer has control over a number of key decisions that will directly affect the quality of writing and the likelihood of its being selected for publication. These decisions involve selection of topic, organizational scheme, audience, and voice of the piece of writing. These interdependent decisions are made as the writer drafts, shapes, and revises the article for submission to a journal. By thinking about the reader or audience, the writer clarifies purpose and topic and tries to visualize the audience.

To illustrate how each of these decisions influences the finished product, I will refer to one article published in *Language Arts* as I discuss these different decision points. The article, "Group Authorship in the Language Arts Classroom," was written by Juliana Yanushefski (1988), a classroom teacher at Port Richmond High School in Staten Island.

Decision 1: What Will the Article Be About?

Selecting a topic for an article often grows out of firsthand experiences in the classroom, wide reading and general interest in an area, specialized training, or concern about a particular issue or problem. Yanushefski's topic comes from her experience in a high school language arts class for students identified as deficient in reading and writing. Guided by current language arts theory, which proposes creating opportunities for students to communicate in meaningful contexts, she attempted to create an environment for learning literacy in her classroom. Her topic emerged from her desire to translate theory into practice and report a firsthand account of such an implementation.

Once the general topic has been selected, writers need to elaborate their thinking on the topic. In fact, Flower and Hayes (1984) divide the composing process into two complementary processes, generating and constructing. In the generating stage of an article, a variety of prewriting and thinking heuristics may be useful. Writers try to get down on paper all the ideas that might become part of an article. Developing fluency on the topic is essential, and such heuristics free up the writer and get the composing process under way. This bank of ideas can be drawn upon as the article is developed. The techniques explained below are frequently mentioned in the literature as being useful to writers in generating ideas.

Brainstorming is a technique that allows the mind to free-associate. Jot down any thoughts that come to mind about the topic. Do not edit. Sometimes the most random thought will lead to an interesting and unpredictable direction.

Clustering involves grouping the ideas and phrases you generated. This technique may be useful in imposing form on random thoughts.

Lists are the starting points for many writers. What are the key points you wish to make? It is easy to prioritize, subsume, and refine the list once it is made.

Journals are used by many successful writers as sources for topics and ideas. Murray (1985) suggests keeping what he calls a daybook. In it are recorded such things as observations of people and places, quotations from other writers, leads for writings, letters, and so on. In such a book, those marvelous ideas that come to us at odd hours can be noted and retrieved for later use.

Freewriting can be helpful in getting past a writer's initial block. Elbow (1973, 1981) suggests that writers force themselves to write without stopping for ten minutes. Frequent freewriting exercises help the writer "get on with it" and not edit ideas prematurely.

Reading, although not usually included in a list of prewriting heuristics, is a useful activity to get started on a topic. When writing as an authority on a topic, it is essential that you know what others in the field have to say on the subject. Even if you are writing a strictly personal reaction piece, reading can be good mental preparation for manipulating language to achieve the desired reaction or effect.

Proett and Gill (1986) describe in detail a number of useful prewriting activities in their book, *The Writing Process in Action*. Such activities help the writer move from thinking about writing to the act of writing.

Having generated a wealth of ideas, images, and phrases about the topic, a writer then begins to focus on the specific content that will be addressed. From a rich source of ideas and insights, the author starts to narrow the topic and give focus to the piece of writing. What aspect of the topic will be addressed? Notice that Yanushefski focuses on using a play-writing activity to actively involve high school students identified as deficient in literacy skills. The focus of the article becomes clear to the reader fairly early in the article. After an effective opening anecdote, Yanushefski sets up the focus of her article:

> Language arts classes at the high school level are generally designed with the express purpose of supplementing the regular English curriculum. The students in language arts programs are identified as having deficiencies in reading and writing. Traditionally, the methods employed in such classes have reflected a "reductionist" or "bottom up" theory. . . . An alternative approach to the high school language arts "lab" is one that views the language arts class as an enrichment program. . . . Such an approach is basically "constructivist" or based on "top down" theory. In this approach, the mastery of subskills is a by-product of the overall involvement in the reading and writing process. (1988, pp. 279–280)

Yanushefski is not going to address all the problems facing high school English teachers. She is going to describe an alternative method of addressing reading/writing skills deficits through involvement in a group dramatic project. The author has set the content parameters and focus for her topic. She has made the first major decision about her article.

Decision 2: How Will the Writing Be Organized?

After deciding upon a topic and determining focus for the writing, the author then moves from what Flower and Hayes (1984) term *generating* to *constructing*. You will need to organize content into related chunks and decide what gets included and what is left out. And, the overall form for the piece of writing will need to be determined.

In searching for a form for your content, think creatively. An examination of recent language arts and reading journals revealed a variety of formats: interviews, question-and-answer sessions, letters, how-to pieces with enumerated steps, examples of students' work with insightful commentaries by the teacher, and case studies. Sondra Perl (1984) suggests that writers first take the topic and attend to what it evokes in them; then, shape through language what is intended. This retrospective structuring of "what's on your mind" is followed by what Perl terms projective structuring, or the ability to craft intentions so that they are intelligible to others. Murray (1985) tells us to let the form find us. Indeed, the material to be presented often dictates the form.

A number of organizational patterns can be "tried on" the ideas. Perhaps the aim is to share a particular teaching activity that has been effective for a class or school. Readers likely will profit most from a step-by-step narration of how such an activity was conducted so that they might replicate it in their own classrooms. A chronological organizational plan might also fit this content. The time order involved might be a single class period or the course of a semester.

Suppose the aim is to make a case for a new approach to an old problem. For example, suppose the author wants to contend that the invented spellings that emerge through children's classroom writing activities should replace the traditional spelling program. A comparative organization plan might be considered. What are the advantages and disadvantages of each program? What are the similarities and differences?

A good organizational plan facilitates the reader's understanding. Since the writer is not present to clarify meaning, the author's intentions must be achieved by careful selection of the order in which ideas appear and the method for their presentation. Effective organization gives movement to the writing and keeps the reader engaged.

In our example article, Yanushefski effectively opens with an anecdote that gets our attention but is left unfinished. We are intrigued from the first line: "And the winner is." She then moves to a brief discussion of theory which strengthens her credibility with the reader. She carefully delineates components of "literary literacy": literacy through reading; literacy through writing; literacy through speaking, listening, and writing; literacy through related arts. Finally, Yanushefski returns to finish the anecdote. Notice how she repeats "And the winner is" in her last subhead. She has brought the reader full circle. The organization is most effective.

Decision 3: Who Is the Audience?

Nowhere is it more important to be aware of audience than when you write for journals. Who are the readers of the journal you have selected? What do they know, and what are they interested in reading about? Many journal manuscripts are rejected simply because they are inappropriate for the journal's readership. Yanushefski directed her article to *Language Arts* whose audience is described, in the directions to preparers of manuscripts for that journal, as teacher-educators and teachers of children in preschool through middle school years. When you look for an outlet for an article, read carefully the directions for style and manuscript preparation, and be sure to note the readership.

As a teacher and reader of journal articles as well as a potential writer, you need to consider what you want to read about and what types of writing you find effective. What compels you to read on once you begin an article? Kirby (1988) suggests that every piece of writing needs to be persuasive—you must persuade the reader to stay with the article and hear you out.

Decision 4: Who Is Speaking?

Is this a practitioner sharing a technique? Is the writer a bemused observer standing back and reflecting? Is this a teacher researcher both involved and detached? Ken Macrorie (1968) suggests that we sit and listen to ourselves speaking. Find an authentic voice as a writer that is appropriate for this writing occasion. Rehearse the piece orally. Talk through the article with a colleague or collaborator. Paper presentations are wonderful mechanisms for discovering voice. Does all this make sense? What tone is conveyed? Does a real voice come through?

Aim for a light touch, humor, or insight. Add your own personality and flair. Notice the voice Yanushefski establishes in our sample article:

> At this point in the project, an unexpected event occurred. Two of the groups found that they were without sufficient cast members to do their plays. . . . I assumed that each of the groups was a separate literary and social environment in competition with the other two groups. My assumption was wrong. (Yanushefski, 1988, p. 286)

The writer here is clearly an insider, but she is a learner in the process as well. The reader watches her discover the things she shares. Notice how the language provides movement in the article. The author is a real, authentic person writing as she would speak. Yanushefski also makes the article come alive by quoting the students in her class: "Let's write a comedy next time." "I don't know. Maybe I'll write a novel."

Work samples are frequently displayed within an article to further clarify or illustrate a key point. Such samples can warm up and make more interesting an otherwise pedantic piece of writing. The reader is drawn into the experience, rather than held at a distance. Kirby and Liner (1981) tell us that good writing is inventive. It says something new or it says something old in a new way.

In conclusion, writers need to make a variety of decisions as they write an article. First, the writer selects a topic. In some instances, this initial selection process requires focusing a general topic to a more manageable and specific topic. A useful metaphor in describing this process is to "picture" one's topic through a succession of progressively narrower lenses. In other instances, the writer begins with a narrow topic and may find some of the prewriting heuristics useful in fleshing out ideas and determining the focus. The second decision regarding how the article will be organized is particularly crucial for a journal article. With keen competition and space constraints in most journals, writing must be tightly organized. The organizational scheme should facilitate understanding of the topic and compel the reader to stay with the writer. Finally, correct decisions regarding audience and voice will determine if the article fits a particular journal because it speaks to its readership. And, if the piece of writing reflects an authentic, genuine perspective on an issue, it will more likely gain the attention and interest of reviewers. The four major decisions discussed in this chapter are not invariant in sequence and are highly interdependent. The harmonious interrelationship of these decisions can improve your writing and keep the reader engaged to the end of your article.

References

Elbow, P. (1973). *Writing without teachers*. New York: Oxford University Press.

Elbow, P. (1981). *Writing with power*. New York: Oxford University Press.

Flower, L.S., & Hayes, J.R. (1984). Problem-solving strategies and the writing process. In R.L. Graves (Ed.), *Rhetoric and composition* (pp. 269–282). Upper Montclair, NJ: Boynton/Cook.

Kirby, D. (1988, February). Remarks at the third annual writing conference of the Greater Houston Area Project.

Kirby, D., & Liner, T. (1981). *Inside out.* Upper Montclair, NJ: Boynton/Cook.

Macrorie, K. (1968). *Writing to be read.* New York: Hayden.

Murray, D.H. (1985). *A writer teaches writing* (2nd ed.). Boston: Houghton Mifflin.

Perl, S. (1984). Understanding composing. In R.L. Graves (Ed.), *Rhetoric and composition* (pp. 304–310). Upper Montclair, NJ: Boynton/Cook.

Proett, J., & Gill, K. (1986). *The writing process in action.* Urbana, IL: National Council of Teachers of English.

Yanushefski, J. (1988). Group authorship in the language arts classroom. *Language Arts, 65,* 279–287.

23 Distancing From and Revising Text

Lea M. McGee
Boston College

Gail E. Tompkins
California State University, Fresno

All experienced, published authors revise and revise again. One well-known children's author, Roald Dahl, claims he rereads and alters his stories at least 150 times. Authors hone the craft of revision because they know that with revision comes quality. Don Murray has argued that "rewriting is the difference between the dilettante and the artist, the amateur and the professional, the unpublished and the published" (1978, p. 85).

Revision Defined

While experienced writers agree on the need to revise, the term *revision* means different things to different writers and researchers. Revision can be simply defined as all changes made in a piece of writing. This definition focuses on the text, the words, sentences, and paragraphs that have been written. It may include major or minor changes, which may or may not alter meaning. This is a behavioral definition of revision, because it focuses on the writer's behavior or changes in the text.

Another definition of revision has evolved from research on cognitive problem-solving processes in writing. Nold (1982) viewed revision as the process authors use to revise or match the written text with their intentions. That is, prior to putting pen to paper, writers have an intended meaning (however vague or specific) that they intend to communicate to a specific audience. Revision occurs when authors check whether their actual written texts match their intended texts. Scardamalia and Bereiter (1983) similarly suggested that during composition, writers create two kinds of text. One text is the representation the writer has of the text as written. The second text is a representation of the text as intended. The intended text includes the whole text—the parts already written and the parts not yet written. Revision, then, is the process of comparing the actual text to the representation of the intended text.

There are several interesting implications of the cognitive problem-solving definition of revision. First, this definition implies that the quality of revision is dependent on the quality of the intended text. If little is planned or thought out prior to writing, then there is little to compare with the actual text. Second, this definition focuses on the writer's thinking rather than on the text or the writer's behavior. Revision begins when the author perceives a mismatch or difference between what has been written and what is intended. Writers might decide to alter the text by revising their writing, or writers might decide to alter their intentions. In this case, revision involves changing thoughts, not changing the actual text.

A third explanation of revision is what we call the three-text definition. Revision, according to this definition, is when writers manipulate three kinds of texts: intended text, actual text, and possible texts. Donald Murray (1978) argued that writing is a process of discovery. He claimed that authors write to discover what they have to say or hope to say. Revision, then, means evaluating what is actually written in light of what was intended, while at the same time remaining open to what could be written. This latter task, searching for possible texts, allows writers to discover what was forgotten, learn what is known, and see what could be. Robert Frost claimed, "For me the initial delight is in the surprise of remembering something I didn't know I knew . . . I have never started a poem yet whose end I knew. Writing a poem is discovering" (cited in Murray, 1978, p. 101).

As experienced writers read their first drafts, they begin to see their topics in a new light. They may discover a new or clearer subject about which to write. They may discover a new path, a new thought to follow to better make their intended point. Writers may get glimpses of more than one possible text, all of which need revising and pruning into shape.

This view of revision does not deny the importance of intended texts. Even when authors know what they will discover from their writing, they nonetheless begin their task with an intention, some idea of what they will write about. Yet it is the discovery of new ideas and new approaches within their writing that clearly draws many authors inward into new, possible texts.

Possible Texts Revealed

Many writers report that their published manuscripts began in quite different forms, with different purposes and voices. As they write and reread their early drafts, writers claim that they learn what it was they wanted to say all along.

One of us reported such an experience as she revised one chapter, "The Literature Connection: How One Teacher Puts Reading and Writing Together" (Tompkins, 1990). Gail began that chapter with the intention of telling teachers the components of a classroom program that combined reading and writing instruction through children's literature. She drafted a chapter that described what a classroom environment ought to include, how to plan a unit around an author or theme, steps in using writing process activities with literature, and activities for supporting responses to literature.

When Gail finished her draft, she laid it aside for a week. When she returned to it, she was struck by the *thou shalt* voice of her piece. She realized that she had produced a comprehensive list of things to do to create a reading-writing classroom, and had even provided a good description of how-to's. But her draft was not about real classrooms. The draft told teachers what to do, but it needed to show one classroom in action. Gail saw that classroom clearly in her mind: she could picture the teacher and the children as they read and wrote each day. She realized that behind her draft, hidden, was a real classroom. She needed to move the teacher, children, and classroom to the front of her piece.

Gail revised her chapter in the form of a teacher's diary, which included a description of each day's activities. All the description of a reading-writing, literature-based program included in Gail's early draft were still there in her revision. But now they were shown in light of a teacher's daily planning, organizing, and evaluating. Rather than tell about a literature-based classroom in action, her chapter showed one.

Finding Possible Texts

In order to find possible texts, such as Gail's revised chapter, writers must be able to distance and detach themselves from their writing. They must strive to read their texts as strangers, as critical and informed readers. Writers must stand back from their texts, detach themselves from their own pages, and examine their writing from different perspectives. Murray (1978) explained that writers need to learn to read their own work so they can differentiate what is actually written on the page from what they wished were there.

When writers are able to distance themselves from their writing, they can see their text with new eyes. They can both see their actual text in relation to their intended text and see beyond their actual text into possible texts. Once writers begin to see a possible text, they have a direction for revision. Revising means seeing alternatives in content, form, structure, voice, and language. Revising means being able to visualize potential choices about what might be said. Once writers can see potential texts, they begin to move about in them, making decisions about what could be added, deleted, changed, or moved (Faigley & Witte, 1984). Skilled, published writers work to perfect the activities of distancing, seeing, and shaping.

Distancing

There are many ways to distance from text. To begin, writers must get a first draft written. A first rough draft, or at least a significant portion of it, can be completed in one sitting. Beginning writers often have difficulty producing a first draft. They frequently feel that their writing is inadequate after writing only a few words, so they begin changing their writing immediately, searching for just the right word (Sommers, 1980). Skilled writers, on the other hand, keep plowing ahead even when they feel their writing is inadequate (Murray, 1985). Experienced writers do not become bogged down in significant revisions or changes as they are first drafting their ideas.

The best way to distance from text is to put time between the writing of the draft and the revising. The longer the time between them, the more distance a writer can achieve. Science-fiction writer Ray Bradbury supposedly puts each manuscript away for a year, and then a year to the day, gets it out and rereads it (cited in Murray, 1982). Most of us do not have that much time to devote to distancing, but distance can be achieved in a week or even a weekend. Inexperienced writers should allow as much time as possible between drafting and revising; they should begin revising when they feel refreshed and eager for a new challenge.

Another way to stand away from text is by putting physical distance between the author and the text. Authors who write upstairs might go downstairs to revise. An author might go into a different room, lie down, and think about something other than writing. A writer might drive to a mall and go shopping, or stare out a window and imagine being at a favorite vacation spot.

A third way to distance from text is to read it in a different form. Writers who compose with a word processor might read the text in printed form. A writer might read the text aloud into a tape recorder and then listen to the tape (Murray, 1985). Writers who draft in pencil or pen may spend some time typing their drafts. A crisp, clean copy makes even the worst writing look better.

Still another way to distance from text is to join a writers' group. A writers' group consists of three to six people who meet at regularly scheduled times to read and critique each other's writing. Members of the group read rough drafts, then comment on the meanings they see emerging and on the problems they had as readers of that text. Writers who are not ready to join a writers' group might find trusted friends to serve as readers. The best readers are friends who are able to share their thoughts, positive and negative, about compositions.

Finally, a last way to distance from text is to read the draft without pencil or pen in hand. A writer should read a draft all the way through, without stopping to correct a misspelling, insert a missing word, or rearrange a few sentences. This reading should be done quickly. A writer might role-play by reading the composition as a specific reader, such as an editor of the journal to which the article will be submitted.

Seeing

Once authors distance or detach from their writing, they begin looking at the text. Writers search for meanings that might emerge, meanings that have begun to emerge, and meanings that ought to emerge. They begin seeing their possible texts. As writers read, they consider whether they have provided enough information, if they have a clear and definite message, if their form works, and if their voice is strong (Murray, 1985).

Murray (1978) recommends three readings, which move the author closer and closer to the text. The first is a quick read for a single dominant meaning. The second reading is in chunks, to see if the main sections support the single dominant meaning and offer a coherent organization. The third reading is a slow one, line by line. All the while, the author searches for what works, what is successful, and what reaches out to a reader.

Sometimes a word or sentence sparks a meaning or suggests a possible text. Then the writer begins moving out from that word or sentence into larger and larger segments of text to shape meaning through rewriting.

Shaping

When writers see what could emerge or what needs to emerge in their writing, then shaping begins. Writers make decisions about moving, changing, adding, or deleting text. Faigley and Witte (1984) compared revising to remodeling a home. Some remodeling requires a little paint, some new carpet, and new wallpaper. Other remodeling requires tearing down load-bearing walls, raising the roof, and rearranging spaces. Only writers who see clearly what kind of remodeling needs to be done on their compositions will know how extensive the job will be.

In shaping, the focus is on content, on making changes that will make the meaning clearer for readers. Shaping involves some editing, some mechanical changes, but the majority of work is on producing clarity of thought and expression. After clarifying the text, then writers return to make spelling, capitalization, punctuation, and grammatical corrections.

Myths about Revision

Inexperienced writers sometimes cling to assumptions about what revising is and how one does it. Six common myths about revising can interfere with good writing.

Myth 1: Revision is just one stage in the writing process. To be able to talk about the process that writers use, theorists have labeled five discrete stages of the writing process, and revision is usually listed as the third stage, the step following drafting. Actually, writers revise throughout the writing process—from the moment an idea enters their heads until they print their final copies. The revising stage provides an opportunity for writers to examine how well their actual text matches their intended one, but it is wrong to assume that this is the only time or even the most important time for revising.

Myth 2: Revision is the same as editing. Revising, as it has been discussed in this chapter, focuses on creating and refining meaning. In contrast, the aim of editing (or proofreading), according to Frank Smith, is not to change the text, but to make what is there "optimally readable" (1982, p. 127). Revising and editing involve different activities for different purposes, even though they often occur simultaneously. As writers reread text to search for clearer meaning, a comma is added, a misspelling is corrected, or a grammatical error is noted. Through proofreading, writers identify mechanical errors to correct, but this is not the same as revising, in which writers search for ways to make the meaning clearer for their readers.

Myth 3: Good writers don't need to revise. Almost all authors revise their writing; in fact, revising is the essence of writing. Strunk and White explain that "few writers are so expert that they can produce what they are after on the first try" (1979, p. 72). Writers should think of revising not as punishment, but as a second chance, an opportunity to explore possible texts.

Myth 4: Writers cannot revise by themselves. Lucky writers have sympathetic and critical readers or supportive writing groups with whom to share their writing. When authors do not know anyone who will read and respond to their writing, they can feel very alone, and the task of writing can seem more difficult. Whether anyone is available to read your writing or not, you must be your own best reader. Writers must learn to distance and detach themselves so they can read their texts from a fresh perspective.

Myth 5: Writers can write and revise their manuscripts in a single day. Good writing takes time, and usually this means more than one day. Writers plan for writing and then over a period of days, weeks, and even months, they write, read their writing, and write again. Crafting a piece of writing takes time. Inexperienced writers often assume that they can write a ten- or fifteen-page article in a weekend or two, but experienced writers take two or three months to write, refine, and polish such an article. It is not the initial drafting of the manuscript that takes the time; it is the distancing and rewriting.

Myth 6: Editors revise for authors. Inexperienced writers sometimes submit a first or second draft of a manuscript to the editor of an educational journal, assuming that the editor will revise the text for the author. This is rarely the case. Editors assume that manuscripts submitted to them are ready (or nearly so) for publication, and their acceptance decisions are made with this assumption in mind. Sometimes editors request that an author make one or two very specific revisions, but usually a manuscript that has not been thoughtfully revised will not be accepted for publication. Sometimes editors suggest directions for revision in their letters of rejection, but it is rare for editors to encourage authors to revise and resubmit their articles. Because few editors have time to critique manuscripts without making publication decisions, authors need to revise their manuscripts before submitting them.

Revision, thus, is a two-step process. First, writers distance themselves from their writing so they can see their text as others might. Second, they shape and refine the content of their text. When writers revise, they compare their actual text to the text they intended to write and consider other possible texts they might write. Revising can be a frustrating part of writing for inexperienced writers, but it should not be thought of as a chore; instead, writers should view revising as an opportunity to explore possible texts.

References

Faigley, L., & Witte, S. (1984). Measuring the effects of revisions on text structure. In R. Beach & L. Bridwell (Eds.), *New directions in composition research* (pp. 95–108). New York: Guildford.

Murray, D.M. (1978). Internal revision: A process of discovery. In C.R. Cooper & L. Odell (Eds.), *Research on composing* (pp. 85–103). Urbana, IL: National Council of Teachers of English.

Murray, D.M. (1982). *Learning by teaching*. Montclair, NJ: Boynton/Cook.

Murray, D.M. (1985). *A writer teaches writing* (2nd ed.). Boston: Houghton Mifflin.

Nold, E. (1982). Revising. In C.H. Frederiksen & J.F. Dominic (Eds.), *Process, development, and communication* (pp. 67–79). Hillsdale, NJ: Erlbaum.

Scardamalia, M., & Bereiter, C. (1983). The development of evaluative, diagnostic, and remedial capabilities in children's composing. In M. Martley (Ed.), *The psychology of written language* (pp. 67–95). New York: John Wiley & Sons.

Smith, F. (1982). *Writing and the writer*. New York: Holt, Rinehart & Winston.

Sommers, N. (1980). Revision strategies of student writers and experienced writers. *College Composition and Communication, 31,* 378–388.

Strunk, W., Jr., & White, E.B. (1979). *The elements of style* (3rd ed.). New York: Macmillan.

Tompkins, G.E. (1990). The literature connection: How one teacher puts reading and writing together. In T. Shanahan (Ed.), *Reading and writing together* (pp. 201–223). Norwood, MA: Christopher-Gordon.

24 Revision: The Heart of Writing

Karen M. Feathers
Wayne State University, Detroit, Michigan

The rough draft is complete. At times it has been hard work to pull and tug words onto paper, while at other times the words flowed easily. The piece now needs revision. But doesn't revision mean changing, adding, even taking words out?

Once writers have struggled to express their ideas in print, they often have a tendency to hang on to every word, phrase, sentence. Elbow (1981) suggests that the hardest thing about revision is believing that your text can undergo major change and cutting and still say what you mean. Revision is, however, an integral part of the writing process. Murray says, "writing is rewriting" (1978, p. 85), and both Murray (1978) and Elbow (1981) consider revision the process by which meaning is truly delineated.

Three kinds of revision are described in this chapter. The first, author-initiated revision, occurs during composing or after writing the rough draft. The second is reader-initiated revision, and it occurs when other readers have responded to the draft with specific suggestions. And third, editor-initiated revisions are changes made in response to suggestions by the editor as potential publisher of the manuscript.

Author-Initiated Revisions

Most people are quite comfortable revising as they write, and do it almost automatically. They reread and make changes—trying new wordings, syntax, and text organization, or crossing out and inserting information as they compose. At some point, however, the initial draft is more or less complete and ready for more formal revision. This process should be viewed as an opportunity for re-vision—a chance to gain a new view of the piece by seeing it through different eyes (Murray, 1982). It is not simply a process of attempting to polish what has been said; instead, it is an ongoing construction of meaning. As Murray explains, "The writing stands apart from the writer and the writer interacts with it, first to find out what the writing has

to say and then to help the writing say it clearly and gracefully"
(1982, p. 5). In order to accomplish this "authorial reading," Rosenblatt
(1989) says that the author must read her or his own text "in the
light of others' needs" (p. 169). In other words, during rereading,
the author must keep the potential reader in mind.

Rereading the Draft

Once the author adopts a stance as a reader of his or her own text,
the question becomes, "What do I look for as I read?" Murray suggests
looking at both content and form (1982). Elbow (1981) proposes that
authors first get their readers and purpose clearly in mind, then find
the main point or center of gravity. Grice (1975) posits four things
to consider:

> Quality—Say what you believe is true and what you can support
> with evidence.
>
> Quantity—Be concise; say enough to make the message clear
> but not more than is required.
>
> Relation—Make the message relevant to your audience.
>
> Manner—Be clear, concise, and orderly; avoid trite expres-
> sions, ambiguity, and redundancy.

These maxims suggest additional questions for authors to ask themselves.

Does the piece say what I intend it to? Is the message clear, or
could organization, grammar, or wording cause confusion or mis-
understanding? Does everything fit together in a logical way? Read
to make sure that the manuscript accurately expresses your thoughts.
Check the organization of the text, making sure that each point is
comprehensible, that one point leads to another, and that connections between points are clear. Check to be sure that the beginning
paragraphs lead the reader into the text and set the context for the
remainder of the article. Make certain that any conclusions are clearly
related to the points made and that the summary ties the text together.

Is the piece focused? Is everything included that should be? Is
everything in the article related to the central focus, or should some
things be eliminated? Authors understand their own message so well
that they sometimes fail to include enough information to ensure
that the reader can construct meaning (Marder, 1982). The author
may use terminology unfamiliar to readers, present information without
explanation, infer connections that readers will not understand, or
assume background knowledge that readers do not have. Check that

the vocabulary is familiar to your audience. Make certain that points are not only stated but also explained. Use charts, diagrams, samples of students' work, and examples to provide clarification.

Is the article interesting? This question goes beyond the issue of an interesting topic. Even a seemingly boring topic can make fascinating reading if it is presented in an interesting way. The issue is not the topic itself, but the presentation. Is the reader's interest aroused in the first few paragraphs and maintained throughout the piece? Some authors write several beginning paragraphs, each time trying to catch the interest of the reader in a different way. Then they read each lead to determine which one works best within the context of the article. A similar procedure can be used with titles, paragraphs within the text, summaries, or concluding paragraphs.

Wording and grammatical choices should also be checked at this time. Is there variety in sentence structure, or do all sentences sound alike? Variety in the types of sentences used will help maintain a reader's interest. Also look carefully at the wording, watching for redundancy and for trite or overused words or phrases.

Revising the Text

Basically, four things can be done to revise a text. First, additions can be made. These changes occur most often if the text is not clear or if a more detailed explanation or additional examples are needed. A single word, whole sentences, even paragraphs or sections can be added. For example, Figure 1 contains several versions of the first paragraph of a text that I coauthored with a teacher who was a graduate student (Clem & Feathers, 1986). Christina drafted the initial piece, and then she and I worked together on the article until its completion.

When Christina and I read the initial draft of the "spider" paper, we decided that the beginning paragraph (1A) didn't tell anything about the context in which Joshua's piece had been written. Yet description of the context was important. We added information (1B) to clarify our message and establish the context for the remainder of the text.

Second, information can be deleted from a draft. At a text level, deletion generally eliminates irrelevant or marginally related information. On a sentence level, deletion is used to streamline sentences so the message is expressed clearly and concisely. In this same example (1A), we had included a conventionally spelled version of Joshua's written message. We decided that most people could understand what Joshua was writing without a translation, so we deleted that information from the revised paragraph (1B).

First draft (1A)

Joshua, age five, writes on a piece of paper:
I LIC SPIDRS CS' SPIDRCR GUD
(I like spiders cause spiders are good).

Second version (1B)

Joshua, age five, writes something on a piece of paper. Later his mother picks up the paper along with many others like it Joshua has left lying around the house. On the paper it says:
I LIC SPIDRS CS' SPIDRCR GUD

Third version (1C)

Joshua is five years old. One day last fall he wrote something on a piece of paper which his mother later found lying on the floor. It said:
I LIC SPIDRS CS' SPIDRCR GUD

Final version (1D)

Joshua is five years old. One day last fall he wrote something on a piece of paper which his mother later found lying on the floor. It said:
I LIC SPIDRS CS' SPIDRCR GUD

Figure 1 First paragraph

Third, substitution can be used to achieve clarity and to rectify redundant or uninteresting wording. New words, phrases, sentences, or paragraphs are substituted for those that are not effective. In the example in Figure 2, an entirely new paragraph (2B) was substituted for the original ending of the article (2A) in order to achieve a different tone—one that was more instructionally oriented instead of research-oriented.

Finally, material within the text may be rearranged. This usually is done to strengthen the focus or provide a more logical flow of information. In Figure 3, the final sentence in our second version of the second paragraph (3B) was moved to the beginning of the first paragraph (3C).

While each of these types of revision have been discussed as if they occur separately, revision often involves a combination of these strategies. For example, Figure 3 shows that in our original draft (3A), the events were told more or less as they occurred, and then were contrasted. As we reconsidered the draft, we didn't like some of the sentences and words used, and we felt that the contrast we wanted to make between the two activities wasn't clear. Our solution was a combination of:

Third version (2A)

　　While further research is needed to explore the way in which children relate the learning of language and content, we find that Joshua has given us valuable insights into this process. As a result of being allowed to make sense of his world in a natural way, Joshua is developing a positive attitude regarding the learning of content and using language to do so. It is this that enables him to write.

Final version (2B)

　　Learning is what the brain does naturally, continually; that is, learning is an extension of a child's everyday experiences. We wish to emphasize that the notion of natural, continual learning is applicable to content as well as to language, and that these two kinds of learning occur simultaneously, reinforcing each other in an environment where the opportunity is made available for the child to freely explore these concepts at will.

Figure 2 Final paragraph

　　deleting to eliminate redundancy,

　　rearranging the information as explained earlier, and

　　rewording the sentences by using addition, deletion, and substitution.

　　The second version (3B) is approximately the same length as the first, and it integrates the contrast between the two activities into two paragraphs instead of presenting it separately (as in 3A). This second version also emphasizes that the second activity was initiated by Joshua, something the first draft did not do. The third and final revision of this section (3C) again moved information from the end of the second paragraph to the beginning of the first paragraph, where it had initially been located.

Reader-Initiated Revisions

"To understand himself, man needs to be understood by another" (Hora, 1959, p. 237). "In learning to use language the only kind of feedback available to us is human response" (Moffett, 1968, pp. 188–189). In these statements, both Hora and Moffett emphasize the importance of feedback from others. Feedback provides a new perspective through which to view the text. It also indicates how successfully an outside reader is receiving the author's intended message.

　　During reader-initiated revision, the author gives the text to other readers and uses their feedback as a basis for revision. One reader who is familiar with the topic might be asked to read for

First draft (3A)

Some structured activities were attempted with Joshua; however, these activities were abandoned because they did not evolve into positive learning experiences. For example, an attempt was made to have Joshua dictate a story about spiders, but he was reluctant to engage in this activity. This dictated story did not contain all the information Joshua had revealed in informal discussions; moreover, it was brief and in rather stilted language.

In a second instance, prompted by a newspaper article on pumpkins, Joshua eagerly began talking about how to roast pumpkin seeds. Paper and pencil were quickly produced to record what he was saying. This time, writing down what Joshua was saying was interpreted as a normal part of the activity—a means of remembering the recipe for roasting pumpkin seeds.

The spider dictation may have been unsuccessful because it was an externally imposed task rather than something generated by Joshua himself. Thus, it may have appeared contrived and artificial. On the other hand, the recipe dictation was purposeful and a natural part of the ongoing activity; and therefore, Joshua willingly took part.

Second version (3B)

In addition to taking advantage of natural, informal moments to gain some insight into Joshua's learning, we also thought we would try to monitor his learning by involving him in some structured activities. For example, an attempt was made to have Joshua dictate a story about spiders, but he was reluctant to engage in this activity, and the resulting dictated story did not contain all the information Joshua had revealed in informal discussions. Moreover, it was brief and in rather stilted language.

On the other hand, some dictations were initiated by Joshua. For example, prompted by a newspaper article on pumpkins, Joshua eagerly began talking about how to roast pumpkin seeds. Paper and pencil were quickly produced to record what he was saying. This time, Joshua seemed to interpret the writing as a normal part of the activity—a means of remembering the recipe for roasting pumpkin seeds, instead of something imposed on the activity from the outside, and he continued willingly with the dictation. Since the structured activities did not evolve into positive learning experiences, they were abandoned in favor of the more naturalistic activities Joshua engaged in on his own.

Third and final version (3C)

Some structured activities were attempted with Joshua; however, these were abandoned because they did not evolve into positive learning experiences. For example, an attempt was made to have Joshua dictate a story about spiders, but he was reluctant to engage in this activity, and the resulting dictated story did not contain all the information Joshua had revealed in informal discussions. Moreover, it was brief and in rather stilted language.

On the other hand, some dictations were initiated by Joshua, and these were included in the study. For example, prompted by a newspaper article on pumpkins, Joshua eagerly began talking about how to roast pumpkin seeds. Paper and pencil were quickly produced to record what he was saying. This time, Joshua seemed to interpret the writing as a normal part of the activity—a means of remembering the recipe for roasting pumpkin seeds and continued willingly with the dictation.

Figure 3 Internal paragraphs

organization, logic, clarity, coherence, and completeness. Another who is familiar with conventions of language, such as grammar and punctuation and spelling, might read to locate problems in these areas. Setting a specific purpose allows readers to focus on one thing as they read, and it allows the author to take advantage of the particular strengths of each reader.

Outside readers need to know where you hope to publish the paper. Because preferred topics and styles of writing vary depending on the publication, readers must know your intended audience so they know how to evaluate the text.

Giving your text to others to read is important, but it can engender negative feelings. It is not unusual to feel nervous, awkward, or even threatened by the prospect of having someone critically read your paper. Remember that whatever the comments from other readers, you as author are in control of the text.

Christina and I gave the spider paper to several people to read, and we received many suggestions. Some we considered and decided not to follow, while others resulted in changes in the text. For example, one reader suggested that we eliminate the example at the beginning of the paper and replace it with a paragraph discussing recent research. Given our intended audience (teachers) and our intended message, we rejected that suggestion.

A second reader, after considering the intended journal for our piece, suggested that we take out the formality, stop focusing on the research aspect, and make the article "more of a story." After the first paragraph, he wrote, "I want more information, NOW!!!" Later, he said, "Tell me more about Joshua's learning and his writing—grab the 'story' side of me." He crossed out the words *study* and *research* wherever they occurred, and asked questions such as: "So what???" "What do you conclude from this?" "Is this relevant? Now I'm wondering what the topic is." Some people might consider these comments blunt and suggest that the reader could have been more tactful or more considerate of our feelings; actually, though, these comments were valuable because they helped us understand how someone else viewed the piece. The comments were also helpful because the reader suggested how the paper needed to be improved.

The first paragraph of our article was changed to make it sound more like a story, resulting in the beginning shown (1C) in Figure 1. The second paragraph of the paper, which had not been changed until this time, also was revised (Figure 4) to better tie it to the example of Joshua's writing and to continue the "story" style.

First, second, and third versions (4A)

This brief text reflects in capsule form both Joshua's learning about spiders and his feelings about spiders developed in the course of studying this topic.

Final version (4B)

This brief text is only one of the many pieces of writing that Joshua produced as he explored the topic of spiders. Like the others, it reflects in capsule form both Joshua's learning about spiders and his feelings about spiders developed over time as he explored this topic.

Figure 4 Second paragraph

A paragraph on current research was eliminated for the same reason, and other references to research were either deleted or reworded. The third paragraph of the article (Figure 5) which, because of its wording, reminded the reader that this was a research project, was revised to fit the "story-telling" style and to delete "research sounding" language. The objective research style (5A) was altered by simply presenting the information using personal pronouns and active voice (5B).

Editor-Initiated Revisions

A third cycle of revision may occur if the article has been submitted to a journal and then returned. The piece may be accepted, but the editor may require changes. In that case, simply make the necessary revisions or discuss them with the editor. On the other hand, the article may be rejected, in which case it might be returned with comments from the reviewers or the editor. Don't be disheartened by a rejected manuscript. Instead, view the suggestions and criticisms as data about revision. The spider paper was rejected initially: reviewers indicated that it was too long, wandered off track, and seemed to have more than one message. Christina and I considered the piece from the editor's perspective and began our third cycle of revision.

The initial paragraph was revised to save space, and Joshua's text was incorporated into the body of the article (1D). Additionally, the original article contained a three-page section discussing the conventions of writing exhibited in Joshua's various writing samples. This section detracted from our major emphasis and was deleted. Another section describing what we had learned was too lengthy. Everything except the core concept was eliminated, thus reducing the section from two pages to a single paragraph.

Third version (5A)

The young child's investigation of the functions of written language is part of his investigation of the world around him. This raises questions about the relationship between children's exploration of their print world and their exploration of the world as information.

In order to investigate this aspect of early literacy, we studied Joshua as he freely explored language and information in the natural setting of his home. To keep the setting as natural as possible, one participant observer was used (his mother) to observe Joshua and to collect the data.

Final version (5B)

We decided to take advantage of Joshua's interest in spiders to see what we might discover about the relationship between children's investigations of the world as information (content) and their use of language to do so. We set out to do some "kid watching": to observe Joshua as he freely explored language and information in the natural setting of his home. Because one of the observers was his mother, it was quite simple and natural to collect samples of Joshua's writings and drawings as well as to expose him to additional information about spiders.

Figure 5 Third paragraph

It was at this point that we changed the final paragraph (Figure 2). The first ending (2A) sounded like the end to a research article. The text was revised to put greater emphasis on the natural and simultaneous learning of content and language (2B).

Our experience taught us that rejection of an article should not be viewed as a final decision, but as an opportunity to further improve the piece. Many published articles were initially rejected, and even well-known authors have their manuscripts rejected. On the other hand, editors' suggestions must not be followed blindly. Another article that I coauthored described an instructional technique and was submitted to a journal whose title included the words *instruction* and *research.* The article was rejected because "it included no research data." In this instance, the article needed to be submitted to a different journal, one more receptive to instructional methods.

Summary

Writing is not so much the translation of thoughts into print as it is the creation of thoughts in print. Similarly, revision is not so much a process of refining, shaping, and polishing as it is a process of taking a new look at our ideas and coming to new conclusions. While we have ideas that are the basis for any piece, it is through revision—through looking anew at our piece—that we discover exactly what it is we want to say and the best way to say it. In the final analysis, revision is the heart of writing.

References

Clem, C., & Feathers, K.M. (1986). I LIC SPIDRS: What one child teaches us about content learning. *Language Arts, 63,* 143–147.

Elbow, P. (1981). *Writing with power.* New York: Oxford University Press.

Grice, P. (1975). Logic and conversation. In P. Cole & J.L. Morgan (Eds.), *Syntax and semantics: Speech acts, Vol. 3* (pp. 45–46). New York: Academic Press.

Hora, T. (1959). Tao, zen and existential psychotherapy. *Psychologia, 2,* 237.

Marder, D. (1982). Revision as discovery and the reduction of entropy. In R.A. Sudol (Ed.), *Revising* (pp. 3–12). Urbana, IL: ERIC Clearinghouse on Reading and Communication Skills and the National Council of Teachers of English.

Moffett, J. (1968). *Teaching the universe of discourse.* Boston: Houghton Mifflin.

Murray, D. (1978). Internal revision: A process of discovery. In C.R. Cooper & L. Odell (Eds.), *Research in composing* (pp. 85–103). Urbana, IL: National Council of Teachers of English.

Murray, D. (1982). *Learning by teaching.* Upper Montclair, NJ: Boynton/Cook.

Rosenblatt, L. (1989). Writing and reading: The transactional theory. In J.M. Mason (Ed.), *Reading and writing connections* (pp. 153–176). Boston: Allyn & Bacon.

25 Rejection: Who Needs It?

Alice K. Swinger
Wright State University, Dayton, Ohio

My writer friends know about rejection. When I wrote asking personal questions about it, responses from across the country streamed in. Gena, Jerry, Jane, Gail, Eileen, Luke, and Marilee told of triumph and trauma. They shared wisdom distilled from years of work. Most of these writers are educators; some write fiction and poetry as well as academic articles and books. Some love it, some don't.

You'll see both patterns and contradictions as they talk about rejection of their work. Chances are, you'll even see contradictions within individuals. I hope so, for ambiguity is part of writing. In their words you'll see struggle for voice, search for truth, and acceptance of marketing realities. That is writing reality. You'll see perseverance. I hope you'll feel perseverance, too, for that will mean you have realized that acceptance of rejection will help you keep writing.

Marilee (Ohio): There's a letter on my desk that's been there for a month or more. Alice wants to know how I handled rejection. She's referring to rejection slips from publishers, yet rejection is rejection. I know, I'm 'spozed to be objective—see the clean lines of demarcation. Hogwash. The mind can try to fool the heart, but the heart knows. It's made of tough stuff, can withstand healthy doses of rejection.

I've not responded to Alice before now because I'm not sure I have truly learned much about responding to rejection. I've not tested myself much lately. Years ago, I vowed to wallpaper my den with the slips: fat, slim, pink, white, printed, scrawled—all some kind of testimony that I did at least write. I also lined up second, third, and fourth markets, though I honestly didn't have the heart to line up twenty-six. After a hundred or so slips, I decided there would be merit in not sending anything out until I vastly improved as a poet and a storyteller. Call those my Moratorium Years.

Then after a few changes, I won some contests, went to more workshops, read a wider market, and finally decided I wasn't going to get too much better. Every day I could read an article in any given magazine that was ten times more boring, ten times wordier, or ten times sleazier than mine. Time to try again. More slips.

Thanks, Marilee. You've set the stage for us. You've said very well what most of us probably feel. Let's hear how others respond to the questions.

How Do You Handle Rejection of Your Manuscripts?

Eileen (Ohio): When I spot the self-addressed, stamped envelope in my mailbox and know that the whole thing, not an acceptance letter, has come back, first the bottom of my stomach drops: I get that sinking feeling like a punch in the stomach if I have invested a lot of myself in the piece.

Jerry (Massachusetts): I'd like to respond to your question, Alice, but succinctly put, I avoid these issues by not writing. I'm in a college that does not support writing and research. There is little or no emphasis on publishing until promotion time. I'm a full professor, and we do not have tenure—so, no writing and no rejection.

Jane (New York): Very lightly. That is, I submit the manuscript to another journal. If two comparable journals reject the manuscript, I revise it if I have the time. If I don't have time, I submit it to ERIC. Due to my schedule, I am sometimes unable to submit the papers they invite, and since my manuscripts are always based on a presentation I have made somewhere, this gives me a good opportunity to show my appreciation to ERIC for their invitations.

Gena (Michigan): I don't think I handle rejection particularly well. I tend to believe everything anyone tells me: when they say something is bad, I believe them. If they say it's good, I believe that, too. If I am ever famous, I'll probably be insufferable. Lately, I've received many near misses. Editors are interested and want to see other things I've written, but ultimately they reject my stuff anyway. This is harder to take than form rejections. All the books say that this is a wonderful sign, but I've been in a blue funk over it. Fortunately, I love the process of writing, and this hasn't affected my output too much. Now for specifics:

1. I keep several projects out so I have acceptance to look forward to, not just one project that gets rejected again and again.

2. If it's a form rejection, I read it once and file it. I put the name of the story and the date it was returned on the form and

put it in the envelope that holds everything about that project. If it is a personal note, I read it quickly, then put it aside and read it later more slowly, giving attention to every word.

3. I sulk for a week. I tell no one and refuse even to discuss writing. Later, in a more detached frame of mind, I reread pertinent comments. If they make sense, I consider rewriting based on them.

Gail (California): Like everyone else, I begin with feelings of disappointment and failure. Rejection hurts. To assuage my ego, I tell myself the reviewers can't recognize a good manuscript when they see one. Then, after a week or so, I decide to do something. I reread the reviews (if any) to see if I can improve the manuscript. If I have not received reviews, I reread the manuscript critically and try to do something to improve it. Then I choose another journal to submit the paper to. I write my papers with more than one journal in mind—in fact, I write the names of three journals on the inside cover of the file folder for that paper. I move to the second or third journal on the list; make editorial changes so that the paper conforms to the writer's guidelines of the new target journal. I send it off again, complete with cover letter and SASE. I think it's important to try again, not to accept defeat. Everybody gets rejections; however, dealing with them gets easier after a few acceptances.

Luke (New Mexico): Last week I had two—TWO!—rejections on the same day. One was the return of a long shot I had taken. I know that magazine has an acceptance rate of one manuscript for every 2,000 submissions. I thought, "Oh, fooey" (or something like that). But I also had two important thoughts: "Now what can I do to have it accepted somewhere else?" and "Where is that somewhere else?" This piece is a new genre—fiction—for me; therefore, I know I must try harder. The other piece had already been rejected and revised more than once. It is written in an unusual style. Not everyone will want it, but whoever takes it will be glad to have it. Rejection is a risk I have to take if I want to try new arenas. I immediately— within fifteen minutes, before I had time to give myself any negative points—took the second piece to a colleague who is an expert on the topic of the manuscript. "Will you read this and tell me who might publish it? Or if you can spot weakness, tell me." With his detached point of view, I'll have new information to help me look at my piece with fresh eyes.

Marilee: When a former friend—far more than a mere friend— just happened to leave his copy of one of my books in the camping gear he had borrowed, I promptly took the manuscripts I was working on and dumped them in the trash with the same energy Lillian Hellman mustered when she threw her typewriter out the window in a fit of despair. It was months before I even considered going back to the typewriter.

It's not that I doubted just whether I should write or not. I doubted whether I should drive, iron, trade cars, or change toothpastes. Even *Honorable Mentions* read like grim reviews. I was at the mercy of old humiliations: standing on the stage in the fifth grade, unable to get a note out of my trumpet; wearing an Indian headband on the school bus and enduring the senior boys shouting war hoops around me, the skinny first grader in the feedsack dress; wrecking the tractor at thirteen and running away from my father's harsh wrath; or even worse, writing a sophomoric theme my freshman year at Ohio State and having to read the professor's red scrawl, "Too sentimental." None of us exactly craves to be laughingly foolish.

All writers don't admit to moments of despair and frustration, as Marilee has. Other respondents offered milder answers to the question, **What do you do with the emotions generated by the rejection?** Eileen writes that she gets on with her life. She thinks writers should begin the next piece when the present one is mailed. She keeps several pieces in progress, so that "if one is on hold, it's not disaster day." Another respondent, knowing that comparable outlets are available, claims not to experience much emotion from rejection. She is angered, however, by "wobbly" explanations or when no reasons are given; journal editors, she thinks, have an obligation to respond to prospective writers. Others drain off emotion by playing—escape reading, horseback riding, cooking, running, canoeing—for a few days. They acknowledge that the disappointment exists, but they know it will pass. Then they go back to the returned manuscript for fresh insights.

What Do You Do with the Manuscript Itself When It Comes Back?

Gail: I find a quiet time to read the rejection letter and the reviews. If I have a busy schedule ahead, I postpone reading the letter and reviews so that they won't ruin my day. When I finally open the letter, I read it quickly just to get the gist of it. I think what I do can be compared to easing oneself into cold water at the swimming pool. Many people jump right in, but I always ease myself in, inch by inch, to adjust to the temperature of the water.

To the question, **What do you do after the initial emotional and physical reactions subside,** most writers say they reread their manuscripts with a constructive point of view. They look for ways to strengthen the work, to make changes, or to adapt it for different journals.

For example, Luke says that when he sees a returned manuscript, he knows his work on that piece isn't finished. "I take risks," he writes, "with style, audience, and topics. I expect some returns. Yet I know that when I write regularly I get fewer rejects, and more acceptances, even if I have ventured into new arenas."

Do these writers plan for the rejection contingency before they mail their manuscripts? Some say they submit articles only to journals they know will accept their work. Others say they make lists and select second-, third-, or even fifth-choice markets. One writer starts with the most prestigious and most appropriate journal and lines up the other choices after that. Another writer has a very detailed plan of action:

Gail: I am aware that many national journals have an 80 to 90% rejection rate, so I know that I have a sizable chance of rejection. However, if I never submit the manuscript, it will never be published. I plan enough time to get the manuscript ready for publication before I send it. I do these things to help ensure my piece will be published:

1. I allow three months to write the paper.

2. I follow the format and guidelines of the journal that I plan to submit the paper to.

3. I have two to three persons read the paper and give critical feedback and suggestions for revision.

4. I let the paper sit after I finish it, and then reread it with a critical eye.

5. I try to show, not tell, when I write. I like to use examples and anecdotes.

How Many of Your Once-Rejected Manuscripts Have Been Published?

Jane: All of them have been published; some with, some without, revision.

Gena: Very few of my ultimately published pieces have not been rejected at least once. I'm poor at targeting markets. Also, in my early writing I revised between rejections. This may have been useful then, but I don't do it anymore.

Gail: That's a hard question for me. I'm not sure. I would guess that about half of them have been published or are now out for review. When I make a plan and follow through, they usually are accepted. It's when I let them sit for a year on my desk that they don't ever get published. Timeliness is important.

Luke: Lots of them [have been published], even some which should be entombed forever in my bottom drawer. Some are still waiting—maybe they are ahead of their time. Some I have cannibalized: the ideas have gone out in other forms. I'm working now on a five-year-old manuscript. I've learned a lot from it. Even if it never smells printer's ink, it will have been worth the time I gave to it.

Marilee: So why do I respond to Alice now? Because I find that none of it matters. Oh, I've not gone through some peak experience at an Esalen workshop or been converted by the preacher in some gospel tent. I just woke up to the way we give our power away: the way we count as wise and true the words of others over our own. This summer I sent out twenty-two manuscripts. None have been accepted—ergo, rejection, right? Wrong. Right words—wrong market, wrong time. Right style and voice—wrong reader. Disappointment, yes. Self-destructive thoughts, no. Midday trip to the dumpster—never again.

What Have You Learned about Rejection?

Jane: I discovered that I have never had a manuscript rejected that wasn't submitted too hurriedly. The manuscripts I prepared carefully were accepted on the first submission. Some time ago, I submitted a manuscript and knew that it was written hurriedly. It was rejected. Apparently, though, the editor remembered it and, much later, wrote to ask me to revise and resubmit the manuscript. It was more luck than I deserved.

Gena: I've learned absolutely nothing about the art of writing from my rejections. I have, however, learned that editors can be as capricious and pigheaded as other humans. Luck, timing, and other intangibles are at work in the process, and it's important to do the best you can at marketing and then forget it. Editors say they want well-written pieces, and to some extent that's true; but they also want something that appeals to their own tastes, prejudices, preconceptions, readership, and space requirements. It's a tall order.

Gail: I've learned that everyone gets rejections. Also that just because one journal doesn't want my article doesn't mean that it's not good. I have to find the right home for it, and if I work at it, I can.

The voices you've heard are writers who have learned that putting ideas on paper, organizing and shaping them, is part of a larger process. Another part of the process is selecting journals to publish the ideas and communicating effectively with the editors of those journals.

That's the story, simply put. But there's more to it than that. Beyond knowing how writing and publishing work, these writers seem to have experienced phases in their understanding of editor's rejection letters.

In early phases of their writing careers, they dread returned manuscripts and feel that their writing abilities are affirmed or denied by them. Later, some learn to cope with the symbols of rejection and turn them into learning tools. Some writers become cautious and select only sure markets, while others develop strong working habits and contingency plans. Some voices hint at real love and respect for the challenges of writing well. Finally they seek the joys from the process and product of writing and accept the discipline and disappointment it takes to keep it in their lives.

Who needs rejection? Some writers of some manuscripts need it some times. No one needs it all the time. Rejection is more acceptable if it is interspersed with acceptance.

VI Teacher Writer Communities

26 Writing Communities: One Historical Perspective

Mary K. Healy
Puente Project, University of California

From my earliest days as a teacher, I have been involved in writing communities. These communities have varied from the public school and university classrooms in which I taught to the Bay Area Writing Project Institute community of English teachers and Mexican American counselors and mentors. What these communities have had in common for me was the transforming nature of the experience of writing and sharing work together, and the pleasure we took in each other's writing development over time. To participate in these communities involved a large measure of risk taking, prodigious amounts of hard work, and a capacity for sustained attention to the work of others. The rewards for such commitment, however, were generous: a more comprehensive sense of the possibilities of my own writing, an increased sense of what works and what doesn't in the writing of others, a growing ability to trust others and share my own work-in-progress, and a deep sense of satisfaction about the accomplishments of everyone in the group.

To illustrate how participation in writing communities affects how writing is taught, I will focus in particular on three of the different writing communities whose evolution I have been part of: the Writing Project summer institute for teachers, a graduate school's teaching-credential program for prospective English teachers, and the Puente Project institute for teachers and counselors of Mexican American/Latino community college students. Through these descriptions, I will show the power of sustained writing in an ongoing community to aid and illuminate teaching and learning.

The Bay Area Writing Project

In the summer of 1974, James Gray, a supervisor of teacher education in Berkeley's School of Education; Cap Lavin, a high school

English teacher who was also director of curriculum in the nearby Tamalpais Union High School District; and Bill Brandt, a professor in Berkeley's rhetoric department, invited me and twenty-four other experienced teachers of writing at levels from junior high through university to attend a "University of California Summer Institute on the Teaching of Writing." Through a yearlong series of meetings, these three had designed this institute to give successful teachers of writing an extended opportunity to demonstrate their teaching approaches and to write together. The schedule they set was ambitious. We would meet Monday through Friday, 9 a.m.–4 p.m., for five weeks.

None of us gathering in Berkeley's summer fog could have predicted that the model which would become known as the Bay Area Writing Project, and eventually the National Writing Project, would evolve from our summer endeavors. All I realized at the time was that I was sitting in a room full of some of the most formidable teacher leaders in the nine San Francisco Bay Area counties. Over half were English department chairs; most had published articles or books on the teaching of English. All were opinionated. And on the first day of this institute, we were becoming more apprehensive by the minute: we had learned that we were going to be steadily writing over the next five weeks and sharing that writing in small writing groups (see Appendix at the end of this chapter for the 1974 Institute assignments).

Our writing began as a genuine exploration—to discover as much as we could about what it meant to write in a range of genres and forms. We wrote all the time, during the two daily teaching demonstrations given by members of the group and then again at home in preparation for the weekly meetings of our small writing groups. Because of the exploratory nature of our task, we attempted to write in ways few of us had in any of our previous schooling. We did a lot of freewriting, consciously holding ourselves back from early editing. We slowly learned to trust how meaning emerged through drafts and response, and we stopped expecting to write polished pieces on the first attempt. We learned the power of our developing sense of audience and how that helped shape what we were writing. We began to write with our writing group in mind, supplying what we thought its members would need. This, in turn, helped to make our writing more focused and explicit.

From this sustained experience, we relearned how to teach writing from the inside out—testing the methods which our colleagues demonstrated against our own immediate responses as writers. Sitting in the institute classroom, we developed more empathy for our students as writers. We experienced, perhaps for the first time, the full complexity of the act of writing. We became intensely aware of the power of the context the teachers in our group created when they taught their demonstration lessons, and how this context affected what we were able to write in response to their assignments. From these experiences we learned to set more realistic and inviting assignments within a larger, more accepting framework of development.

The work in our writing groups taught us to respond more tactfully and sensitively to our students' drafts, and to appreciate in new ways our pupils' achievements, no matter how minimal. Because the groups stayed together throughout the institute, their members grew close, trust developed, and the writing became increasingly honest and genuine. Risks could be taken and were allowed to develop, with sufficient time for response, reflection, and revision.

As one summer participant put it:

> I have re-discovered the sweet agony of writing. As a teacher of composition, I had almost forgotten the beauty of discovery through writing. Except [for] the few times I read to my students, I was too busy becoming an expert in editing my students' papers.
>
> When I had to write for other English teachers this summer, I was terrified. I had thought of every excuse possible including the fact I had worked all school year and was mentally exhausted. As I painfully approached the writing task of points of view, Josephine Miles' theory that writing is not a "once thing" but an art that is perfected by continuous work prompts me on.
>
> I have concluded that teachers of English . . . must write more. I am convinced that if we write more, our assignments would take on new dimensions and perhaps help rescue many of our students.

Very quickly during that intense summer we learned the power of modeling writing behaviors for our students. Watching each other struggle, day after day, with the assignments we were given as part of the teaching demonstrations helped us to understand the powerful function of teachers writing with their students. Just as we had rarely seen other teachers writing before the institute, very few of our students had opportunities to see any adults writing.

What evolved out of our institute community of writers became one of the central principles of the Bay Area Writing Project: that teachers of writing themselves must write—regularly and extensively—

and that they must reflect on their own processes and learn from them. It followed that our growing knowledge of our own highly idiosyncratic writing processes must inform our planning for our students; no longer could we envision teaching one process for all students to follow. Finally, we realized that effective inservice sessions for teachers must include sufficient time for them to experience the frustrations and pleasures of writing within a trusting group.

The Bay Area Writing Project became the lead agency for the formation of the National Writing Project, which over the next seventeen years grew to include 157 sites across the country. Through this national development, the crucial importance of *doing* writing, not just reading or talking *about* it, was emphasized. Teachers wrote in their summer institutes, and they wrote in the after-school inservice sessions they led. Increasingly, teachers trained in these institutes were writing for publication: monographs in the Writing Project publication series, texts on the teaching of writing, articles in professional journals, pieces in mass-circulation magazines. In many areas, the writing groups formed during the summer institutes continued to meet during the academic year. These writing communities became a necessary part of these teachers' professional and personal lives.

The English Credential Program

From 1984 through 1987, I worked with the University of California (Berkeley) Graduate School of Education's one-year teacher-preparation program for post-B.A. students who desired a California teaching credential in English for Grades 7–12. Like the Bay Area Writing Project, whose central tenets it exemplified, the program encouraged the student teachers to develop as a community of writers through its organization into small (twelve to sixteen students) yearlong seminar groups, who took all their credential classes together. A basic program belief was that prospective teachers must themselves experience—over a sustained period of time—the teaching methods they are encouraged to use in their student teaching assignments. Because of this core belief, the credential program emphasized immersion in writing, including extensive log keeping, observation writing, and most important, writing across a range of genres for small response groups of other students.

While the majority of students who were admitted to the program had been successful undergraduate English majors, most had not written extensively on self-chosen topics in a range of genres before. Perhaps most surprising was that they rarely had experienced reading successive drafts of their writing to a supportive and responsive small group. Because of their exposure to the beneficial effects of ongoing writing groups in the credential program, many of the students were able to effectively start such groups in their own classrooms. So out of their own sustained experience in a writing community, they were empowered to set up writing communities of their own. In addition, they had learned the crucial importance of modeling—not just talking about—for their students the behaviors of writing, responding, and revising.

From their positive experiences in their credential program writing groups, they also had been able to muster the courage to delay evaluation and grading of their students' papers until sufficient time had been spent on reflection and revision. What had happened over time in their small writing groups had shown them that in order to increase students' writing development, things had to slow way down in the classroom. They could trust this now only because they had experienced it themselves.

The Puente Project

The Puente (*bridge* in Spanish) Project, founded in 1981 by Felix Galaviz and Patricia McGrath and now operating in twenty-five California community colleges, is a writing, counseling, and mentoring program for underprepared Mexican American/Latino students. Run by a Puente English teacher and Mexican American counselor on each campus, the project was designed to prevent students from dropping out of school and to prepare them to successfully transfer to four-year institutions. Since 1983, I have worked with Pat and Felix in Puente Summer Institutes to prepare these teams of teachers and counselors to begin their programs.

The academic core of Puente is a rigorous, two-semester sequence of writing courses—developmental writing and English 1A (the college-level transfer class)—taught by the Puente English teacher with the in-class collaboration of the Puente counselor who has selected their cadre of students. The ability of the counselor and teacher to collaborate and develop a sense of community within the class has been crucial to the project's success. This ability is fostered through the writing community that develops during Puente's intensive, residential training institutes. Puente team training is sustained and extensive, beginning with an initial ten-day institute to enable the teams to start the program on their campuses, followed by a five-day residential Phase II Institute halfway through the program, and supplemented by twice yearly two-day regional conferences. The development of writing communities is central to all this training.

Conclusion

What has been the result of the development of these writing communities? Once teachers began examining their own writing processes and revealing those processes to their students, it was a natural progression to examine other aspects of what went on in their classrooms. As teachers raised questions about their own writing processes and the writing processes of others in their writing groups, they naturally extended that to encouraging their students to question their own processes.

Once a teacher becomes a teacher writer, there is no going back. From my own experience I know that regular writing changes how teachers talk about writing with their students. We become more sympathetic and understanding on the one hand, because we know what writing feels like and how obstinate and unpredictable our own writing processes are. On the other hand, once we write regularly, we also know that nothing will ever happen unless someone actually does put words down on paper, so we work hard to create a climate that will allow our students to risk completing at least a first draft!

Finally, the involvement of teachers in their own writing communities has encouraged the growth of the writer researcher scholar teacher—in other words, it is now accepted that teachers will do what they teach, will share regularly what they do with other teachers, and will reenvision teaching as an active exploration, with their students as companions, of complex, evolving practices and processes.

Appendix

University of California
1974 Summer Institute on the Teaching of Writing

Schedule of Activities

I. Writing:

    a. During the five weeks participants will write papers in several forms, points of view, etc., presented as sample/ model assignments.

or

    b. Continue on a work-in-progress story, play, profile, novel, series of poems, journalism of some scope and length, etc.

    c. All participants: Other miscellaneous writing that may be part of a participant's presentation or lesson or part of a presentation by one of the guest consultants or staff members.

(Participants will choose some material written for a.-b.-c. above to read aloud and discuss during the Friday reading/writing groups.)

    d. Position paper: A personal statement on the teaching of writing, reflecting your experience as a classroom teacher of writing and your experience in the Summer Writing Institute. (Maximum two to five pages, single-spaced. Try to get in by the last week. Position papers will be read to the group during the last two days of the Institute.)

II. Curriculum Projects: Work on at least *one* of the following curriculum projects:

    a. The detailed development of a composition course.

    b. Preparation of text materials on writing for possible publication.

    c. A carefully developed plan for research to be undertaken during the 1974–1975 school year by the participants—field research.

    d. A specific unit in composition designed for a definite grade-level with a progression of activities extending over a minimum period of six weeks.

    e. Sample units or lessons of instruction in writing about literature: Grades 7–9, Grades 10–12, Grades 13–14.

    f. A critical synthesis of several approaches to the teaching of composition—Gibson, Moffett, Macrorie, Miles, Christensen, others—to be done in several short papers or one longer essay.

    g. Development of materials for students with severe language disabilities.

    h. Development of materials for students with problems of dialect or for students for whom English is a second language.

    i. Setting up a way to evaluate ability and progress to write—tailored to the participant's own school and its objectives in composition.

III. Symposium/panel participation . . . on particular problems in the teaching of writing of general interest.

IV. Teaching demonstrations: Presentations to the group of a personal approach to the teaching of writing, specific classroom practices, demonstration lessons, etc.

V. Reading:

    a. Reading and discussion of core articles: Miles, Booth, Gibson, Christensen, Ong, Moffett, etc.

    b. Reading in composition materials not yet read, examination of new composition texts, reading materials written by staff and participants.

VI. Evaluation: Familiarity with evaluation procedures, e.g., Subject A evaluation, Drake Composition Project, National Assessment, Advanced Placement, etc.

Point-of-View Assignment

Further explicit instructions for the point-of-view assignment were given by one of the codirectors, Cap Lavin.

Start with an experience and write about it from three different points of view:

    1. Monologue, interior or dramatic (stream of consciousness)

    2. First person point of view

    3. Third person point of view (anonymous narration)

27 A Writer's Community: How Teachers Can Form Writing Groups

Russel K. Durst
University of Cincinnati

If you are stuck writing or trying to figure something out, there is nothing better than finding one person, or more, to talk to. If they don't agree or have trouble understanding, so much the better—so long as their minds are not closed.

Peter Elbow (1973)

Can people write productively in writing groups? For me, the more apt question is: Can people write *without* groups? Or better yet, why would they want to? For nearly ten years now, I have been a writing-group member and an advocate of using groups for students, teacher researchers, and anyone interested in writing. Back in graduate school, my writing group saw me through a dissertation, course papers, and several published essays. The group at my first job after graduate school helped with my early attempts at making it as a publishing academic. My present writing group has seen me through a number of articles, book reviews, and grant proposals. Over the years, I have helped group members with thousands of pages of their own writing.

All these experiences, I am convinced, have combined to make me a better writer, a better reader, and a better teacher. Whatever kind of writing you want to do, I believe that being part of a writing group can help. Accordingly, in this chapter I will discuss, by giving examples from my experiences as a writing-group member and founder, some of the benefits of belonging to a writing group, lay out a possible framework for forming a writing group, and describe how such a group operates.

Benefits of a Writing Group

I write because I like to, but also because I have to. It comes with the territory. Tenure, promotion, recognition in my field—in other words, professional survival—all require substantial publication and grant getting. For most elementary, secondary, and community college teachers, however, writing is not a necessary part of the job. On the contrary, the responsibilities of their jobs generally work *against* finding time and energy for writing. And, of course, there are few job-related rewards for being a teacher who writes.

But increasingly and in spite of the difficulties, teachers *are* writing. I believe a major reason for this development is the intrinsic reward that writing offers, the excitement and sense of belonging to a larger community that comes from writing. Sure, being part of a writing group can help you become a better writer, get more writing done, and get more enjoyment out of writing, and these are sufficient reasons to join or form such a group. But just as important, being part of a writing group can help you build an intellectual community, or transform your existing community into one that is more alive, more productive, more reflective, and more engaged with what is going on nationally in the teaching of English.

There are at least as many types of writing groups as there are types of writers. In the midwestern city where I live, there are poetry groups, fiction groups, fantasy groups, science fiction groups, children's book groups, playwriting groups, research writing groups, gay writing groups, and a great many mixed groups. In the early 1970s when Peter Elbow introduced what he called the teacherless writing class, his version of the writing group, he argued that each group should be as diverse as possible, with people bringing in for discussion whatever genre they happened to be writing in at the moment. The formation of more specialized groups was perhaps inevitable as the idea caught on with, for example, my crowd: tenure-driven professors afflicted with academic tunnel vision in their particular fields. My own writing group consists of five such professors, all literacy researchers, and the writing we do examines issues in the teaching and learning of written language. We all write articles and essays on reading and writing, and we generally read and attempt to write for the same journals in composition, reading, and language arts. Within the field of literacy, however, our interests and approaches vary considerably. We include an ethnographer, a psycholinguist, a multicultural specialist, a quantitative researcher, and a postmodern theorist. One of us directs a college writing center; one runs a reading center for young children; one administers a freshman English program; one coordinates a federally-funded longitudinal study in several elementary schools; and one is editing a literature textbook series. So while we might not seem that diverse to an outsider, to ourselves we seem as diverse as the field of English education itself. And this diversity, the different perspectives on research and teaching, is one of the things that makes the group so interesting and useful for us.

Though we are all busier than we would like to be, our group tries to meet every two weeks. We meet on the same weekday evening at the same time, because establishing routines about writing is very important for writing groups. Although Elbow recommends that each group member produce some writing for every meeting, at our meetings we usually discuss drafts by one or two group members; any more writing to discuss and we would be there all night. Pieces we have worked on range from two-page conference paper proposals to 250-page research reports, but we generally work on drafts of articles which run from twenty to forty typewritten pages. We also sometimes bring in starter ideas, partial drafts, or even freewrites of pieces we are still in the thinking stages on, to see if people find the idea itself promising enough to pursue or if they have ideas for where the piece might go. And we occasionally bring in repeat performances, drafts that have already gone through the group once but that we would like more feedback on, perhaps a very careful, sentence-level reading of an article that is just about ready to go to a journal.

Our rule is that you have to get your draft to the group one day before the meeting, though all of us have violated this rule on occasion. Our meetings usually last about two hours. We are all friends, so we invariably spend the first few minutes having small talk and enjoying refreshments, but the bulk of the meeting finds us engaged in serious discussion. The writer begins by talking briefly about the draft under scrutiny, though not much needs to be said. This is because we describe the audience, purpose, and desired destination of the piece in a note that comes with the draft. Then, one by one, each person gives personal reactions to the work. We do not have a general discussion. Instead, each person gives the writer feedback on the piece; after everybody has given their feedback, the writer asks questions, attempts to clarify comments, and generally tries to make sense of the new information.

Our feedback comes in three parts. We try to be very specific, saying first what we liked about the piece; then where we had problems, didn't understand, got sidetracked or distracted; and, finally, how we think the piece could be improved. This three-part response format is structured enough to ensure that the big issues get discussed, but flexible enough to allow readers freedom to wander a bit in their responses. If a piece is in an early stage of development, still fairly rough, then we try to pay less attention to sentence-level concerns and focus instead on more global matters of organization, development, argument, or on specific aspects of content that seem particularly provocative, suggestive, or problematic.

When I submit a draft to the group for feedback, I am eager to hear what my colleagues have to say, in large part because I know how much I have benefited from their comments in the past. My eagerness overshadows whatever anxiety I might feel at the prospect of having my work critiqued by my peers. I know that the criticisms, if they come (and they generally do), will be gently given and balanced by positive comments. The group process works well precisely because it involves getting the reactions of a *range* of readers, each with their own interests, preferences, idiosyncrasies, and areas of expertise— a microcosm of the "real" audiences all of us are aiming for. The group must be doing something right: in our three years of existence, almost every piece we have worked on has been accepted for publication by a refereed journal.

Forming a Writing Group

Setting up a writing group is a fairly straightforward process; I've done it three times now, and each time I was surprised by how easy it was. I suppose the reason it's easy is that there is so much demand for the support, the structure, and the response a group provides. Vast numbers of people are out there trying to write, many of whom feel isolated or blocked or both, wishing they could get more feedback on their writing. Others would like to write but are marking time, wishing for an opportunity, perhaps an environment that is more supportive of writing. Or perhaps they wrote best in a school-like situation where they knew they would be expected to produce some writing every few weeks or so. For many writers, an external deadline—knowing some writing must be produced for the group by Thursday—is an enormous help.

There are no ironclad rules to follow when starting a writing group; many radically different approaches can be and have been successful, but there are some useful suggestions that I can make, based on the work of composition specialists like Peter Elbow (1973), Anne Ruggles Gere (1987), Donald Murray (1982), and Roger Whitlock

(1987), and on my own experiences as an organizer and member of writing groups.

A first question to ask is, do you want to set up your own group, or is there an existing group that could better meet your needs? The answer to this question will depend on the type of group you are interested in, and on the type of person you are. If you want to be in a very specialized group, such as people writing articles on education, or fantasy writers, and you don't know enough people to start your own group of that particular type, then you may want to find an existing group. If you are not much of an organizer and wish to get into a structure that has already been established, then an existing group is probably for you. To find out about existing groups, you will have to do some checking around. A community newspaper might list writing groups, or the writing program at a local college may have some leads for you.

If, however, you want to be part of a group of people doing different kinds of writing, or if you like the idea of beginning on the ground floor and learning along with others who haven't been involved in a writing group before, then starting a group can be a very exciting prospect indeed. I would personally recommend this approach, in part because though it means doing a fair amount of rooting around for members and helping to organize them into an effective group of writers and readers, it can also be less intimidating and more comfortable than joining an ongoing group of more experienced writers.

Once you have decided to form a writing group, the question becomes, who should you ask to join the group? The best answer I can give is to seek out people who are interested in writing and who you think can get along reasonably well together. It is probably not worth taking a great deal of time to decide whom to invite into your writing group, as long as the eventual group members are willing to work at making the group a success. In any case, the membership may shift initially as some people decide they don't really want to write or don't like the new demands on their time. There is no proven formula for determining group success. It may be helpful to include a range of personalities: an extrovert, a critical type, a tactful person, an organizer, and so on. Peter Elbow cautions against dominators, people who like to hear themselves talk or who are unnerved by and cannot tolerate silence. Nothing so quickly destroys group morale as a nonstop talker who usurps the floor and won't let others have their say. But Elbow also says that, when a group fails because one member dominates and the others lose interest and gradually fade away, it is not really the fault of the talkative one. Rather, members who passively let the person talk, who do not assume responsibility for the success of the group and get the talkative person to quiet down a bit, must take the largest share of the blame. So in putting together a writing group, ask people you like, people you respect, people you haven't really gotten to know but who seem interesting. Put up signs or put advertisements in local papers, but make it clear to interested people that this is a *writing* group, not a social circle.

There is no optimum number of people to have in a writing group. Three seems like a realistic minimum, though two people giving each other feedback may well make for a better writing situation than one person working alone. Seven or eight seems like a good maximum number to start with, especially since not all members may last for long, although I have heard of successful groups with as many as fifteen members. In such large groups, however, you won't get many opportunities to have your own work discussed in much detail, and these big groups lack the intimacy that is a pleasant feature of the smaller group. In my own group, we started with three because that was all we could get, but that number worked well. After a year, we added a fourth member, a newly hired professor in my department, and that worked even better. Now we are five, and that number is also working well, but we are not eager to get much bigger than five.

How often should people share their writing in writing groups? As Donald Murray has said, writing effectively depends to a great extent on establishing routines. To become a fluid, productive writer, you must accustom yourself to writing on a regular basis; it's best always to have something in the hopper. Routines help a writer develop momentum, and momentum is needed to get any serious writing done. Taking a writing class with required assignments is one way of making sure that you write; there's nothing like a deadline. But classes, valuable as they can be, only last from ten to fifteen weeks. While I recommend taking classes (which are, of course, a fertile breeding ground for writing groups), a long-term way to establish a writing routine and to develop momentum is by joining or forming a writing group for which you need to produce and share some writing every few weeks—that is, at every meeting. For this reason, every member of a writing group should bring some writing to each meeting.

In our own group, where we are generally writing fairly long pieces, twenty-five pages or more, we have found it impossible to discuss more than two or three pieces in one meeting. Therefore, each person brings something to read about every other meeting.

This means that there are times when we write without the benefit of feedback from the group, as well as times when we are not writing as regularly as we might like. We are not completely comfortable with this situation. It might be advisable, therefore, to establish a new group with the expectation that each member will have some writing for discussion at each meeting. While this stipulation puts more demands on group members, it also enforces greater productivity than would likely be found in a more laissez-faire situation. Remember that the purpose of the group is to get people to write. It doesn't particularly matter *what* people write—a poem, a short story, a letter of complaint, a book prospectus, a newspaper article, an essay on literature, an op-ed piece, some initial ideas for a piece, whatever they like. And it doesn't matter how long a piece members write, as long as they do write and accustom themselves to getting words down on paper.

Working in a Writing Group

I have learned from my own experience, and the experts seem to concur, that writing groups generally work best when they are run according to a clear set of guidelines. These guidelines should not be seen as coming down from on high, rigid rules to be followed at the risk of being smitten. Instead, each group should work their guidelines out themselves, given their own situation; it is best to do this working out of guidelines in an informed way, based on what others have had success with in the past. Accordingly, what I will do here is lay out a possible format for a writing group, one based largely on the work of Peter Elbow, made more specific by Roger Whitlock in his work at the University of Hawaii, and further developed by our own writing group at the University of Cincinnati. These guidelines have been used in forming writing groups composed of professors, as well as with groups of teachers doing intensive summer writing project training and with response groups of students taking writing courses. The following guidelines, therefore, offer suggestions on how to set up and establish working procedures for a writing group.

Although Elbow recommends meeting every week, I have found that for all but the most dedicated writers, a reasonable amount of time for a writing group is between two and three hours every couple of weeks. More than that and people may find the meetings, which tend to be fairly intense, too draining. Less than that and people may find the meetings insubstantial. As I mentioned before, the group should pick a standing day of the week and time of day for the meetings, in order to establish a sense of routine.

If every group member brings in a piece of writing to be discussed at every meeting, then the total group time should be divided by the number of members, to ensure that everyone gets the same amount of time for feedback. If the group has seven members who each bring in some writing, and the group spends twenty minutes on each person, then the meeting will last for about two-and-a-half hours. If the group is not conscientious about the amount of time spent on each person, a situation may well develop in which certain more adventurous, more productive, or more assertive group members receive the lion's share of group time, while others move, perhaps happily, into the background. Because the group is intended to get *everyone* writing, insisting on an equal amount of feedback time for all members is critical. Generally speaking, twenty minutes total time spent on each writer's contribution is adequate, which means that in a group of five, four people would each talk for about four minutes on each piece. While more time could easily be spent on most, if not all, pieces, it works best to move relatively quickly through each individual member's contribution for the meeting, get everyone involved, and establish a comfortable pace with momentum. A time-keeper may be necessary to ensure that things move along appropriately and that everybody gets the opportunity to share their writing.

Before beginning, the group should decide what order to go in, so that valuable time is not spent discussing this relatively trivial issue. A simple clockwise or counterclockwise order is generally best. Writers should take a few minutes, if possible before they even come to the meeting, to select some specific aspects of their piece that they might like feedback on. If people are bringing in mainly short pieces, then it is very advisable to read papers aloud, twice if time permits. If possible, members should make copies of their writing for the rest of the group. But even when the group decides to provide copies of each person's work for everyone, reading aloud is still a valuable procedure. In reading the piece aloud, the writer is able to get a very different sense of the writing than can be obtained from reading a piece silently; the writing is experienced more vividly, the strengths and weaknesses revealed more dramatically. In hearing the piece read aloud, the reader, even if he or she reads silently along as well, can experience the piece more fully, noting sudden shifts, powerful phrasings, and problematic ones. Remember, though, that reading pieces aloud may add considerably to the amount of time needed. For pieces longer than ten or fifteen pages, reading aloud may be too time-consuming and may slow the pace of the group. One possible strategy is for the writer of a long piece to read an excerpt to the group. At any rate, each group must decide for itself how to deal with the issue of whether or not to read aloud, and if so, how to do it.

If the writer has read his or her piece aloud, group members should spend a moment reflecting, reexamining the piece, jotting down notes, gathering their thoughts, and otherwise planning their responses. If people have done the reading beforehand, they can skip this moment of reflection and move right into the key work of the writing group: the feedback process. And a few words need to be said about how best to give writers feedback on their pieces in a writing-group situation. It generally works best to have one person at a time give a response, as opposed to having an open discussion of each piece of writing. This way the writer gets a chance to hear everybody's reactions in an organized manner and to keep track of what each group member has said. Also, in an open discussion, the writer tends to speak and participate more and to listen less, and this is not necessarily a good thing. The most valuable thing the writer can do at this point is to take in the reactions of the group members. As Peter Elbow says, "To improve your writing, you don't need advice about what changes to make; you don't need theories of what is good and bad writing. You need movies of people's minds while they read your words" (1973, p. 77). The writer should mainly listen to what others have to say.

Probably the most important point to keep in mind in giving feedback is that your task as a group member is not to criticize or to take the writer to task for what the writing did or did not accomplish. Such criticism suggests that you are attempting to take on the role of a teacher or expert, descending from on high to lay down the laws of writing. On the contrary, it works best to approach the task of responding *as a reader*, simply giving the writer one person's honest reactions to the piece. What did you like? What did you find particularly effective, interesting, unusual, provocative? What surprised you? What words or phrases jumped out at you? How effective was the opening of the piece in making you want to continue reading? Were there enough specifics to keep you interested and informed? Was the piece organized in a way that made sense and seemed appropriate? Was the ending powerful? Did the writer lose you at any point? Did you learn anything interesting from the piece? Were there any parts of the writing that could use further development? Were there any parts that seemed superfluous or even got in the way of your reading? The list of possible questions is infinite; whatever catches your attention in reading the piece can be discussed or asked about, if the matter is of sufficient importance. This last point is key. Don't bother with the trivial. Talk about the important points.

All responders should remember that they are not evaluating the writer or giving the piece a grade. Rather, they are responding to the piece as a reader, as someone who may or may not find it interesting, entertaining, shocking, powerful. As long as you approach the response process as a reader, nothing you say can be wrong; you are simply giving your own reactions as the reader.

In a similar vein, writers are urged not to quarrel with their group members' responses. Simply take in what everyone has to say, and suppress the urge to say, in response to a comment, "But I did that right here on Page 2!" Don't get defensive. Don't make excuses. Don't get hostile. If the writer needs to participate at all, it should be to ask for clarification of readers' comments or to ask for feedback about specific aspects of the piece about which the writer feels there are problems or uncertainties. The writer doesn't need to incorporate all the suggestions group members make, or to make all the changes, or to concede all the problems that everyone brings up. But the writer should note them all, mentally or in writing, consider them carefully, and accept those comments both positive and negative that will be of most help in revising. Perhaps now it is clearer why a relatively brief response time for each writer's contribution usually works better than having unlimited time for response to a piece. It's much easier for a writer to make sense of fifteen or twenty minutes of feedback than to sort through sixty minutes' worth of comments. Also, the more restricted time forces group members to discuss only their most salient responses.

In addition to giving each other feedback on drafts, a writing group can do other kinds of activities that lead to increased professional participation and development and that are interesting and enjoyable as well. The group can actually write together during meetings; for example, people might practice different ways of writing leads on a topic agreed upon in advance. A group might even collaborate on an extended piece of writing; such collaborative publications are getting more and more common. Or members might read an interesting book or article and write a response to it, with each person reading his or her response at the meeting as a prelude to a larger discussion. Besides the intrinsic value of such activities, it is worthwhile occasionally to do something other than respond to rough drafts, just to vary the group's routine and keep things lively.

The full value of writing groups can only be realized after you have participated in a group for a period of time, given and received feedback, and revised your writing based on that feedback. But to a writer like myself, who used to struggle alone but now has the support of a community of trusted peers, the advantages of a writing group are many. Belonging to a group helps you move away from the traditional—but largely inaccurate and often paralyzing—notion of the lonely writer ensconced in a book-lined study, working in isolation, operating without benefit of feedback, finally emerging from the study with a completed work. The writer working alone is a romantic notion. It is also a fiction, one that has put many people off writing, made them feel they could never produce a worthwhile piece of writing, though with some good feedback they could. A writing group can provide that feedback intensively, systematically, and in a supportive but challenging atmosphere. Writing groups create an environment as conducive to writing as any you could find. Group members who are, like you, working writers can give you a range of reactions, not just the perspective you receive when you ask only one individual, a friend or colleague, to read your work. Moreover, the group itself may well make you a more productive writer, since you will have to produce writing on a regular schedule. Along the way, you will get into the habit of writing regularly, indispensable for becoming an accomplished writer. You will also become more adept at giving feedback to other writers, which eventually feeds back into your own writing and makes you a more skillful writer and reviser. Writing groups, because they provide routines and responses from other writers, work in supporting the writing development of their members.

References

Elbow, P. (1973). *Writing without teachers*. New York: Oxford University Press.

Gere, A.R. (1987). *Writing groups*. Urbana, IL: National Council of Teachers of English.

Murray, D. (1982). *Learning by teaching*. Montclair, NJ: Boynton/Cook.

Whitlock, R. (1987). *Making writing groups work: Modifying Elbow's teacherless writing group for the classroom*. Paper presented at the annual meeting of the Conference on College Composition and Communication, Atlanta, GA.

28 Collaborative Writing as an Option

Jill Dillard
Summit Elementary School, Cincinnati, Ohio

Karin L. Dahl
The Ohio State University, Columbus

How do writers collaborate? Are two heads better than one? We were curious and decided to see what we could find out. We tried collaborative writing for ourselves and contacted others who had written together.

Learning to Collaborate

Our own experience began with a sense of the story we wanted to tell; we had taught a reading-writing course together and wanted to share the experience (Dillard & Dahl, 1986). We also knew who we wanted to reach with our message: our audience was classroom teachers. What we didn't know was how to write together. Each of us made separate preparations: one generated a freewrite that got the ideas flowing and the other wrote a list of concepts and ideas that needed to be included. Uncertain about how two partners got the text written, we talked about our options. "Do you want to write or do I? Do we both write at the same time?" Neither of us knew how to get started, but within seconds, our concerns didn't matter. We were in the thick of it. One of us picked up the pen! We dictated together, each adding to the other's thoughts. We used both the freewrite and the list to guide our unfolding text.

"Talk-write" became our initial way of collaborating. But as we continued working together over several sessions, it grew more and more inefficient. Almost every sentence required a decision, and we found ourselves talking more than writing. Sometimes we got off the subject altogether. Because we were friends who were working together, all kinds of topics lured us away. When one said, "Now let's put the part in about Penny and her question," the other answered, "Oh by the way, Penny called yesterday and said she was trying some new strategies with her students." We were off the task—the conversation turned to news and shared experiences.

Collaboration, as it evolved for us, turned out to be a series of give-and-take sessions. Ownership of ideas and chunks of text became an issue and needed to be discussed. Each of us became a sponsor of a particular idea we thought should be included. For example, one wanted to explain a range of conference formats; we compromised and included only one. The other wanted to provide an overview of the course we were writing about, but the overview failed to capture a reader's interest. Instead, we wrote a series of leads without describing the course.

Since each of us remembered relatively good progress when working alone, we turned to separate writing as a second approach in learning how to write together. We each took sections of the outline and wrote that portion of the text. When we came together, however, our text was rougher than we had anticipated. The chunks didn't match in style, and they emphasized points the outline didn't include. Each of us was discovering new meanings as we wrote separately, thinking of new things to say that our initial plans hadn't included. While we were excited by the new ideas, we recognized we would have to generate the text together before we could work separately on specific parts.

We developed more ways to keep going and shifted back and forth from drafting on paper to writing together at the word processor. When scrunched together at the terminal, we learned to talk aloud as we wrote to provide an understanding of the joint text being produced. When working on paper, we dictated sentences and talked about what was to come next.

Four strategies in particular helped us with our collaborative talking and writing. "Rather Than" was a way to vary sentence structure so every sentence didn't begin in the same way. One of us would say "rather than" when spotting a series of sentences that were too similar. Then the other would use that phrase to think of new ways to begin the sentence which would lend the needed variation. Sometimes this strategy helped us think of new connections for the idea in that part of the text, and thus we generated a more elaborated version.

A second strategy, which we called "This or That," allowed us to decide between equally good options. We would say, "Shall we tell about the phone call as a turning point or shall it be listed within a group of events?" We would each write a version to see what the alternatives looked like. "This or That" gave us an opportunity to generate options and decide after they were written which one was more interesting.

The third strategy, "Something Something," helped us with word choices. Often during talk-write, we did well with the generation of ideas but got stuck on choosing the precise words. Rather than stop the forward movement of the emerging text, we simply wrote "something something" as a placeholder for the words we couldn't find and kept going. We learned it was more important to keep the synergy than it was to work out details.

"Good Garbage," our fourth strategy, was an effort to save unrelated parts of the text. We often found ourselves with sections we liked but that didn't quite fit the point we were making. With the computer, we moved these sections to the end of the text by typing a row of asterisks and depositing the good garbage after it. In almost every case, the leftover text was recycled and moved back into our piece. The scraps became useful and turned out to be just what we needed when the draft neared completion.

We also learned to live with differences in our drafting processes. One of us was comfortable with a fast-draft style, and the other was used to polishing as the text developed. "How can it be good, if it's this rough now?" the polisher would ask. "Don't read, just write," the other would answer. Differences also included different abilities. Initially, we felt guilty when one would produce something and the other would not. Later, we came to see that our talents complemented each other, one being better at generating alternatives and the other at revising and shaping the manuscript as a whole. We learned to accept our different roles.

When our draft was complete, we sent it to other readers, expecting that a few tidy revisions would be suggested. Instead, our readers had troubling things to say. "Try being more chummy," one commented; "Make it more academic," said another. We had to decide what we wanted to tell and how to listen to these outsiders. We generated chummy sections and rewrote others; we cited some references and decided to share our story rather than write an academic report. Another cycle of critiquing from different readers brought more suggestions. "Add examples." "Can you reconstruct your conversation?" We revised, and revised again.

At the end we discovered we had learned a number of things in learning to collaborate. We found a "we" voice, different from our separate voices. We learned there is a kind of magic in collaboration—two people create something that each would not generate working alone. We learned to be patient about time. What we thought would take four months took twice as long. And we found being friends made it easier. There was compromise, cooperation, and a level of trust that made collaboration work.

Learning from Other Collaborators

Our experience made us all the more interested in the writing of other collaborators. We contacted five pairs of well-known writers and asked how they went about writing together. We asked about their purposes, sought their advice, and drew from their responses some additional strategies. Our first pair was Andrea Lunsford and Lisa Ede, two professors who have studied how writers collaborate and written about their own techniques (Lunsford & Ede, 1985). Lunsford described the central reason for collaboration: "There is a richness of thought that comes from collaboration. When we work together, we discover new meanings."

Jane Hansen and Donald Graves shared with us the techniques they used in two of their pieces, "The Author's Chair" (1983) and "Do You Know What Backstrung Means?" (1986). Graves described how they focused their pieces around an image. "You have to decide what you want to teach. In your lead you have to bring the reader in from the standpoint of what you want the reader to want." Hansen talked about how they shared ideas and drafts, each reworking parts of the piece once the central focus was established.

Chris Clark and Robert Yinger, two researchers who investigate teacher thinking, emphasized the importance of friendship in collaboration. "What precedes any co-writing is sense making and working together. . . . It is valuable and necessary for teachers who hope to write together to do other work together first," Clark advised.

Lucy Schultz and Chet Laine, professors who have worked extensively with evaluation issues in writing, described their strategies for collaborating. Schultz explained, "Sometimes we start by dividing up the subject or topic and just quickly writing about it. Chet will take one segment and I'll take another. We work with each other's zero drafts. Each one adds to the other's and we end up learning from each other."

Cora Five and Martha Rosen, two collaborating teachers who contributed a chapter in *Breaking Ground* (Five & Rosen, 1985), both described how they worked together to achieve one voice. Their efforts involved rereading and revising their separate drafts in order to fit them together. Five explained, "We revised by trying to combine our writing styles. Sentences from my paragraphs were often re-written into Martha's paragraphs or vice versa."

The interviews, taken together, indicated that collaborators cope with a number of similar issues. Their strategies and suggestions provide information for people using collaboration as a writing and learning tool.

Suggestions and Patterns for Writing Collaboratively

Getting started. Most of the writers found collaboration seemed like a natural step in their relationships. In each instance, they previously had worked together, either as teachers or researchers, and shared an experience. They enjoyed exchanging ideas with each other and talking about their projects. The next step was to combine ideas and words on paper.

Generating the text. These pairs of writers used a variety of techniques to get the text written. Lunsford and Ede began by talking through their ideas thoroughly, thrashing out all of the possibilities and problems. Once the ideas were expressed, they divided up the work and each wrote separate sections. Next, they revised each other's work, ex-changing drafts and rewriting freely. With successive revisions, drafts were exchanged again and again. The final draft represented both authors' work and the best of their thinking together.

In contrast, Clark and Yinger produced their text by dictating it into a machine. Both partners took turns "talking text," each in-serting additional ideas into the other's remarks. Once the dictation was typed, both revised the text and talked about what needed to be changed.

A third pattern was to generate text together at the word processor. Laine and Schultz alternated typing and talking, with the text ap-pearing on the screen in front of them. Often this led to revision of the printed-out text and to separate assignments to solve problems.

Acquiring a "we" voice. Some collaborators decided that one of the two writers would be the dominant one for a particular piece and be responsible for reworking it into one style. Others found they could suppress some of their individuality and learn to write in compatible ways. The "we" voice was reached most often through discussion and through successive revision for collaborators working across a series of writing projects.

Conferencing together. Conferencing was an integral part of the development of each team's writing, from the beginning all the way through to publication. Most mentioned lots of talking before writing began, and others stressed the importance of the immediate response from their partner. Some pairs conferenced about trouble spots in the draft and worked on the wording of transitions together. Others told how they learned to be tough with each other and throw out parts that didn't work. Conferences for each pair included the generation of ideas and the negotiation of differences.

Developing joint ownership. Within the act of collaboration, the wordings, sentences, and paragraphs become a synthesis of both writers' thoughts and feelings. The writers we interviewed not only cared about their message and their writing, but also about their relationship. "If you worry about that [ownership], you can't do it," Graves cautioned. Collaboration calls for listening, sharing, and being responsive to each other.

Establishing a time line. Joint writing frequently takes a great deal of time. As Laine explained, "It is clearly not faster to collaborate"; Graves remarked, "It takes three times as long to do a joint piece, maybe longer." The collaborators found that deadlines required by publishers and due dates established by journals spurred them on. As Hansen explained, "A deadline forces you to get the whole article focused quickly." Other deadlines are also helpful. Clark talked about arbitrary deadlines writers establish for themselves, and Rosen and Five reported keeping the internal deadlines they had set so they would not disappoint each other with unkept promises. Most collaborators accepted the extensive time involved and found the several kinds of deadlines served them effectively.

Deciding first authorship. Every collaborating pair had to decide whose name came first on the final manuscript. Some writers who collaborated across a number of projects simply traded off, alternating the name listed first. Other pairs weighed a variety of factors: who worked most on the piece, who needed the publication, who was invited to do the piece. Sometimes the first name decision was related to expertise and knowledge of the topic; other times it depended on who wrote the first draft. While writers thought differently about how to handle the name issue, Graves's suggestion to "discuss it early" appeared to be valuable advice.

Working together. Our interviews indicated that working together has advantages but can also bring with it some difficulties. We learned writers are real people. They deal with the complexities of every day just as everyone else does. Some have children, and some have their work interrupted while a leaky roof or a plumbing problem causes a crisis. Even when the collaborators are friends, the venture can be uneven. If one is doing more of the work than the other, Clark suggested that writers "slow down with patience instead of resentment." Sometimes writers live in different towns, and collaboration is even more difficult. Writers from separate locations learn to schedule time to write together during the year.

Besides learning to deal with the frustrations of collaboration, these writers also talked about enjoying their deepening relationships. As Lunsford put it, "The process of collaborating has been interesting personally. It has cemented our friendship." For many of the writers, the support and reinforcement the buddy system provided allowed them to take bigger risks as writers and to learn from each other.

Writing strategies. When we shared the strategies that grew out of our collaboration, we found other writers developed strategies, too.

For example, "Lean Forward, Lean Back" was Clark and Yinger's creation. Yinger described it as two phases of their writing process. "Lean Forward" was the intense writing phase of their work, when the two authors dealt with writing the analytic portion of their articles. "Lean Back" was the speculation and theorizing portion of their writing when the two, perhaps with hands behind their heads and feet propped up, enjoyed the experience of thinking about what it all meant.

"Capture That" was a brainstorming strategy that Schultz and Laine used when thinking through an article. They would talk at length, each throwing out ideas that could be included. Then, when a particularly rich idea surfaced, one would quickly try to capture it on the word processor before the idea faded.

"Being Together" functioned literally as a heuristic for Lunsford and Ede. When they had the luxury of being together, having journeyed from their distant universities, they discovered the ideas and the wordings they needed for their current piece. The intensive work that a two-day session together allowed seemed to be a discovery strategy in itself.

Final Reflections

Clearly there are common threads in our experience and that of other writers. Almost every set of writers made the point that collaboration comes about from a relationship where common professional experiences make the need to write together urgent. Collaboration happens when there are stories to tell. Interestingly, all of our collaborators accommodated each other, in one way or another, by working out the relationship. Whether it meant slowing down the pace of writing, sticking to a schedule, or being sensitive to the other's ideas, all found adjustments needed to be made. Friendship seemed to be the enabling factor. Writers found their friendship expanded as they shared the experience of collaborating.

A look into our own collaborative effort and the experiences of other writers taught us that people write collaboratively in a number of ways. By writing together, writers come to recognize different viewpoints and skills and discover the ups and downs in a joint writing process. But most important, we found collaboration is not only a way to learn from each other, it is a way to learn "with" each other. It's an option worth trying!

References

Dillard, J., & Dahl, K. (1986). Learning through teaching in a reading/writing classroom. *Language Arts, 63,* 692–697.

Five, C., & Rosen, M. (1985). Children re-create history in their own voices. In J. Hansen, T. Newkirk, & D. Graves (Eds.), *Breaking ground.* Portsmouth, NH: Heinemann.

Graves, D., & Hansen, J. (1983). The author's chair. *Language Arts, 60,* 176–183.

Hansen, J., & Graves, D. (1986). Do you know what backstrung means? *Reading Teacher, 39,* 807–812.

Lunsford, A., & Ede, L. (1985). Collaboration and compromise: The fine art of writing with a friend. In T. Waldrep (Ed.), *Writers on writing, volume II.* New York: Random House.

29 Creating Communities for Teacher Research

Marilyn Cochran-Smith and Susan L. Lytle
University of Pennsylvania, Philadelphia

As a profession, teaching is primarily defined by what teachers do when they are not with other teachers. When teachers are evaluated, it is individual classroom performance that is scrutinized. When contracts are negotiated, it is amount of instructional time that is often a key issue. In fact, when teachers are out of their classrooms or talking to other teachers, they are often perceived by administrators, parents, and sometimes even by teachers themselves as *not* working. The isolation of teachers at all stages of their careers is well-documented, and it is clear that the daily rhythms of schools typically provide little time for teachers to talk, reflect, and share ideas with colleagues.

On the other hand, teacher research is by definition a collaborative and social activity that requires opportunities for sustained and substantive intellectual exchange among colleagues. It also requires time within the school day to perform the fundamental tasks that researchers in all other professions take for granted: observing and documenting phenomena, conducting interviews, and gathering artifacts and supporting data. Tacit images of teaching as a solo performance carried out on the classroom stage work against the institutionalization of inquiry both as an integral part of teaching and as a way for teachers to interact professionally.

Defining Teacher Research

We have found it useful to take as a working definition for teacher research, *systematic, intentional inquiry by teachers about their own school and classroom work*. We base this definition in part on the work of

---

Lawrence Stenhouse (1985), who defines research in general as "systematic, self-critical enquiry," and in part on an ongoing survey of the literature of teacher writing (see, for example, Goswami & Stillman, 1987). This literature includes articles written by teachers, in-house collections of teachers' work-in-progress, monographs about teachers' classroom experiences, as well as published and unpublished teachers' journals and essays. With this definition we emphasize that there already exists a wide array of writing by teachers that is appropriately regarded as research.

Although its roots are in the action research of the 1950s, the current teacher research movement remains in many ways on the margins of both the teaching and research communities. Furthermore, there has been debate about its methods and its status as research (Cochran-Smith & Lytle, 1990b). In its recent iterations, teacher research has been thought of primarily as classroom-based studies teachers conduct of their own practice; this work resembles university-based research in methods, forms, and reporting conventions. Equating teacher research with classroom studies puts limits on what we can learn from teachers about their work. A broader perspective (Lytle & Cochran-Smith, 1990) helps to legitimate teacher inquiry as a critical dimension of the activity of teaching. It allows us to reclaim and reexamine more of the existing literature on teaching which is written by teachers themselves, and it enables us to make distinctions about a variety of teacher researcher texts and the contexts in which they are produced and used.

Many teachers have written about their work in forms that can, we have argued, be appropriately regarded as research. We have proposed four categories as a tentative typology of teacher research that acknowledges a wider range of teachers' writing. In the first we include teachers' journals, published and unpublished. In the second category we place both brief and book-length essays in which teachers analyze their own classrooms or schools and consider issues related to learners, curricula, and school organization. The third category includes accounts of teachers' oral inquiries and discussions, convened specifically for reflection and questioning. These are usually preserved in the form of written transcriptions or notes. Our final category includes small- and larger-scale classroom studies based on documentation and analysis procedures similar to those of university-based classroom research.

We believe that as teachers' research accumulates and is more widely disseminated, it will represent a radical challenge to our current assumptions about the relationships of theory and practice, schools and universities, and inquiry and reform (Cochran-Smith & Lytle, in press). Despite its potential, however, there is also widespread agreement that there are no obvious and simple ways to create the conditions that support teacher research; in fact, there are major obstacles that constrain this activity in schools and make it difficult to redefine teaching as a form of inquiry. In working with groups of preservice and inservice teachers, it has been our experience that overcoming these obstacles requires the building and sustaining of intellectual communities of teacher researchers, or networks of individuals who enter with other teachers into "a common search" for meaning in their work lives (Westerhoff, 1987) and who regard their research as part of larger efforts to transform teaching, learning, and schooling.

Creating Communities for Teacher Research: A Conceptual Framework

Drawing on our own work, we would like to propose a framework for analyzing and evaluating the work of communities for teacher research, according to four perspectives: the ways in which communities organize time, use talk, construct texts, and interpret the tasks of teaching and schooling (Cochran-Smith & Lytle, 1990a). A framework based on time, talk, text, and task provides a way for groups of teachers to plan their collaborative work and raise questions about the cultures of school and university organizations as sites of inquiry.

Organizing Time

In schools, teachers and students are organized according to whether they are on time, behind time, out of time, saving time, serving time, or moving double time. Clearly time is a central dimension in the work lives of teachers. It is also one of the most critical factors in the formation and maintenance of learning communities for teacher research and writing. Unlike other professions that are organized to support research activities, teaching is a profession where it is extraordinarily difficult to find enough time even to collect data, and almost impossible to find time to reflect, reread, or share with colleagues.

When groups of teachers come together as researchers, they need sufficient chunks of time in which to work, and they also need sufficient longevity as a group over time (Little, 1987). When the pace of a community's work is unhurried, and when members of the group make a commitment to work through complicated issues over time, then ideas have a chance to incubate and develop, trust builds in the group, and participants feel comfortable raising sensitive issues and risking self-revelation. These ways of organizing time are frequently identified in the feminist literature as critical for fostering collaborative ways of knowing and constructing knowledge (Belenky, Clinchy, Goldberger, & Tarule, 1986). Over time, communities that support teacher research develop their own histories and in a certain sense, their own culture—a common discourse, shared experiences that function as touchstones, and a set of procedures that provide structure and form for continued experience. Longevity makes it possible for teacher researchers to engage in inquiry that is both systematic and spontaneous.

On the other hand, maintaining teacher research communities over relatively long periods of time also presents a number of challenges. How can a group meet the needs of both new and experienced members? Can a group become too large or too small? What happens to a group as members come and go? How can a group avoid becoming locked into procedures and continue to be receptive to critique and change, even when many members feel satisfied with the status quo? What are the ways teacher researcher groups can be increasingly responsive to special interests without fragmenting the organization? If teacher researcher groups are to be more than the latest educational fad or the newest theme for staff development programs, they need to be analyzed and reconceptualized as enduring structures subject to many of the same problems as other voluntary organizations that exist over time.

One of the most salient issues is how much control teachers have over their time. Forming and maintaining communities that support teacher research within schools require attending to the constraints and conflicts around the construction and interpretation of time by both teachers and administrators. In relation to teacher research communities, the issue of control of teachers' time involves redistributing some of the time during the school day already allotted for other purposes, adding to the contracted amounts of time for research purposes, as well as enabling teachers to make different arrangements for class preparation and meeting times. For example, in Crossroads, a charter school-within-a-school at Gratz High School in Philadelphia, eight teachers have reorganized the school day so they share students and planning periods in order to construct an integrated interdisciplinary curriculum. By redistributing time across the school day, they have reframed and reconstructed their own teaching lives and significantly altered the learning opportunities of their students. As part of the continuous cycle of inventing, enacting, and evaluating the curriculum, they collect, share, and interpret data about the effects of these innovations (Fecho, in press).

Doing teacher research cannot simply be another task added to the already crowded teacher's day. It has become increasingly evident from our work with teacher researchers that building communities requires that teachers have more discretion over how they spend in-classroom and out-of-classroom time. Increased control over time enables teachers to engage in research by analyzing data gathered in their own classrooms, as well as by documenting learning in other settings. If teacher groups are to become communities, participants will have to integrate research more fully into the ongoing activities of the school day and work out some of the difficult issues associated with the politics of time.

Using Talk

A second critical factor in the formation and maintenance of learning communities for teacher research and writing is talk—particular ways of describing, discussing, and debating teaching. In communities that support teacher research, groups of teachers engage in joint construction of knowledge through conversation. Through talk they make their tacit knowledge more visible, call into question assumptions about common practice, and generate data that make possible the consideration of alternatives. Teacher research is not limited to classroom studies carried out by teachers, but also includes essays, journals, and oral inquiries. Oral inquiry, which we define as teachers' self-conscious and often self-critical attempts to make sense of their daily work by talking about it in planned and formally structured ways, is one type of teacher research, one that is only beginning to be recognized as a research process. Some teacher research groups regularly conduct oral inquiries, such as reflections on practice or descriptive reviews of students (Carini, 1986), literature studies (Edelsky, 1988), and doubting/believing discussions (Elbow, 1973). Other communities do not use formal oral inquiry formats, but they do talk in distinctive ways about their teaching.

In communities that support teacher research, all talk does not contribute directly to the joint construction of knowledge about teaching. Rather, teachers swap classroom stories, share specific ideas, seek each other's advice, and trade opinions about issues and problems in their own schools and the larger educational arena. In most professional contexts, these exchanges are typically considered "small talk," implying that they are pleasant but unimportant relative to the "big talk" or more serious purposes for which the group has convened. In communities that support teacher research, these smaller conversations have an important function: they create and sustain the interpersonal relationships necessary for the larger project, the joint construction of knowledge. When teachers describe encounters with individual students or the responses of their classes to particular texts or activities, for example, they provide rich information about their day-to-day work and the ways they construct their worlds inside and outside their classrooms. Stories swapped casually acquire more significance when recalled in a different context; advice sought and received may solve an immediate problem, but it may also percolate for a time and then reappear as a different kind of question. In communities for research, teachers use small talk to enter into each other's frames of reference.

Two interrelated ways of talking about teaching are central to building communities for teacher research, both in and out of school. The first way is similar to Geertz's (1973) notion of thick description, in which he emphasizes that what researchers often call "data" are really their own constructions of what others are saying, doing, and meaning. In teachers' communities, this kind of rich descriptive talk helps make visible and accessible the day-to-day events, norms, and practices of teaching and learning, and the ways that different teachers, students, administrators, and families understand them. Talk of this kind transforms what is ordinarily regarded as "just teaching" (Little, 1989) into multilayered portraits of school life that depend on diverse and sometimes conflicting interpretations. Structured formats such as Prospect School's Documentary Processes (Carini, 1986) are particularly powerful ways to make explicit what is often implicit, to remember by drawing on past experiences, to formulate analogies between seemingly unrelated concepts and experiences, and to construct from disparate data patterns in students' learning. When teachers' conversations build thick description, they conjointly uncover relationships between concrete cases and more general issues and constructs.

The second way of talking about teaching that is central to building communities for teacher research is broadly termed *critique*. In using this term to describe teacher researchers' talk, we call attention to conversations in which teachers question common practice, deliberate about what is regarded as expert knowledge, examine underlying assumptions, interrogate educational categories, and attempt to uncover the values and interests served by the common arrangements and structures of schooling. This way of talking makes problematic much of what is usually taken for granted about teaching and learning.

In teacher research communities, making teaching problematic means calling into question labels, practices, and processes that are so ingrained in our language and metaphors for teaching and learning that they have become reified. The givens of schooling comprise a long list, including reading groups, rostering, inservicing, tracking, abilities, disabilities, mastery, retention, promotion, giftedness, disadvantage, special needs, departmentalization, 47-minute periods, coverage, standards, Carnegie units, detention, teacher-proof instructional materials, and homework. Making the givens of education problematic requires asking interpretive questions, which rarely take the form, "What's the best way to teach reading to first graders?" or "Is this child reading 'on grade level'?" Instead they are phrased, "What do reading and learning to read mean in this classroom?" or "Under what circumstances does this particular child ask for which kinds of help?" Talking like this is a way for teacher research communities to "learn to struggle collectively" (Lieberman, 1986), a process which is rarely aimed at, or ends in, conclusions.

Using Texts

A third factor is the critical role of texts in forming and maintaining communities for teacher research. Communities use a wide range of texts, not all of which are published or disseminated, that are essential to teachers' individual and collective gathering, recording, and analyzing data. Texts include teachers' writing in the form of journals, essays, and studies, as well as selections from the extensive theoretical and research literature in the fields related to teaching and learning. Texts used by teachers in their communities also include the written records of teachers' deliberations, informal writing used to facilitate the talk of teacher groups, transcripts of classroom interactions and interviews, notes made of classroom observations, as well as drafts of teachers' plans and work-in-progress. In addition, teachers have access to students' work, including writing, drawing, and other materials; school forms, documents, and records; demographic data; and curriculum guidelines and materials. While some schools and districts collect some of these texts for management and research purposes, teachers in research communities regard all of these texts as potential data and attempt to examine their interrelationships from the perspective of the classroom teacher.

Communities play a critical role in making texts accessible and usable by teachers. Each separate piece of teacher research can inform not only subsequent activities in an individual teacher's classroom, but also potentially informs and is informed by all teacher research, past and present. As the number and modes of communication among teacher research communities increase, it is more likely that the full potential of teacher research to inform the profession will be realized. Teacher research, like all forms of knowledge-building, educational or otherwise, is a fundamentally social and constructive activity which depends upon the dissemination and use of texts. In the teacher researcher community, the generation and critical use of texts make teachers' inquiries accessible to other teachers. Further evidence for this collective and cumulative power within the community occurs when members generate and then use texts about their own work.

When a wide range of texts are used over time, teacher research communities function as discourse communities. The concept of discourse community draws on the everyday meaning of *community* as a group with common goals and interests, as well as on the notions of *interpretive community* and *speech community* (Harris, 1989). *Interpretive community* refers to a network of people with similar meaning perspectives, while *speech community* refers to a group of people who engage in face-to-face interaction within a specific context. Teacher research communities often function as discourse communities in all three of the ways suggested by Harris: they are "real groupings of writers and readers," they share a kind of larger mission, and they become networks of "citations and allusions," which refer to texts both within the speech community and outside of it. Teacher researchers are often part of several of the discourse communities of their profession—the school, the school system, the union, the university. Thus they are "always committed to a number of conflicting beliefs and practices" (Harris, 1989, p. 19). This means that teacher research communities are not, and should not be, grounded in consensus, but rather they are sites of critical reflection on the discourses themselves.

Teachers' writing is beginning to reach new audiences. The publication and dissemination efforts of teacher research communities are effectively widening the discourse about schools and schooling to include the knowledge and perspectives of teachers, long disenfranchised from the professional and academic processes of building the knowledge base of teaching. When teachers publish and present their work at regional and national levels, they demonstrate the power of their writing to make the familiar strange, to link teachers' work, and to challenge the status quo (Lytle & Cochran-Smith, 1991).

Defining the Tasks of Teaching

We think that communities for teacher research may have particular ways of spending time, talking, and using texts. In our experience, they are also committed to a common task, which is, ultimately, the radical reform of schooling. Underlying this task is a set of assumptions about teaching, learning, and organizations. One critical assumption of participants in teacher research communities is that teaching is primarily an intellectual activity that hinges on what Zumwalt (1982) calls the "deliberative" ability to reflect on and make wise decisions about practice. Teaching is regarded as a complicated and intentional activity requiring a great breadth and depth of professional knowledge and judgment in conditions that are inherently uncertain (Shulman, 1986). In contrast to a more technical view that teaching hinges on the use of particular techniques applied in various situations, a deliberative view of teaching regards teachers as professionals who use their knowledge to construct perspectives, choose actions, manage dilemmas, interpret and create curricula, make strategic choices, and to a large extent define their own teaching responsibilities. Teacher researchers regard these tasks as opportunities for systematic, intentional inquiry and regard the inquiries of others as opportunities for rethinking their own assumptions and practices.

When teachers participate in communities that support research and writing, they often reconstruct their classrooms and begin to offer different invitations to their students to learn and know. In other words, thinking of teaching as research also means regarding learning as constructive, meaning-centered, and social, making central the reciprocal relationship between theories about teaching and theories about learning. Often teachers who are actively researching their own practices provide opportunities for their students to become similarly engaged (Johnston, 1990; Schwartz, 1988). This means that what goes on in the classrooms of teacher researchers may be quantitatively different from what typically happens in classrooms. These researching teachers create classroom environments in which there are researching students (Goswami, Branscombe, & Schwartz, in press): students ask, not just answer questions; pose, not just solve problems; and help to construct curriculum out of their own linguistic and cultural resources, rather than just receive preselected and predesigned information. Britton (1987) reminds us that "every lesson should be for the teacher, an inquiry, some further discovery, a quiet form of research" (p. 13). Our point here is that in every classroom where teachers are learners and all learners are teachers, there is a radical, but quiet, kind of school reform in process.

In teacher research communities, the task of teachers is not simply to produce research, as some have argued is true in the academic research community. Rather, the commitment of teacher researchers is change—in their own classrooms, schools, districts, and professional organizations. At the base of this commitment is a deep and often passionately enacted responsibility to students' learning and life chances.

Thus, we suggest that there may be powerful connections between teacher research and school reform. When teachers work together in communities, they are in a position to identify and help establish priorities for school policy and practice that need to be reexamined. Creating and supporting these communities ensure that the agenda for school change is informed by insiders' perspectives on everyday school life.

Conclusion

There has been a growing effort over the past decade to provide organizational structures that enable groups of teachers to come together to talk and write about their work, learn from one another, and address curricular and instructional issues. Innovative arrangements include in-school and school-university structures such as cross-visitation, teacher study groups, schools-within-schools, writing projects, student teacher-cooperating teacher discussion groups, and on-site courses and seminars that focus on teacher inquiry. These arrangements also include teacher groups that meet outside of the auspices of schools or school systems, projects or programs that are based on school-university collaborations, and local, regional, or national networks that provide forums for teachers to exchange ideas with colleagues from across the country. All of these structures have in common the purpose of enabling teachers to reflect on their work, and some of them are intended explicitly to encourage teacher research and writing.

We think it is extremely important that teachers conduct research on their own practices and write about this work for their own colleagues as well as for wider educational communities. What is clearly missing from the literature on teaching are the voices of teachers themselves, the questions teachers ask, the ways teachers use writing and intentional talk in their work lives, and the interpretive frames teachers use to understand and improve their own classroom practices. But we also recognize that it is extremely difficult for teachers to write about their work in isolation from their colleagues, from groups of teachers whose talk and writing support their research. In communities that support teacher research and writing, part of the ongoing agenda is both systematic reflection about the work of the group itself and exchange through writing and conversation with other groups about ways to make communities successful.

References

Belenky, M.F., Clinchy, B.M., Goldberger, N.R., & Tarule, J.M. (1986). *Women's ways of knowing.* New York: Basic Books.

Britton, J. (1987). A quiet form of research. In D. Goswami & P. Stillman (Eds.), *Reclaiming the classroom* (pp. 13–19). Upper Montclair, NJ: Boynton/Cook.

Carini, P. (1986). *Prospect's documentary processes.* Unpublished manuscript.

Cochran-Smith, M., & Lytle, S.L. (1990a). *Communities for teacher research: Fringe or forefront?* Paper presented at the annual meeting of the American Educational Research Association, Boston.

Cochran-Smith, M., & Lytle, S.L. (1990b). Teacher research and research on teaching: The issues that divide. *Educational Researcher, 19,* 2–11.

Cochran-Smith, M., & Lytle, S.L. (in press). *Inside/outside: Teachers, research, and knowledge.* New York: Teachers College Press.

Edelsky, C. (1988). Living in the author's world: Analyzing the author's craft. *The California Reader, 21,* 14–17.

Elbow, P. (1973). *Writing without teachers.* New York: Oxford University Press.

Fecho, R. (in press). Reading as a teacher. In M. Cochran-Smith & S.L. Lytle (Eds.), *Inside/outside: Teachers, research, and knowledge.* New York: Teachers College Press.

Geertz, C. (1973). *The interpretation of cultures.* New York: Basic Books.

Goswami, D., & Stillman, P. (Eds.). (1987). *Reclaiming the classroom.* Upper Montclair, NJ: Boynton/Cook.

Goswami, D., Branscombe, A., & Schwartz, J. (in press). *Students teaching, teachers learning.* Portsmouth, NH: Heinemann.

Harris, J. (1989). The idea of community in the study of writing. *College Composition and Communication, 40,* 11–22.

Johnston, P. (1990). *A shift in paradigm: As teachers become researchers so goes the curriculum.* Paper presented at the Ethnography and Education Forum, Philadelphia.

Lieberman, A. (1986). *Rethinking school improvement.* New York: Teachers College Press.

Little, J.W. (1987). Teachers as colleagues. In V. Richardson-Koehler (Ed.), *Educators' handbook* (pp. 491–518). New York: Longman.

Little, J.W. (1989). *The persistence of privacy: Autonomy and initiative in teachers' professional relations.* Paper presented at the annual meeting of the American Educational Research Association, San Francisco.

Lytle, S., & Cochran-Smith, M. (1990). Learning from teacher research: A working typology. *Teachers College Record, 92,* 83–104.

Lytle, S., & Cochran-Smith, M. (1991). *Teacher research as a way of knowing.* Paper presented at the annual meeting of the American Educational Research Association, Chicago.

Schwartz, J. (1988). The drudgery and the discovery: Students as research partners. *English Journal, 77*(2), 37–40.

Shulman, L. (1986). Those who understand: Knowledge growth in teaching. *Educational Researcher, 15,* 4–14.

Stenhouse, L. (1985). Research as a basis for teaching. In J. Rudduck & D. Hopkins (Eds.), *Research as a basis for teaching.* London: Heinemann.

Westerhoff, J.H. (1987). The teacher as pilgrim. In F.S. Bolin & J.M. Falk (Eds.), *Teacher renewal* (pp. 190–201). New York: Teachers College Press.

Zumwalt, K. (1982). Research on teaching: Policy implications for teacher education. In A. Lieberman & M. McLaughlin (Eds.), *Policymaking in education (81st yearbook of National Society for the Study of Education)* (pp. 215–248). Chicago: University of Chicago Press.

Editor

Karin L. Dahl is an associate professor of language arts in the Language, Literature, and Reading Program at The Ohio State University. She teaches graduate courses in language arts and conducts research in the ways that inner-city children interpret and make sense of their early reading and writing instruction in school. She has published articles about this research in *Language Arts* and *Journal of Reading Behavior.* Dahl currently chairs the NCTE Committee on Professional Writing Networks for Teachers and Supervisors.

Contributors

Chris M. Anson is an associate professor of English at the University of Minnesota.

Patricia J. Austin teaches in the Department of Education at Tulane University, New Orleans. She is currently a columnist for *Reading: Exploration and Discovery* and has served as associate editor for *Louisiana Philosophy of Education Journal.*

Renée Casbergue is an assistant professor in the Department of Education at Tulane University in New Orleans. She is coeditor of *Reading: Exploration and Discovery,* an IRA affiliate journal.

Marilyn Cochran-Smith is an assistant professor in the Graduate School of Education, University of Pennsylvania, and author of *The Making of a Reader.*

Chris Crowe, an assistant professor of English and director of the University Honors Program, teaches composition and creative writing at Brigham Young University, Hawaii Campus.

Margaret A. Deitrich is an associate professor at Austin Peay State University in Clarksville, Tennessee.

Jill Dillard is a resource teacher in Summit Elementary School, Cincinnati, and a fellow in the Ohio Writing Project.

Ken Donelson is former coeditor of *English Journal.* He currently is professor of English education at Arizona State University at Tempe.

Russel K. Durst is an associate professor in the English Department at the University of Cincinnati, where he serves as director of the Writing Center.

Karen M. Feathers is an associate professor in the Teacher Education Department at Wayne State University in Detroit, Michigan.

Cora Lee Five teaches in the Scarsdale Public Schools and is author of *Special Voices,* a just-released book about her experiences as a teacher researcher.

Alan M. Frager is an associate professor at Miami University in Oxford, Ohio, and editor of *College Reading Association Monographs.*

Nancy Gorrell is a teacher at Morristown High School, Morristown, New Jersey, and has published several articles in *English Journal.* She was chosen New Jersey State Teacher of the Year, 1991–92.

Mary K. Healy is research and training director of the Puente Project in the Office of the President, University of California. She also coedits the NCTE journal *English Education.*

Thelma Kibler is an assistant professor of language arts and English education at New Mexico State University. She is currently writing about literacy concerns for second-language learners.

Susan L. Lytle is an assistant professor in the Graduate School of Education, University of Pennsylvania.

Bruce Maylath teaches in the composition and communication program at the University of Minnesota.

Lea M. McGee is an associate professor at Boston College, and associate editor of *Journal of Reading Behavior.*

Vera E. Milz is an elementary teacher in Conant Elementary School, Bloomfield Hills, Michigan, and author of numerous articles appearing in *Language Arts.*

Rick Monroe is a teacher in Woodinville High School, near Seattle, Washington.

Ben F. Nelms is current editor of *English Journal* and an associate professor at Florida State University in Gainesville

Thomas Newkirk is professor of English at the University of New Hampshire, where he directs the New Hampshire Writing Program. His most recent book is *Listening In: What Children Say about Books (and Other Things).*

Doris L. Prater is an associate professor in the School of Education, University of Houston, Clear Lake. She serves as director of the Greater Houston Area Writing Project.

Tom Romano, formerly of Edgewood High School in Trenton, Ohio, now teaches at Utah State University in Logan. He is the author of *Clearing the Way: Working with Teenage Writers.*

Jay Simmons received his doctorate from the University of New Hampshire in 1991 and teaches in the Oyster River schools in Durham, New Hampshire.

Alice K. Swinger, professor at Wright State University and former editor for *Ohio English Language Arts Bulletin,* is now editor of *United States Board for Young People Newsletter.*

William H. Teale is current editor of *Language Arts* and a professor at the University of Texas, San Antonio.

Gail E. Tompkins is an associate professor of reading and language arts at California State University, Fresno, and author of *Teaching Writing:*

Balancing Process and Product. Previously, she was director of the Oklahoma Writing Project; she is now associated with the San Joaquin Valley Writing Project.

Eileen Tway's chapter is being published posthumously. She was a professor at Miami University in Oxford, Ohio, where she encouraged and provided support for writers. In addition to serving as a columnist for *Language Arts,* she was a mentor for the NCTE Committee on Professional Writing Networks for Teachers and Supervisors.

Betty Van Ryder is a teacher in the Advanced Learning Center, Yakima Public Schools, Yakima, Washington, and an adjunct professor at Central Washington University.

Rod Winters is a teacher in Orchard Hill Elementary School, Cedar Falls, Iowa.